ROPE
BURNS

IAN PROBERT

ROPE BURNS

ONE MAN'S RELUCTANT
OBSESSION WITH BOXING

First published by Pitch Publishing, 2016

Pitch Publishing
A2 Yeoman Gate
Yeoman Way
Worthing
Sussex
BN13 3QZ

www.pitchpublishing.co.uk
info@pitchpublishing.co.uk

A CIP catalogue record is available for this book
from the British Library.

ISBN 978-1-78531-200-7

Typesetting and origination by Pitch Publishing
Printed by Bell & Bain, Glasgow, Scotland

Contents

Foreword

BACK in 1996 everybody was talking about Nick Hornby. His new novel *High Fidelity* was a big hit and *Fever Pitch*, an autobiographical account of life as an Arsenal supporter, was being made into a movie. At the time I had an agent who was determined that I was to follow in Hornby's footsteps. She wanted me to write a book about my experiences as a boxing writer. The result was *Rope Burns*, which crawled on to the shelves in 1998.

The book was written not without a great deal of resistance on my part. Not least of which was the fact that I had made a conscious decision to distance myself from the sport. There were myriad reasons why I wanted to do this. As well as the fact that I had other ambitions and didn't want to just be seen as a person who could only write about people hitting each other, I was also deeply troubled by boxing itself. Although my close quarters involvement with the sport only spanned a very brief period I had already seen enough of the harm it could do. I'd seen a boxer named Rod Douglas suffer brain damage during a fight that ended his career on the day before his 26th birthday. Even worse, I'd been deeply distressed by what happened to Michael Watson after his tragic fight with Chris Eubank. These were both people whom I could call friends. One was a man who had frequently been a guest at my small Islington flat when we were both younger. The other came to my thirtieth birthday party. How could I sit and watch as boxing caused such damage to people I knew?

So I abandoned boxing. I went and got a job in one branch of publishing after another. I wrote about music, about technology, about murder even. Many different subjects, most of them long forgotten about. I also started writing books, one of which an embarrassingly lightweight title written on commission over a drunken weekend. This, surprisingly, became a hit in the US and was eventually made into a small independent film. Its success, however, was enough to get agents sniffing around me. And at the urging of one of these people *Rope Burns* was dragged kicking and screaming into the world.

When I awoke the day after its publication to find the book at number 12 in the nascent Amazon charts I began to believe my own hype. Perhaps, I thought, I really *was* the next Nick Hornby. I began plotting my next bestseller. However, it was not to be. Despite that fact that the book received some very positive reviews, *Rope Burns* slipped steadily down the rankings. Within a year or so it was to be forgotten forevermore.

Forgotten, that is, until four or five years ago when I suddenly began receiving messages from admirers of the book. I wouldn't go so far as to call them fans but they'd read the book, liked it and felt the need to tell me they'd liked it. The internet had made it relatively easy for them to track me down. Some of these fans were writers and journalists who had read the book as kids and – even though I find this hard to believe – apparently been inspired by it. Then in 2014 I heard that Glyn Leach, respected editor of the British-based *Boxing Monthly* magazine, had unexpectedly died. Having briefly been the editor of that title myself and having worked closely with Glyn for about a year I went along to pay my respects.

There I met faces from the past. Boxers, managers, writers and friends whom I had not seen for close to a quarter of a century. Perhaps it was the emotion of that sad occasion but sitting a pub later crammed full of 'boxing people' both young and old, I felt strangely loved. People were coming up to me and treating me like a long lost brother. People I'd never met seemed to know who I was. For the first time in over two decades I began to think about boxing.

FOREWORD

Then a lot of threads seemed to untangle themselves at once. Several people contacted me asking if I'd be interested in writing about boxing for them. I wrote a piece for the magazine I once edited, *Boxing Monthly*. I'm not exaggerating if I told you that you could have knocked me over with a featherweight if someone had said that I'd ever see my name listed in that hallowed title again. I was also persuaded to meet a real, live, living, breathing, eating, sleeping boxer named Frank Buglioni. And when I nervously entered an east London gym to discover him sweating it out on an exercise bike I was instantly transported to 1987 and Michael Watson. Even more inevitably I fell instantly in love with him.

So here then is *Rope Burns* – the story of a very much younger me's very reluctant obsession with boxing. Despite the fact that I still have a number of copies on my bookshelf I must admit to rarely looking at it over the years. I think of it as a diary. And like most diaries it is a huge source of discomfort and embarrassment to the person who wrote it. But strangely enough, it's only part one of that journal. The second part I'm writing right now. It deals with what happened when I decided to go back and revisit my past. And like all aspects of the sport that is not a sport I'm calling it *Dangerous*.

Ian Probert

Introduction

SOONER or later I'm going to have to get around to admitting to myself that there is a certain inevitability to my relationship with the sport of boxing. As ludicrous as it may seem, boxing follows me around. It's like a big brother: it watches what I'm doing, it keeps a beady eye on my every movement and throws in a crafty kidney punch whenever the referee isn't looking.

Sometimes, in my darkest moments, it appears from nowhere as a saviour holding a burning sword, but at other times boxing is like an embarrassing item of clothing that you come across in the wardrobe – a leather jacket or a pair of trousers that you bought on the cheap years ago from somewhere like Portobello Market – which you might, for whatever reason, slip into and parade in front of the mirror and wonder what on earth had possessed you to think that you ever looked cool wearing it.

Ninety-nine-point-nine per cent of the time boxing keeps a discreet distance from me and I try to keep as far away from it as circumstances permit, boxing lets me get on with my life and for a while I even forget that it exists; but every now and then it leaps out at me and catches me unawares. I suppose if I were looking for any proof of boxing's omnipresence I only have to examine what I'm doing now: freshly-bathed and clean-shaven and sitting in front of a computer keyboard and – you will probably find this difficult to believe – trying hard (not that hard) to avoid writing about boxing.

INTRODUCTION

A few years ago in another life, I came across a book on the sport by an American novelist named Joyce Carol Oates. A slim volume, as they say, I discovered the book in the two or three shelves of old review copies and trade magazines that constituted the *Sunday Sport*'s sporting reference library (how I came to be working – as boxing correspondent – for David Sullivan's tawdry soft-porn tabloid, is, I am quite sure you understand, another story). The book was called, appropriately enough, *Joyce Carol Oates On Boxing*, and she began well. One particular sentence seemed to leap out from the page at me; it read, if I remember correctly, 'One of the primary things boxing is about is lying.' It was a statement that I would only really begin to understand many, many years later, after a number of unsuccessful and quite pointless attempts to rid myself of the sport's grip on my life.

Boxing has been there to share my lowest lows and highest highs. It has shaken its head in mirth as I tried to become the next David Hockney; it has pointed its finger sternly at me and watched me descend into a bottomless pit of drug-taking and destitution, and it has allowed me to become one of its own – not a protagonist, I hasten to add, but nevertheless a 'boxing man', which, as you shall learn, is an epithet not to be taken lightly.

What exactly is a 'boxing man'? At its simplest level, it's a term often utilised by those who work within the sport to describe those who work within the sport. It's used by trainers, managers and promoters, and by the man who holds the spit bucket; it can also be found in the vocabulary of fans, free-loaders and anyone who decides to attach themselves to the shirt tails of what has too often been described as 'show business with blood'. Most of all, to be nominated a 'boxing man' signifies entry into an exclusive club whose membership, while comprising some of the richest and most powerful people in the world, finds room to incorporate a number of the saddest, most desperate examples of humanity that you will ever come across. All of these people have one thing in common: from the journalists who make their living writing about the exploits of boxers, to the numerous courtiers with which a professional boxer will surround himself – they are all liars.

To suggest that one might be a liar is, however, not necessarily always the truth; just if I was to claim that boxing's contribution to my life came entirely uninvited – there exists, I am bound to admit, far too much evidence to the contrary. If this book is about anything, it is about a reluctant love affair, a love affair in which both partners were forced to endure long periods of severe doubt and aching reticence, before eventually growing to just about tolerate one another on a visit-each-other-twice-a-year-including-weddings-and-funerals sort of basis. It is the story of a partnership with more fall-outs and reconciliations than Burton and Taylor, a union one part adrenaline and five parts smelling salts. An unwilling coalition that quite literally changed my life.

Part One

Me and
David Hockney

1
The Alpha

I WAS 12 years old when boxing came to me. It was early in the morning and I was lying in bed waiting for the alarm clock to ring when suddenly my father rushed into the room in a state of great agitation. 'He's won!' he exclaimed. 'I can't believe it – he's only gone and won!'

The 'he' in question was Muhammad Ali and what he had won was his heavyweight title back from George Foreman in the celebrated 'Rumble in the Jungle'. I have to confess that I had seldom seen my father so excited; the only other occasions when this happened came usually as a result of some form of misbehaviour on my part. But here he was, his great big body trembling and a stupid grin stretched across his face: Muhammad Ali had won! Muhammad Ali had won!

It would be 15 years later, and I would be living in a north London squat watching the fight on a stolen video recorder with an alcoholic drug dealer before I would finally comprehend the true significance of Ali's amazing victory but even so I couldn't help noticing that something strange was happening in my room. For a brief moment my father seemed to forget that I was his son and I seemed to forget that he was my father; in his rush to communicate his excitement to someone – to anyone – he had come to me because he just had to talk about what had happened. For the first time in our lives we seemed to connect.

It would have been difficult for anybody not to get caught up in his mood. I remember throwing back the bed sheets and jumping around with my arms waving about in the air: Muhammad Ali had won! The Greatest was the greatest once more! There was, however, a fairly large part of me that detected the distinct aroma of rat. After all, to anyone brought up in the 1960s, Muhammad Ali was supposed to win, wasn't he? Indeed, in terms of iconic value, in those days Muhammad Ali was boxing in the same way that the Beatles were music and Georgie Best was football. Everybody knew who Muhammad Ali was, everyone recognised his face, and everyone knew that he was the best at boxing. At school, for example, I had a friend who, in addition to being the hardest in our year, was also a talented mimic. He could do Cliff Richard, pulling his lip up just like Cliff does, and he could do Freddie Starr's impersonation of Elvis, pulling his lip up just like Freddie does. He could also do Muhammad Ali, 'I am theee Greatessst!' he would proclaim to girlish titters. 'I'm a baaad man!'

At the time home was not a happy place. My father had a job with British Aerospace in Bristol which left him perpetually tired and ill-tempered. He worked three rotating fortnightly shifts, sorting through punch cards and rewinding spools of magnetic tape in the vast, cavernous computer department which nowadays probably wouldn't be even half as powerful as the laptop I am writing this on. His first shift – the early shift – lasted from seven in the morning until three in the afternoon, he would do this for two weeks and then change to the next shift, which was nights – ten in the evening until eight in the morning; a fortnight later that he would move on to the late shift – two in the afternoon until ten at night, and then it was back to the early shift. He did this for years and years, and the upshot of this exhausting schedule was that his internal clock was always up the creek.

The routine also affected the rest of the family: my younger brother and elder sister and I developed what psychologists would refer to as cyclical behavioural patterns. For two weeks, when my father was on the early shift, home life by most people's standards would be fairly nondescript. We would usually get up in the morning just as he was leaving for work and when we came home he would be sitting watching television or cooking our tea, which we would generally eat on our knees during *Magpie* or something. When the time came for the night shift, however, things would change dramatically: in the morning we would get up just as he was returning, bleary-eyed, from work, and when we came home from school he would be still asleep, forcing us to creep around the house like burglars. This situation was especially bad on Saturdays, when, with him sleeping upstairs, we would be compelled to watch Tiswas with the volume of the TV at an impossibly low level. Prematurely awakening my father was not a wise thing to do; although we did not know it at the time, he had developed an unhealthy dependence on the sleeping pills that his doctor liberally doled out to him in an effort to assuage his fucked up internal clock; his wrath could be awesome. Ali himself would have thought twice about tangling with my father.

The late shift came as a something of reward for what we had been forced to endure over the past two weeks. Then my father would generally stay in bed until after we had gone to school and would already be out of the house by the time we got home. With my mother also working shifts as a nurse, it meant that we had the run of the place; we could play records, watch whatever we wanted on the TV and stay up to whatever time we liked. My sister could entertain her boyfriends and I was able have school friends around.

At school I was an outsider. I was an outsider primarily because I had a northern accent and everyone else had Bristolian accents. We had moved to Bristol in 1972, after an abortive attempt to emigrate to Australia. Prior to this we had been living in Burnley, Lancashire – the birthplace of my mother, a small town erected by the Victorians to accommodate the miners and textile workers that the gentry had imported to service the pits and mills. Many of my relatives were miners, and I can still recall them coming home covered from head to toe in black coal dust in the days when it was considered an impossibly flamboyant luxury even to have an inside toilet. They would wash the muck that covered their fingers and eyelids and crawled inside their nostrils in a tin bath that rested on a hand-made rag carpet in front of the fireplace.

If all this seems unnecessarily parochial, it's because in Burnley it was and still is unnecessarily parochial. As today it was all cobblestones and Black Jacks and liquorice sticks and working men's clubs that didn't allow women inside. If you don't believe me ask John Cooper-Clarke, the self-styled 'Punk Poet' from Manchester, a stone's throw away from my place of birth. To this day he devotes a substantial portion of his comedy routine to Burnley. 'Anyone here from Burnley?' he will ask as I find myself cringing in the audience. 'In Burnley they still point at aeroplanes,' he will say.

At some point around the beginning of the 1970s, to their eternal credit, my parents decided they wanted out. We were living in a two-up-two-down terraced house that brought a whole new meaning to the word 'minimalist' and they came to the conclusion that it was time to move on to sunnier climes. They filled in the forms and we all went off to interviews at Australia House in Manchester; we also managed to stoke up the rage of our neighbours by becoming the first people in the street to sell their house to a family of Pakistanis.

But then something went wrong. A week or so before we were due to leave for Perth where, according to the nice lady at the interview, perpetual sunshine and the delights of Australian Rules football awaited my arrival, my mother received a letter telling her that she had failed the medical because of high blood pressure. Having no desire to infest their country with sufferers of this dangerously contagious condition, the Australian Immigration Board politely asked us if it wouldn't be too much of an inconvenience if we kept our distance for a generation or so.

This unexpected rebuff clearly presented one or two problems for the family. Having already sold the house, there would soon be nowhere for us to live. With my father having already given up his job at the local factory, this meant that things were looking bleak.

ROPE BURNS

In the end my father had no option but to return to Bristol, the place where he had been born and raised, and where he had fostered the strange country bumpkin-esque accent that made him an outsider in Burnley. He took us there in a battered old Ford estate, which had enough room inside to store all the family's possessions. Upon our arrival we were taken in by his father until we could find somewhere to live. He was employed as the caretaker in a block of high-rise flats, in the Redcliffe area of Bristol, where I made my first acquaintance with the word 'gert' (pronounced, with feeling, 'gurdhh').

For those of you who have never come across this word it means, as was explained to me by the first friend that I made in Bristol, well, it means gert. Bristolians use the word all the time: Are you coming down the gert pub? What's the gert time? What's on the gert telly tonight? It comes as second nature to them and yet none of them seem to have the slightest idea of its meaning. For a nine-year-old Burnley lad still in short pants the word had earth-shattering implications: to me it signified the enormous cultural gulf that existed in the 200 or so miles separating my home town from Bristol. Furthermore, my inability to add the word to my vocabulary immediately had me down as something a little peculiar among my new schoolmates. I found myself admiring my sister, who almost from the day we arrived in Bristol, was able to turn on and turn off the Bristolian accent at will. She had no difficulty saying 'gert' and was thriving because of it.

I had one or two problems settling into my new school. For a start it was fiercely Catholic, and I had yet to encounter religion in Burnley. Of course, I had been told there was a God and I knew that his house was somewhere in the clouds, and I knew that when it rained God was crying. But in Burnley the people we mixed with had little time for religion; they apparently had more pressing concerns on their minds. Catholicism totally bemused me, I would stare agog at the daily rituals that we were forced to endure in the school chapel and wonder if the world was going mad. Luckily, Dame Fortune smiled upon me one afternoon when I was hit by a car on the way home from school.

The car was a write-off but I emerged from the wreckage with a few bruises, a fractured collarbone and a ready-made excuse for stopping off school.

Some months after arriving in Bristol my parents scraped together the deposit and bought us a nice little semi-detached and we moved out of my grandfather's. The house sat on top of a steep hill in a lower middle-class area of the city known as Horfield. Our neighbours were a downmarket Margo and Jerry from *The Good Life*. While I contemplated the prospect of my third school in a year, my father started his job at BAC and my mother was forced to look for work to help pay the mortgage. She got a job as a trainee nurse and we all settled into a routine.

%. %. %. %.

I was feeling miserable and lost when boxing decided to pay me its second visit. By now, I was in the third year of senior school and just beginning to notice girls and feel self-conscious in the showers. Despite much effort I had still been unable to come to terms with the Bristolian accent, and while my sister was now completely fluent in the dialect, people at school still asked me if I was from *Coronation Street*. One morning I happened to bump into Clive Rutter, the aforementioned school tough guy and famous impersonator, and for no apparent reason asked him if he was planning to watch the Muhammad Ali-Joe Frazier fight that was being broadcast on TV later that evening. Clive looked at me strangely, like he was seeing me for the first time and said, 'You're not into gert boxing are you?'

The truth is, I wasn't really. I'd only heard about the fight because my father had been talking about it for weeks. Anxious to impress, I proceeded to tell Clive all I knew about it: how Ali had been beaten by Frazier and then beat him in the re-match and had then gone on to defeat the mighty George Foreman; how Frazier was a shot fighter who had only earned his re-match with Ali because the champion's management thought that he was a soft touch. You could tell Clive was impressed. We met again during morning break and continued our conversation in the playground. I could feel eyes burning into my neck. What was the hardest boy in the school doing talking to that kid with the strange voice? By lunchtime I was with Clive and his mates smoking my first cigarette in the bushes of the school playing fields. With merely the slightest of nudges – and without me realising it – boxing had somehow managed to transform my standing within the school.

Prior to this I had been viewed with distrust by my classmates. Unable to say 'gert', I had kept myself to myself and tried as best I could to concentrate on my school work. This attitude was not appreciated by my peers. Not only was I seen as a bit of a smart-arse, I was also seen as a bit of a smart-arse who spoke differently to everyone else. I got into many after school fights because of this and I can still remember the terrible trembling feeling that overpowers your whole body as you sit in class watching the fingers of the clock creep slowly towards home-time. It is when I am at ringside watching the fighters enter the ring that the memory is at its clearest.

At first, being slightly bigger than most of my classmates, I was able to look after myself fairly well. But later, when, by a fiendishly cruel twist of genetics, the onset of puberty was delayed for some two years, my vanquished opponents gained their revenge. Powered by free-flowing hormones that had added facial hair and a good two or three inches to their height, our skirmishes became as a flyweight to a middleweight. Bumps and bruises and blackened eyes became a regular part of my school uniform.

Puberty finally arrived at about the same time that I befriended Clive. It was like my hormones had been waiting around for something worth coming out for. The results of our chemical association, however, were fairly catastrophic. In time-honoured teenage tradition, I became a different person overnight: sullen, moody, loudmouthed and determined to break as many rules as possible – it was as if I had taken a sip from Dr Jekyll's deadly medicinal compound. As a consequence of this belated unveiling of my alter-ego, my schoolwork suffered badly, I began playing truant and received awful school reports (which, courtesy of my father's erratic working hours I was usually able to intercept before they reached him). My height, however, did finally begin to make pace with my contemporaries and I was able to renew my various squabbles on a more even footing.

I did a good job in hiding this character transformation from my parents; they had kind of ambitions for me and were hoping that I would be the first member of the family ever to go to university. They would have been horrified if they had known what I was really up to with my new-found friends. When the time to take my O Levels came I had to practically plead with many of the teachers to be allowed to take the exams. Already they saw me as a bit of a waste of time, someone who had gone off the rails. 'You're probably good enough to pass,' they would trill, 'but you've got too much work to catch up on.' It was my hitherto unrecognised abilities as a salesman that finally won them over, qualities which would hold me in good stead later on in life. Incredibly, I managed to persuade them to let me sit eight O Levels – the maximum number in our school, I did this with the added incentive of a crisp £10 note for every one that I passed courtesy of my father. Even he seemed disappointed that he wasn't handing over more of his hard-earned cash, when two months later he reluctantly pressed £20 into my palm.

I left school and my father got me an interview at BAC as an apprentice engineer. I failed the interview and he and my mother drove me down to the Job Centre, where I picked out the card that seemed most appropriate to me. The year was 1978 and Ali had just won back the title he had lost a year earlier to Leon Spinks; after the fight he had announced his retirement. He was a chubby 36 years of age. As I prepared to step into adulthood I was aware that I was witnessing the end of an era; with Ali gone, boxing would never be the same again.

First Rule Of Boxing: Boxers Never Retire

When a boxer announces that he is about to retire, it is to be taken as seriously as a royal consort's wedding vows. Boxers simply do not retire. There are, of course, exceptions to this rule; Rocky Marciano, for instance, retired unbeaten after 49 fights, while the ferocious Marvin Hagler never fought again after his shattering 1987 loss to 'Sugar' Ray Leonard (Marciano, it must be admitted, was apparently toying with the idea of a comeback shortly before his untimely death in 1969). Generally, however, boxers never retire. While it is a fairly indisputable fact that at some point in a boxer's career he will be compelled to announce his retirement, very few can escape the allure of the square ring.

There is an element of symbolism in the act of a once-great champion taking, as it were, a vacation from his vacation from the ring. His reflexes, timing and boxing ability shot to pieces, tradition maintains that the old-timer be fed to the New Kid On The Block, the Hungry Young Lion who is waiting in the wings to batter his own version of reality into the former king. In this way the torch is passed and boxing writers get the chance to use lots of clichés in their attempts to apply a sense of history to the whole brutal ritual. It is possible to follow this bloodline all the way back to the first heavyweight champion, John L. Sullivan back in 1892. Thus, a 38-year-old Larry Holmes comes out of retirement in 1988 to take a battering from a young, raging Mike Tyson; a physically sick Muhammad Ali returns from two years of inactivity in 1980 to get stopped for the first time in his career by his former sparring partner, Larry Holmes; a dazzlingly inventive Cassius Clay gives an outclassed Floyd Patterson a walloping for 12 rounds in 1965; a 21-year-old Floyd Patterson stops a 40-something Archie Moore in five rounds in 1956; devastating puncher Rocky Marciano knocks out Joe Louis who is out of retirement to pay a tax bill in 1951, etc.

If a boxer is extremely lucky he will get a good ten years out of his career before he is forced to retire. Sometimes, however, he can be riding on the crest of a wave and still be compelled to call it a day. This is one of the many things that sets boxing apart from normal life as we know it. A boxer can be at the very peak of his profession; he can be champion of the world and be paid millions of dollars for what he does, yet within the space of less than an hour he can become something that you would scrape from the bottom of your shoe.

Consider this scenario: you get up one morning and take the tube to work – let's say you work in a bank – and on your arrival the manager strolls into the middle of the office, and, while everyone is watching, casually informs you that you've been sacked. He orders you to leave the office straight away, and tells you that even though you've been working in the bank for the last decade, you will not receive a penny for your loyalty or troubles. As you exit the building crestfallen you see that half of your workmates are in tears and the other half are cheering wildly and maybe throwing a few personal insults in your direction. This is what can happen when a boxer loses a fight and yet still cannot find it in himself to let go. The difference is that when he participates in the ritual he is practically naked and millions of eyes all over the world are there to watch his humiliation. Furthermore, he will be sharing a 20-foot-odd wide roped enclosure with a man who is trying to beat him into unconsciousness.

So why do boxers come back when history tells them that they are doomed? Is it pride? Arrogance? Stupidity? The truth is it's probably all of these things. More importantly, though, they come back to fight because it's what they do; it's how they define themselves. In the immortal words of Gloria Gaynor: they just never can say goodbye.

2

Seven (Not Out)

THE job I applied for was something called an architectural technician. The pay was £21 a week and involved the one thing that I was probably ever good at. All my life I had been drawing: first Disney characters, then Marvel comic characters and eventually, elaborate pencil sketches of boxers.

On my bedroom walls were home-made drawings of all the current stars of the day: Roberto Duran, the little street mugger from Panama who had once knocked out a horse with his fists; Larry Holmes, Muhammad Ali's disgruntled successor to the heavyweight title; John Conteh, the handsome English middleweight from Liverpool who later fell victim to the bottle. They were all there.

At school I had the reputation of being someone who was, as they say in Bristol, 'the best drawler'. It was a position that was fiercely contested, my closest rival being a young black boy named Errol, who could produce amazingly accurate sketches of naked women in a matter of seconds. Being able to draw held certain advantages, not least of which was that it earned you the instant respect of our tyrannical art teacher, Mr Batterbury, and the right to sit in his art room at lunchtime listening to his big stereo speakers before an elite congregation of nubile teenage girls who had been similarly invited by him.

SEVEN (NOT OUT)

For reasons best known to himself, Mr Batterbury did not allow many boys to enter into his domain.

I began the job in the winter of 1978, and found myself working in the drawing office of an architectural practice known as PMW, near Park Street, which to this day is a Bristolian equivalent of Knightsbridge. I dressed as smartly as I could and took the bus into work every morning and before I received my first salary cheque I was hating it. A couple of days after starting there one of the architects had casually informed me that I was a 'pleb'. Not knowing what the word meant I had cheerfully nodded in approval and told him that it was very nice of him to say so.

It was only when I later looked up its meaning in the dictionary that I realised the accuracy of his comment. Ostensibly, I was supposed to be working as a trainee draughts-man, making corrections to architectural drawings and doing time-consuming tasks like working out how many bricks were needed for hospital extensions in places like Frome, one of the many middle-class suburbs of Bristol (as one of the architects advised me, 'Frome wasn't built in a day'). The reality of the job, however, was somewhat different.

At PMW I was soon to discover that there was a clearly defined and well instituted pecking order. At the top of the tree sat the partners; they were usually in their 40s or 50s and frequently spent their days in meeting rooms over wine and sandwiches. They lived in six-bedroom houses in the leafy suburbs of the city and were to be avoided at all costs. Unless you were driven by ambition, becoming overly familiar with a partner was not to be recommended as it meant they were likely to remember your name whenever they were looking for someone to do 'a little job' for them. A partner's 'little job' could mean anything from cleaning the windows of the office to lugging furniture up three flights of stairs, to purveying messages to groups of Irish navvies on a mud-soaked building site in the middle of nowhere.

Resting a couple of notches below the partners were the associate partners. These would never see 40 again and lived in large semi-detached Georgian houses in Clifton or Redland – the artier parts of Bristol. They had no compunction in achieving first-name terms with their superiors, and would spend their weekends graciously losing at golf with a partner of their choice. They had pot-bellies and thinning hair and drove Citroën IIcvs, sometimes with plastic eyelashes glued to the headlights. Associates were serious and had lofty ambitions. They talked about things like post-modernism, Michael Graves and Le Corbusier. At lunch times they combined forces over the Guardian crossword. Believe it or not, some really did wear red spotted bow ties.

Hovering some way below the associates were the junior architects. Most of these were only a year or so out of university and still had pimples; the tasks they were given to undertake – office conversions, extensions, etc. – were more or less appropriate to their experience. A junior architect was usually in his mid-20s (an architectural degree takes seven years to complete) and sported a fluffy beard. He listened to bands like Supertramp, ELO and Dire Straits, read books by Douglas Adams and still wore flares.

Along with people like Mandy the Print Girl and any one of the troupe of black cleaners that came into the office at night, at the bottom of the ladder sat the architectural technicians like me. A technician could be any age and existed solely to do the dirty washing – the boring, mundane, nuts-and-bolts stuff that the creative types in the office couldn't really be bothered with. Once you were a technician, you were a technician – nothing more, nothing less; there was no room for ambition. You sat at your drawing board and plotted the latest damp proof course and scratched away the ink from someone else's drawing.

Worst of all, being a technician meant that you were sometimes compelled to work in the print room. This was an 8ft by 12ft cupboard that housed the photocopier and dyeline machine. The dyeline machine was an ammonia-fired monstrosity that was used to produce copies of architectural drawings, which would then be sent to clients and contractors.

With eyes watering and throat scorched, I spent weeks and weeks alone in that room.

PMW had a cricket team which played once a week during the summer evenings in something called the Bristol Construction League. They took their cricket very seriously, turning out in immaculate starched whites and carrying cricket bats that would have taken me six months to afford. Soon after I joined the company they were short of players and I was asked if I would like a game. Hitching a lift to the ground in one of the associate's cars, I entered the field wearing a pair of faded blue jeans and a purple shirt and was immediately relegated to a spot on the distant boundary. In general, the games lasted 40 overs; each team would bat for 20 overs and then take their place in the field. Prior to the game the order of batting would be pinned to the office notice board. This was the first PMW team sheet to bear my name:

Bristol Construction League
12 August 1978
1. Peerless (partner)
2. Burns (partner)
3. Golding (partner)
4. Preston (associate)
5. Brown (associate)
6. Bartlett (associate)
7. Butler (architect)
8. Jessup (architect)
9. Hardy (structural engineer)
10. Pierce (mechanical engineer)
11. Probert (technician)

From a seat in the pavilion I watched as Peerless and Burns took to the crease looking confident if a little overweight. In their peaked caps and glowing white linens it was obvious that they meant business. An over later, both men were out and I found myself asking why they had been allowed to open the batting when they were obviously so ill-suited to the task. My question was received with tuts and grunts and sidelong glances from my disapproving looking colleagues. The third partner to drag his bulk to the crease fared slightly better, he managed to score five before being run out as he waddled down the pitch chasing an extra. Preston, Brown and Bartlett's resistance was just as ineffective: they scored a combined total of nine before they were removed and Butler and Jessup took their place.

Being younger, fitter, and possibly having played cricket before, Butler and Jessup fared remarkably well, scoring some 70 runs in a partnership that lasted over half of the innings before Jessup was caught in the slips. His respective replacements, Hardy and Pierce, reverted to form: in scoring a tally of four runs they proved, however, that they were definite partner material. Then it was my turn. In the 19th over, with eight balls remaining, I was given a pair of pads, some gloves and a plastic thing to stick down my trousers. I took to the crease and prodded out my bat and scored two runs. Then I stuck it out once more and got another. By the time the innings was over I had managed the grand total of seven runs – the third highest tally of the game. The team scoresheet recorded this act for posterity and I looked forward to a glittering career as opening batsman for PMW. In the pub afterwards I was congratulated and plied with pint after pint of best bitter by my new team-mates. When the team sheet was pinned on to the notice board a week later it read:

Bristol Construction League
19 August 1978
1. Peerless (partner)
2. Burns (partner)
3. Golding (partner)
4. Preston (associate)
5. Brown (associate)
6. Bartlett (associate)
7. Butler (architect)
8. Jessup (architect)
9. Hardy (structural engineer)
10. Probert (technician)
11. Pierce (mechanical engineer)

SEVEN (NOT OUT)

※ ※ ※ ※

I stayed at PMW for over a year and found myself becoming sucked into the lifestyle. After a hard day in the Print Room I would invariably end up socialising with my workmates in the local pub. I began to dress like them, all woollen sleeveless sweaters and pinstripe flares; I even toyed with the idea of growing a moustache. As I turned 17 I was looking like a 25-year-old and had the ambitions of someone of that age. Although I was still living at home and so forced to creep about the house one weekend in three, I looked forward to the day when I could get myself a little car, find a steady girlfriend, secure myself a nice little council flat. The part of me that once liked to snick off school and smoke Number 10s seemed to go into hiding. I could still feel it inside me, but the routine of work had made me comfortable. But then boxing chose to put in its third appearance and everything was to change.

※ ※ ※ ※

'Richard tells me that you do drawings of boxers,' said Stephen Burns one day after he had mysteriously summoned me into his office. Burns was a quantity surveyor by trade, but he was also a partner; it was only the second time that I had been granted access to such a hallowed location and I suspected the worse. 'My son is, um, very keen on boxing,' he continued. 'Have you perhaps heard of a boxer named Alan Minter?'

Of course I had. Minter was an English fighter from the East End of London. It was said that he came from gypsy stock, but what was certain was that he fought with an intensity which suggested he hated the whole world. He was by no means a classic fighter like Ali, he could not dance and he could not shimmy and he certainly did not quote poetry. He was handsome but ugly and was frequently boring to watch – on one occasion one of his fights was stopped by the referee because nobody could be bothered to throw any punches. Nevertheless, Minter was, however, British middleweight champion and, at the time, one of the most popular sporting figures in the country. He'd even been on *Superstars*.

Stephen Burns went on to explain that he wanted to give his son a special present for his 16th birthday; he asked me if I'd be interested in drawing a portrait of the boxer for him. For this he would pay me £25. It was more than a week's wages. I said yes.

The picture took a couple of evenings to complete. After finding a photograph in a magazine, I spent my evenings carefully copying it in 2B pencil. When I was finished I mounted the drawing on a piece of board and gave it to Burns. 'You should go to art college,' he said as he handed me a cheque.

You should go to art college. For weeks afterwards I could not get the words out of my head. You should go to art college. What did it mean? What was an art college? Burns' casual statement seemed to light some kind of touch paper inside me. I decided to do a little investigation.

The first thing I did was to ask my father what he knew of the matter. 'It's where they take drugs and things,' he proclaimed. 'It's where they splash paint all over the walls and go to orgies.' As I think back to what I would have said had I been in his position, I cannot help but conclude that I might have handled the situation somewhat differently. Although his prognosis had naturally been intended to deter me from pursuing such foolish ideas; it had, of course, quite the opposite effect.

Second Rule Of Boxing: Know Your Opponent's Name

Just as one would surely endeavour to discover as much as possible about the job for which one is applying, it is to a boxer's distinct advantage that he be able to remember his opponent's name when stepping between the ropes. The history of boxing is littered with former champions who have come a cropper in underestimating their opponents. The most famous modern example of such a circumstance being, of course, James 'Buster' Douglas' stunning upset over the apparently invincible Mike Tyson in 1990. On that occasion Tyson was guilty of one of boxing's cardinal sins: he had begun to believe his own publicity.

Except under exceptional circumstances, a professional prize-fighter's career path usually follows one well-trodden route. Generally, he will have begun to box while in his early teens (although some start as young as five or six), joining a local amateur club and having perhaps a dozen or so fights (although in exceptional cases some fighters will have more than a hundred amateur bouts). If he shows promise and reaches national level he will invariably catch the eye of a promoter or manager and be offered a professional contract. On average, boxers turn pro in their early 20s; if successful they can look forward to a decade or so of ring activity. These days, it is a rarity for a boxer to participate in more than 50 fights during his career, which is in stark contrast to how the sport was run earlier in the century, when boxers would often contest hundreds of bouts in careers that could span up to three decades. If a modern fighter is unlucky enough not to possess a knockout punch, thus being unable to bring a premature conclusion to his contests, he can look forward to spending a combined total of around 300 hours in the ring with a variety of opponents, many of whom are hell bent on knocking his head off.

A boxer's first three or four professional contests are some of the most important he will ever have in his life. Usually fed a collection of no-hopers and has-beens, he will be expected to handle his opponents with style and panache – all the better if he can manage to render them unconscious. To become a marketable commodity it is almost essential that his early record be liberally splattered with knockouts and stoppages. If he is to catch the eye it is necessary that his CV bears strong evidence of precocity: that feeling of latent talent waiting to be unleashed upon the world of people who punch other people for a living. Should, however, a boxer lose a fight so early in his career it is often an insurmountable obstacle for him to overcome. If he is lucky or, for example, suffered the loss due to an injury, he may be allowed a re-match with the boxer responsible for taking away the '0' part of his record, in which case it is of paramount importance that he avenges his defeat. If he fails to do so, there is every likelihood that he will become a journeyman, a term that is used to describe a boxer who is principally used to furnish the records of other fighters for a derisory fee.

With the next stage of a boxer's development comes a conveyor belt lined with inferior imported opposition, or, as ex-middleweight champion Nigel Benn once put it, 'Mexican road sweepers'. This motley crew make a partial living travelling around the world losing fights; they are sacrificial lambs with a three-figure pay cheque. They come via Belgium, Africa, Italy and France; Sheffield, Barnsley and Luton. For every boxer who achieves even limited success in the business, there are hundreds of Mexican road sweepers in every corner of the globe. Most of them have other jobs and do the fighting purely as a moderately paid hobby; others, however, have more dubious credentials – on rare occasions there proves to be some foundation in Hollywood's gangsters-and-thugs depiction of the sport.

By the time a fighter has had his first dozen or so fights, it is possible to gain a reasonably accurate assessment of his potential for success. In addition to a local – and possibly national – following, he will usually by now have gained a nickname and possibly had his head shaven in an attempt to look meaner. If he's white and looks boyish he will be called something like Billy 'The Kid' Walker; if he is black and punches powerfully, he becomes Nigel the 'Dark Destroyer' Benn, or 'Iron' Mike Tyson; if he's from Africa he's 'The African Lion'; if he's fast on his feet he's 'The Dancing Master'. If, however, the boxer in question is a boring fighter, an extravagant nom-de-plume will often be adopted in an attempt to disguise this deficiency; thus the creation of Bernard 'The Executioner' Hopkins, 'Slugger' O'Toole (real name, would you believe it, Fidel Castro Smith!), Renaldo 'Mr Reindeer' Snipes and the ultimate boxing oxymoron, Johnny 'The Entertainer' Nelson.

SEVEN (NOT OUT)

By this stage a fighter is usually ready to dip his toe into deeper waters and meet fighters who, like him, still have ambition. For spectators, these confrontations represent the true spirit of boxing. They can be savage, brutal and exhilarating affairs with strings of zeros being the reward for those who prevail. If a boxer manages to get this far he will soon be ready to fight for a title. Although nowadays there are quite literally hundreds of different titles available to a fighter, there is still a certain amount of kudos attached to owning one. More importantly, however, without a title it is almost impossible to attract television coverage and the vast amounts of revenue that this medium offers.

Should a boxer manage to win a national title – and, better still, look good in doing so – the opportunity to contest a version of the world title is usually only a few fights away. To facilitate this, the boxer's manager and promoter may combine their efforts to select the weakest current champion from one of the five or six governing bodies that have sprung up since the days when there were only eight weight divisions with one champion in each (there are now 13). In an attempt to gain home advantage, a large sum of money will then be offered to the champion of their choice, who, although realising that he is putting his position in severe jeopardy by defending his title overseas, will often have difficulty in refusing a fee that can run to several hundred thousand pounds.

Being businessmen, it is unusual for boxing managers and promoters to misjudge their investment. More often than not, their man will suffice to become a world champion in order that they may reap the benefits of the effort that they have put into guiding his career. For the next three or four fights they will strive to find him easy opposition, these will include faded former world champions and mediocre local fighters, the new champion may also find himself renewing his acquaintance with a few Mexican road sweepers.

However, it is at this time that a fighter is at his most vulnerable. Since winning the title his life will have changed beyond recognition. He will have money, fast cars, designer suits, designer women and a legion of hangers-on, all of whom are making a healthy living from the champ by simply telling him how good he is. If the boxer manages to hold on to the title for several years he will begin to consider himself invincible. By now he will have been victorious in some 30 or so contests; having defeated everyone that has been put in front of him, he may actually believe that there is nobody on the planet capable of beating him.

%% %% %% %%

'I am the baddest man on the planet… I simply refuse to feel pain… I cannot be beaten.' These are, of course, the words of 'Iron' Mike Tyson, the fighter who, at the age of 19, became the youngest man ever to win a version of the heavyweight title. Right from his amateur days everyone knew he was something special; Tyson looked and fought like he came from a different era. With his 16-inch neck and Neanderthal gait, it was once remarked that Tyson's punches even sounded different to everyone else's.

In the ring Tyson was literally an animal: opponents would often fall victim to his brutal attacks before the sound of the opening bell had faded. Many – as in the case of Michael Spinks and our own Frank Bruno – would find their knees trembling and their arms turning to jelly long before they had even climbed on to the ring apron.

Tyson was an exceptional talent. He was the person that boxing had been looking for since Ali had decided to put his enormous charisma out to pasture at the end of the 1970s. In many respects he was the perfect fighter for the MTV generation: his fights seldom went more than three or four rounds and could normally be programmed into a time slot comparable in length to the average Prince video. By the time Tyson was 20 he was famous all over the world and was well on the way to his first $50m. However, when he stepped into a Tokyo boxing ring to defend his titles in the early hours of 11

SEVEN (NOT OUT)

February 1990, the weight of all that cash was proving a little too hard for him to bear.

The man he was fighting that night in Tokyo could have been anybody, for the truth of the matter was that Tyson had been fighting anybodys for the last four years. His name, as I mentioned earlier, was James 'Buster' Douglas and he had earned his shot at the title primarily because he had no chance of winning. Tyson prepared for the contest by doing what he had been doing for a long time. He partied, he drank, he hardly went to the gym and he partied some more. Tyson scarcely bothered to even look at videos of his opponent in action and he lost the fight. He lost the fight because he knew he could not lose. He lost the fight because he knew that he would win. He lost the fight because he did not bother to learn the name of his opponent: his life was never the same again.

3

Advice from a Falling Idol

S O I'm standing at the bar and Alan says to me, 'How long you been doing this for then, kid?' And I say, 'Not long but I don't plan to do it forever, you know.' And he says, 'Really – What do you want to do?' And I say, 'Well don't laugh but I want to be an artist.' To which he replies, 'I wouldn't do that if I were you – I had a mate tried to do that, waste of time.'

Boxing was back in business with visit number four, except that on this occasion the advice that it was attempting to provide could not have been more graphic in its presentation. The year was 1980 and while people all over the country were busy kicking in shop windows and setting fire to parked cars in a mass display of public dissatisfaction with Margaret Thatcher's blue-tinted vision of Britain, I was wearing a purple suit and doing my level best to pick the pockets of the bourgeoisie. Standing beside me, his face a mess of cuts and bruises from the hammering he had taken a few days earlier from Marvin Hagler, was freshly-deposed world middleweight champion Alan Minter.

If I may call a brief recess here, I feel it only fair to explain that this was the first occasion that I had ever encountered a living, breathing professional boxer in, as it were, the flesh. He was a little smaller than I, skinnier than he looked on TV and wearing a dinner jacket. I was a trite overawed to say the least, but if I were a believer in fate, in Karma – in Mystic Meg – I would be forced to admit that I should have made some effort to heed his words. Boxing – in the form of Alan Minter – appeared to be telling me to put my foot on the brakes, to take stock of what I was doing with my life. To take a moment or two to consider the implications of a decision I had made four months earlier. Unfortunately, at the time I had absolutely no way of interpreting this message or, for that matter, of even knowing that a message was perhaps being sent.

From being asked to do a £25 drawing for one of the partners at the architects' office I had somehow resolved to become a famous artist. It's the sort of leap of faith that you're apt to make when you're young, I suppose. The idea, of course, held much appeal: first of all, there was money in it; secondly, if you became successful you would get invited to lots of celebrity bashes; thirdly, and more importantly, prior to becoming a famous artist it was necessary that you go to art college for four years, where you could apparently take lots of drugs, splash paint on walls and got to lots of orgies. So it was that early in 1979, filled with a sense of destiny, I packed in my job at the architects' office and found work as a waiter in Bristol's Grand Hotel.

It goes without saying, it must be said, that working as a waiter is not always an essential pre-requisite for becoming a famous artist – although there have been many notable names in the field who have taken that route: Modigliani, Francis Bacon and Rolf Harris, to name but three – the vast majority of famous artists seem to manage quite well enough on the other side of the bar. Becoming a waiter was, however, quite necessary for me.

Earlier that year I had taken my drawings of boxers down to the art college at Bower Ashton, on the outskirts of Bristol. There, a man with a beard told me that, although it was obvious I could draw, I was a little young and needed to go away and practise my craft. I was advised to spend a year in the life drawing room, learn painting techniques and get myself an A Level in art, without which, entry into an art college was impossible. I mulled over these suggestions in my mind – most of which seemed relatively straightforward. Life drawing classes, I discovered, were held two evenings a week at a museum in Park Street; painting techniques could be gleaned from any number of the books that I found on the shelves of the local library; getting myself an A Level in art, however, would be slightly more problematic.

I found the solution to this dilemma by doing something that many people, at some point in their lives, have dreamed of having the opportunity to do – I went back to school. I went back to school having sampled the delights of working in the adult world and armed with the knowledge that the old cliché about schooldays being the best days of your life is probably true.

I paid my former art teacher Mr Batterbury and his two giant stereo speakers a visit and told them of my predicament. After pondering the situation for a few moments the art teacher made me an offer: he would permit me to return to school for the remaining four months of the school year and, if I proved able to cram two years' work into that period, I would be allowed to sit the exam. Without hesitation I agreed to his kind proposal.

My father was not a happy man when I revealed my plans to him one afternoon after he had just come off the early shift. 'You must be out of your tiny mind!' he raged. 'You've got a good job with prospects and you're going to give it up to become one of those arty-farty people!'

The atmosphere in the house was uncomfortable for several weeks after my bombshell but eventually my father appeared to come round to the idea. He would allow me to pursue my crazy scheme if I agreed to continue paying the £6 a week house-keeping money that my salary at PMW had enabled me to contribute to the household balance of payments. I nodded my head in agreement, skimmed the jobs pages of the *Bristol Evening Post*, and began my career as a wine waiter.

For those of you who have never been attended to by a wine waiter in a large hotel, I have three words of advice: watch your wallet. I was to discover that along with telephone salesmen, chartered accountants, Great Train Robbers, American presidents and – of course – boxers, wine waiters are among the biggest thieves and liars in the known universe. To my great surprise, however, I was also to discover that I had very little problem in stepping into the shoes of such a person.

The Grand Hotel was an enormous, sprawling Georgian building in the middle of the city. It was the poshest hotel in Bristol and inside was not unlike the one that Jack Nicholson had ended up demolishing in The Shining. Working there required a purple nylon waiter's suit with black lapels, a sensible haircut, a corkscrew and the ability to address anybody as 'Sir'. The pay was £8 per ten-hour evening shift which meant that if I did five shifts a week I would be earning almost twice as much as I did in my former career. On my first night there I was introduced to Bob, a fellow wine waiter who had been working at the hotel for about 30 years. Small, balding and serious, Bob was given the task of looking after me until I got the hang of the job – learned the ropes, so to speak. 'The money's not much here,' grumbled my charge as he led me through one of the three huge banqueting halls that I would be working in, 'but there are ways and means of making a bit more.'

Bob's 'ways and means', it transpired, were as follows: the Grand Hotel employed some 20 or so wine waiters. On any given night each waiter was responsible for three or four tables that seated parties of between 20 and 30 people. The waiter's job was to ensure that his clients were given a steady supply of overpriced wine and other beverages. This meant that on some nights he could be in charge of over 100 people, with the responsibility of ensuring that the money for all their drinking and merriment was collected at the end of the night and handed in to the head barman, and on the understanding that any discrepancies were to be made up from the waiter's own pocket. This procedure was usually carried out in the early hours of the morning after one's clientele had been partying away for some seven or eight hours. Being too full of expensive cheap Beaujolais to notice that the cost of an extra bottle or two of wine and half-a-dozen brandies had been added to their bills they usually paid up without question. It was a loophole that had been exploited for many generations and one which enabled the waiters to go home with considerably more than the £8 that the hotel paid them for their attendance.

I can recall being completely appalled when this practice was first explained to me. Despite the distant memory of a minor bout of shoplifting at a local sweet shop that had gone badly wrong when I was a kid living in Burnley, I considered myself at the time to be a person of upstanding morality. During my first week in the job I refused to have anything to do with the scheme. However, when my colleagues began ignoring me and elbowing one another in the ribs whenever I passed by, I realised that to gain their acceptance I would have to become a thief. My debut performance in that role netted me an extra £17; when added to the £8 that the hotel paid me it meant that I was rich. For the first time in my life I had money in my pocket.

As my new-found wealth looked around for a lifestyle to support I began to enjoy the new job. The work may have been tiring and stressful but it came not without a certain touch of glamour. Once or twice a week there would be after dinner speeches; minor celebrities such as Ian Botham, Leslie Crowther (would you believe he's the filthiest, dirtiest stand-up comedian I have ever witnessed?) and Ray Reardon would be paid not insubstantial sums of money to entertain revellers with their anecdotes; sometimes even royalty would pay the hotel a visit. With the acolytes and hangers-on that their presence attracted, came rich pickings for the men in purple suits. In view of the fact that the majority of my clients treated me with the respect that one might afford a pubic hair in a bowl of snuff, I began to see myself as a latter day Robin Hood. Somehow, I got it into my head that I was stealing from the rich to give to the poor. Unfortunately, I did not so much warm to the task as take a blow torch to my misplaced convictions. Soon I was taking home at least £40 a night, eventually my nocturnal activities were netting me over £300 a week.

The summer of 1980 became a blur as I acclimatised to the routine of practising my drawing at school during the day before heading off to rip off a few rich kids in the evenings. My return to school after a gap of almost two years had been greeted with bemusement from those members of my year who had stayed on for the sixth form. Clive Rutter was still there, handy as ever with his fists and still keen to talk about boxing, but many things had changed, or rather, I had changed. For those of you, as I mentioned earlier, who have ever dreamed of going back to school, allow me to give you the benefit of my experience: don't bother – it ain't all it's cracked up to be. While it is doubtless the fantasy of many men to spend their days surrounded by an assortment of fresh-faced teenage girls dressed in school uniforms, it's still school – the food's lousy and there isn't a pub in sight.

It was not long before I found myself taking days off from my re-education so that I could do an extra shift at the hotel. As the autumn approached my artistic ambitions were rinsed away by the flood of distractions that the roll of pound notes in my pocket brought forth. By the time that I heard that Alan Minter would be appearing at the hotel as an after-dinner speaker I already knew what it meant to win a world title belt. With wealth came new friends and new habits; with riches came women and opportunity. In truth, nobody in our school had ever been on the kind of pocket money that I was on, and my rediscovered schoolmates were soon treating me like a long lost sibling. There was a price to be paid, of course.

There is a certain sense of linearity in boxing's decision to elect Alan Minter as spokesman in its fourth attempt to change the course of my life. After all, it was because of Minter that I was now spending my evenings uncorking bottles and robbing the landed gentry. We met at a time when he was possibly at the lowest ebb in his life. He had just had his world title ripped away from him in three utterly brutal rounds by Marvin Hagler, the boxer who would go on to dominate the middleweight division for most of the 1980s. After the fight there had been rioting at the Royal Albert Hall, drunken supporters of Minter had hurled bottles, glasses and – bizarrely – bags of sweets at the American, in violent scenes that were shown on live television, prompting the banning of alcohol at future fight venues. Furthermore, Minter had been accused of fuelling emotions and prejudices in a statement he had made at a press conference on the eve of the fight. He had told reporters that he would 'never lose to a black man' and had taken a severe beating in the ring for his ill-judged proclamation.

Minter had been world champion when he had originally been invited to the hotel. His intention had probably been to do what any champion will do after a fight – he had planned to celebrate. He would drink champagne, perhaps even take a smoke, pose for photographs, shake hands with local dignitaries and get kissed by models. However, the Minter who turned up to mumble a few words into a microphone that night was a devastated figure. In his eyes you could see the hunted, wounded look that is often present in those who have suffered severe personal tragedy. His face still held the stitches that had pierced the torn and weeping flesh around his eyes in a futile attempt to repair the damage caused by Hagler's twisting punches. He spoke with the voice of a little boy lost, shell-shocked, hunting for sympathy, desperate for something that might erase the memory of what he had so recently been forced to endure.

I was given Minter's table (of course) to look after and forced my hand into his as he stared forlornly at the carpet. As with most boxers the grip was weak, almost feminine. Although I knew that Minter would not be remotely interested in the fact that I had recently sold a pencil sketch of him for £25, I told him the story anyway. Later at the bar I collared him again and he was able to present me with boxing's opinions as to my artistic ambitions. Before we finished our conversation I asked him one question, 'Are you going to fight Hagler again?'

'Sure,' he grunted, carefully avoiding my eyes, 'we'll get it organised and I'll get the bastard next time.'

Minter never did fight the bastard again. In fact, he would never even box at anything approaching world-class level. Like many boxers who suffer a devastating defeat, Minter was never the same fighter. Within a year he had lost his British title and within two he had retired. I know for a fact that Minter does not remember our first encounter, I'm also fairly sure that he does not recall the second and third times that we met – although on those occasions the circumstances were somewhat different and Minter wasn't really Alan Minter any more. He was someone else, someone who looked pretty much like Alan Minter used to look, but nevertheless a different person. He was an ex-fighter struggling to come terms with the fact that he was an ex-fighter; the fame, the rush of achievement and the five-figure paycheques long gone.

Third Rule Of Boxing: Hold On To Your Money!

A quick question:

Who – apart from Ian Beale and Pauline Fowler, the battle-hardened former Miss Brahms from *Are You Being Served?* – is the longest serving cast member on the popular BBC soap *EastEnders*? A strange question to be asking at this point in the proceedings, I readily admit, but a pertinent one nevertheless. I'll not hold you in suspense for too long. Even if you have a life and are, therefore, totally unfamiliar with the mythical hinterland of Albert Square and its character-set of cockles-and-muscles-how's-your-father-duvet-jumping-Cockney-sparrows, it is not my intention to tease.

No, it's not Poison Pat, the heavyweight drama queen who married one of The Comedians and, according to recent plot revelations, is now sharing her bed with someone in dire need of Viagra (damn! I've gone and done it! I was determined to make it through this book without referring to the wonder drug that has become the buzzword of the late 20th century!). Nor is it either of the Mitchell brothers, those insipid psycho twins, who, despite obvious physical deficiencies, have somehow managed to work their way through the entire female cast of the show. It's Harry Holland.

Who the hell, I hear you ask, is Harry Holland? I'll tell you.

Now into middle-age, Harry Holland is one of British fight game's longest established boxing promoters. Since the late 1970s he has been staging regular boxing events in London; indeed, fight fans have a particular soft spot for Holland's promotions at Battersea Town Hall which, although seldom featuring big-name boxers and never transmitted on television, are usually guaranteed to thrill. As well as this, Harry Holland is also a boxing manager , having been responsible for guiding the careers of the exciting welterweight Rocky Kelly and the indomitable super-middleweight Andy Till. And, if this were not enough, Holland has, for more than a decade, been the Queen's Vic's most loyal customer.

Take a look next time you're channel hopping: Harry is the stocky fellow with greying hair who can often be observed in the corner of the pub exchanging pleasantries with Big Ron while Grant and Tiffany indulge in another screaming match. Harry can also regularly be seen in the café, munching on a sandwich and sipping at a lukewarm coffee as Ricky and Bianca take turns practising their Mockney accents. Last but not least, when he's not loitering with intent in these two locations, Harry Holland is apt to stroll up and down the market, occasionally stopping off at Mark's fruit and veg stall to purchase an apple.

So why does Harry waste his days working as a television soap extra when there are obviously so many more important things he could be doing with his time? Why does one of this country's most widely respected boxing promoters choose to sit in the bar of the Queen Vic mouthing non-existent phrases to non-existent people?

The answer can best be summed up in one word: money. For, like the boxers that he manages and promotes, Harry needs the cash. He needs the cash because, although his shows are undeniably among the most popular local boxing events in modern times, it is rare for him to make profit. Harry is not Frank Warren, sitting pretty with a multi-million-pound contract with Sky; nor is he Don King, the controversial American promoter who actually owns his own television station. Harry's success or failure is solely dependant on the number of tickets he sells; and even on a good night there is very little left in the coffers when the purses, the site fees, the doctor's fees and the board's fees have been paid.

%% %% %% %%

Boxers and the substantial sums of money that they are capable of generating have an unfortunate habit of parting company after what is often only the briefest of acquaintances. Quite why this should happen is something that few of them ever come close to understanding, despite an inherent willingness to hand over large portions of their earnings to people who claim to be able to prevent them from falling victim to this unhappy scenario. For some this may entail the engagement of a posse of highly paid financial advisors, managers and agents in a quest to discover the reason why their bank balances are so often printed in red ink rather than black. For others, it may mean selling their soul to the devil.

Like the acting business, the world of professional boxing distributes its riches unevenly. In the same way that for every Meryl Streep or Julia Roberts there are a thousand nameless actresses wiping tables in bars and cafés who dream of a walk-on part in *Emmerdale*, there are far too many boxers who must share their most dangerous of occupations with other trades. For many, the pressure of combining a job as a milkman, a fireman, or a telephone engineer, with the bumps and bruises of unarmed combat will prove to be too much of an obstacle to overcome. Curiously, however, should a boxer manage to find an exit to this unhappy circumstance, his rise to stardom is often characterised by a total inability to remember how hard life was before his name started appearing at the top of fight posters.

Boxers like to spend money. Having fought their way up, in many cases, from abject poverty, they spend their cash with the enthusiasm of someone who has just turned up six numbers plus the bonus ball. They buy cars, and more cars, and even bigger cars. They buy houses, and more houses, and houses with swimming pools and private discos. They buy huge flashy stereos with lots of flickering lights, and they buy televisions with screens that are bigger than most people's kitchens. It is often only when the spending spree is finally over that they will shrug their shoulders and realise that they'd better get back into that ring fast and earn some more cash.

Some boxers become quite good at spending money. Indeed, the endless list of boxers who became so good at spending their money that they eventually ran out if it, is graced with the names of some of the biggest earners in the history of any sport or pastime. Among the many boxers who have experienced what it is like to be woken up one morning by the bailiff, are all-time greats such as Joe Louis, the fabulous 'Brown Bomber' of the pre-war era, who was forced to try to make a living as a wrestler before ending his days employed as a greeter at a Las Vegas casino; Roberto Duran, who, despite fighting at the highest level for over three decades, is yet to win his ongoing battle with insolvency; and 'Sugar' Ray Robinson, reckoned to be the ring's finest exponent by many experts, who was compelled to fight on well into middle-age in a futile attempt to appease the Taxman. And let us not forget that modern prince of the big-spenders Mike Tyson, who, at the time of writing, has allegedly managed to work his way through some $150m; an achievement which I'm sure you'll agree certainly takes some doing – even for someone with a penchant for giving away Rolls-Royces when he is bored of them.

In reality, however, boxers tend to squander their fortunes because they are not accountants. They do so because the only figures that they truly understand are usually wearing boxing gloves. They spend because they refuse to read the small print and remain blissfully unaware that the glittering baubles dangled before them are so often made of pyrite. They fail to realise that their six-figure salaries are seldom what they seem.

A boxer's take home pay is often a bitter disappointment for a man who has just done so much more than dance for his dinner. When the appropriate governing body, the manager, the agent, the trainer, the cuts-man, the sparring partners, the referee, the judges, the ring announcer and the spit-bucket holder have all taken their cut, six figure purses have an alarming habit of turning into four figure purses. And if supporting the lifestyles of this rogue's gallery of acolytes is not enough to be thinking about, there is always the Inland Revenue waiting to grab their slice of the pie.

And yet in a sense there is a certain poetic justice involved when a boxer finishes his career and realises that after all the hard work, all the pain, all the disappointment and all the punches he has to take in the course of his career, he is no better off than he was on the day that he first decided to pull on that pair of glowing crimson gloves. The Americans like to call it completion. For even though it is in a boxer's nature to be a keen student of history, he will seldom find a way to stop himself from making the same mistakes as his over-indulgent predecessors.

4

A Kind of Hold

NOW that we've got to know each other a little, I hope you won't mind if I introduce you to a friend of mine. A very good friend who I'm sure that you've heard of. He's a fair bit older than the majority of people I usually choose to hang around with – a good few years, in fact – and, in all honesty, of all the people that I choose to hang around with he's someone whom I actually end up hanging around with the least.

It doesn't help, of course, that in the couple of decades or so that we've been acquainted we've only actually bumped into each other on three separate occasions. It also doesn't really help that he has never even been told my name and that if I walked past him in the street there would be no earthly possibility of him ever recognising me. As far as I'm concerned, however, he's still a friend.

His name's Muhammad though he used to be called Cassius. His place of residence is somewhere on the other side of the Atlantic and he has lived a life that I cannot possibly even begin to imagine. He has dined with kings and sipped with presidents; he has scaled impossible peaks and stared death and disaster between the eyes on so many occasions. He is black and I am white. He is rich and I am poorish. He is oldish and I am youngish. We have nothing in common. Yet somehow there is a part of me that feels in some small way responsible for the manner in which he has conducted his life.

I know that if I look across from my keyboard I will see a shelf that contains, let's see, one, two, three, four, five... 14 books devoted exclusively to the subject of Muhammad Ali (including two copies of *The Greatest* by Richard Durham, one unsigned the other signed), and two copies of *Muhammad Ali: His Life and Times* by Thomas Hauser (one unsigned the other signed). I also know that if I go into the spare room I will find an entire shelf that is straining under the weight of videos that contain recordings of the vast majority of his professional contests (and it still irks me when I think about the half dozen or so of his fights that I do not possess, even though these date from early on in his career and are impossible to get hold of). Clearly this strange preoccupation of mine is not a healthy one.

I can at least console myself that I've managed to control this fixation to some extent: although I'm more likely to remember the date when Muhammad Ali won his first world title than I am for the majority of my friends' birthdays, I have never felt compelled to be like him. I'm not, I am relieved to say, like the sad young man who once appeared on TV's *Stars in their Eyes* dressed in black leather, sporting a toupee carefully crafted to be the mirror image of his idol's receding forehead, and then proceeded to give a note perfect rendition of Gary Numan's 'Are "Friends" Electric?' Furthermore, I've never to the best of my knowledge been compelled to run around telling everyone within earshot how great I am; I've also seldom felt the urge to write crappy poetry and try to predict the exact stanza in which the reader will become bored and go off and make himself a cup of tea; and I've certainly never been gripped by any great desire to remove most of my clothing and allow George Foreman to use my ribcage as a snare drum. Nevertheless, the man that is Muhammad Ali has at certain times in my life occupied a disturbingly disproportionate portion of my thoughts. Which is why, just as the death of Lennon or Joplin or Morrison or Cobain or Diana undoubtedly meant so much to so many people, I cannot describe it as a particularly pleasant experience when I found myself attending the funeral of a friend.

%, %, %, %,

By now you should not be remotely surprised to learn that one fine evening back in 1980 on a night off from the waiting job I somehow conspired to find myself perched on a stool in front of a small television set in my local pub watching a delayed ITV transmission of Muhammad Ali's foolhardy attempt to win a fourth world title. Of course, it did not matter to me at the time that I had already learned the result of the fight in the newspapers and, were it not for the fact that I, like too many others, was what can only be described as bewitched by Ali's enormous charisma, it should have been no particular revelation to discover that The Greatest turned out to be just as mortal as the rest of us. Apparently, he was human after all: as capable of bleeding, of bruising, and of succumbing to the debilitating effects of Father Time as the man who had served me the beer that I was having great difficulty swallowing.

Naturally, the benefit of hindsight allows me to contemplate the dismemberment of the Ali legend with a sense of reluctant and undeserved smugness. One does not have to be a boxing expert in order to be able to look back at the circumstances surrounding this invidious spectacle and conclude that Ali had no possible chance of winning the fight. He was 38 by then and for the past couple of years newspaper picture editors had been taking an almost puerile delight in regularly demonstrating to their readers that the body beautiful was not what it used to be. Like those pictures of Elvis taken in the months leading up to his death, in which the bloated singer, with vacant George A. Romero stare, slouches on to stage wrapped in sequins and rolls of blubber, photographs of the new – enhanced – Ali were appearing in the tabloids on an almost weekly basis. There was New Ali sitting at the ring apron of some title fight or other, accompanied by a dwindling entourage and a stomach that could have belonged to a pregnant woman. There was

A KIND OF HOLD

New Ali at the dinner table, filling his cheeks with food in the way that Satchmo would once fill his own with air. It was clear that the Ali we were all familiar with was no more; the person who was once described as the most beautiful man in the world had mutated into something else. Ali had become Fat Ali, an apparition which, in another era, would perhaps not have been out of place being wheeled on to Chris Evans' *TFI Friday* ('My name's Barry from Dorchester and I'm a fat… Muhammad Ali!').

No longer forced to endure the endless torture of early morning runs, gym callisthenics and constant sparring sessions, in two years out of the ring Ali had developed rather too much of a liking for the burgers that he had taken to endorsing on television. In horticultural terms, he had gone to seed. However, unlike his former victim George Foreman, whose unexpectedly successful ring comeback in the late-1980s was, if we are to believe the boxer, fuelled by a mountain of Big Macs, it was apparent that Ali's extra weight would provide no additional advantages when the lure of the ring – as it inevitably would – became too much for his ego to bear.

This is not to say that Ali did not do a good job in extending his own rather extravagant interpretation of reality. Indeed, even the most qualified of observers –Ali's trainer Angelo Dundee among them – found themselves rubbing their eyes in wonderment when he began training for his doomed attempt to wrench the heavyweight title from his accomplished successor Larry Holmes. As the extra poundage was sweated away and the Fat Ali persona was exposed as an apparent impostor, fans and critics alike found themselves drawn inexorably into the dream. The rebirth of Ali may have been achieved, as we were to learn later, with the help of prescribed diet pills that left him dangerously dehydrated, not to mention the odd flask or two of black hair dye, but it seemed at the time as if the master conjuror had somehow managed to transform himself back into the beautiful, dazzling young athlete whose streamlined features had made his the most recognisable face on planet earth. By the time that he was ready to climb back into the ring and receive the hiding of a lifetime, Ali's weight was exactly as it had been when he had first fought Sonny Liston back in 1964. More than the 'rope-a-dope' in Zaire, more than the 'Ali Shuffle' or the 'Butterfly' punch that put down Liston in their second fight, this astonishing re-attainment of youth was the fighter's greatest feat of illusion.

Personally, I had no doubts at the time as to who would win the fight: even though I was not naïve enough to consider broadcasting my ill-conceived loyalties to the illusion, deep down I was sure that Ali would prevail. There was no logical reasoning behind this conclusion; it was not as though one could run an eye down the statistics for the fight and pinpoint any particular flaw in Holmes's not inconsiderable armoury. Although he was by no means The Greatest, Holmes was set to become one of history's more distinguished heavyweight champions. At 30 he was in his prime and, were it not for the fact that it was his misfortune to have been appointed the impossible task of filling the tasselled boots of the man who had once employed him as a sparring partner, Holmes would certainly have become one of the premier stars of the 1980s. Yet somehow it seemed to me that Ali would find a way to beat his protégé; it might take a miracle, but then Ali always seemed to have first refusal whenever anybody up there was doling out miracles.

Almost two decades on from that dreadful evening there are several memories that stubbornly refuse to fade. For any trivia fans out there I can inform you that the beer I was endeavouring to drink as the massacre ensued cost the princely sum of 37 new pence a pint. Similarly, I can divulge that a packet of 20 cigarettes was available at the bar for under 50p. Even more trainspotterrishly, I can reveal that the pub's solitary arcade machine was one of those table-top versions of Galaxians, featuring the usual collection of badly rendered sprites descending through a beer-clouded space and accompanied by an assortment of pings, whistles, fizzes and pops, at a cost to your pocket of ten new pence a game. If you are wondering why I appear determined to waddle in this paddling pool of consumerist nostalgia I need merely point out that Muhammad Ali, in payment for what was, admittedly, to be the worst night of his life, was collecting a fee of $8m. In modern day terms Ali's purse for the fight was in excess of $30m, a truly staggering amount of money for a portly middle-aged ex-champ whose talents had been in steady decline since the early 1970s.

Another reminder, for those of you out there who weren't around when Ali was busy putting us all under his spell, of just how enormous a name his was. Ali was the superstars' superstar: bigger, bolder, brasher, louder, prettier and better paid than any athlete or entertainer in history. (It is worth reflecting that almost 20 years on, Lennox Lewis, the British/Canadian WBC heavyweight champion who rightly qualifies as being one of the premier fighters in the world today, is at the time of writing due to receive a purse of only $5m for his heavyweight unification fight with Evander Holyfield, a contest which, as well as being the most important fight of Lewis's entire career, is also one of the most important fights of the whole of the 1990s).

The evening was also memorable in that it was the first occasion I can recall someone using the word 'fuck' during a televised primetime sporting event. At the beginning of round ten, as Muhammad Ali slumps into his stool and prepares to drag his heaving body back into the centre of the ring to be used as target practise by a saddened and visibly embarrassed Larry Holmes, the diminutive figure of Angelo Dundee could clearly be heard telling Drew 'Bundini' Brown, 'Fuck you! No! I'm stopping it!' as the other man implores Ali to resume participation in the beating that is placing the boxer's life in considerable jeopardy. It was also the first (and only) time that I can recall a television boxing commentator actually pleading for a fighter to hit the canvas, 'Come on Ali… Either throw a punch or go down! He really can't linger like this… It's quite pathetic!' cried the weary voice of Reg Gutteridge who, like the rest of us, was clearly not enjoying the spectacle of Ali's public execution.

Boxing completists will already be aware that the only stoppage defeat of Ali's long career was not, in fact, his last fight. The dubious honour of being the last man to defeat The Greatest belongs to Canada's Trevor Berbick, Commonwealth champion at the time but himself a future holder of the WBC heavyweight title (indeed, as well as Larry Holmes, it is Berbick who provides a precarious link between the Ali era and the Mike Tyson era, being in the opposite corner on that night in 1987 in which Tyson became boxing's youngest ever heavyweight champion). In real terms, however, the Holmes fight was the last hurrah. It was the final full stop at the end of the last sentence of the closing chapter of a story that had managed to both illuminate and transcend boxing.

At the risk of appearing overly sentimental, those images of Ali's public pain and humiliation were enough to send me scurrying into the toilets with tears welling up in my eyes. I was a skinny 18-year-old by then and to this day I cannot find any rational justification for my reaction. Although it was true that Ali had been around in both the background and foreground of much of my life, it has to be said that he was well down on the list of what I considered important at the time. He wasn't female, he didn't come in a glass and there were certainly no portraits of Queen Elizabeth II printed about his torso. However, in common with countless people in every corner of the globe, whatever special quality or combination of special qualities it was that Ali possessed was somehow able to touch some deeper part of me; a part of me which the usual mixture of instinct and social conditioning ensured was usually happily hidden away.

Before we descend too far into the realms of Beechy Colclough breakfast television psychology it is worth noting that the only other occasions that I have cried in adulthood were prompted by two considerably less compelling spectacles. If you really want to know, it is my sad duty to inform you that for some completely inexplicable reason I burst into tears during an episode of the TV mini-series *Rich Man Poor Man* when Tom Jordache, one of the main characters, played by a youthful Nick Nolte, was buried at sea after being gunned down by Falconetti's henchmen; I also found myself unable to stifle a sob during the funeral of Damon Grant, younger brother of Barry from the long-running Channel 4 soap *Brookside*!

Some 20 years after the horrors of Ali's final curtain call, the fighter still has a kind of hold over me that I cannot really explain. I am not alone in this, of course: even the most cynical and world-weary of those who follow, write about or indulge in the sport of boxing tend to come over all misty-eyed whenever Ali's name happens to crop up in conversation. Yet while it is certain that Ali as a twentieth century icon seems to exemplify the more positive and heroic aspects of boxing, there have been many fighters – some of whom I have known personally – who have completely failed to move me in circumstances which should have had even the most stony-faced of us reaching for the Kleenex.

Yet Ali was not without his flaws. The occasional unfor-givable cruelty that he bestowed upon his ring opponents is often buried away in the hyperbole surrounding his battles with the US government and his human rights campaigning. Moreover, not only did Ali sometimes appear to take pleasure in humiliating and, one might even argue, actually physically torturing opponents who were patently inferior athletes (his contests against Floyd Patterson and Ernie Terrell are particularly brutal examples of this spiteful and malicious aspect of Ali's personality) but the personal insults that he meted out to rival Joe Frazier were apparently sufficient to reduce the great heavyweight champion's children to tears.

Ali's ambiguous treatment of women also left much to be desired: during his infamous 1974 appearance on the BBC's *Parkinson* show, for example, the newly-recrowned heavyweight champion arranged for a group of Muslim women to sit out in the audience as an example of how the female form should be, in his words, 'properly dressed'. Clad in simple cotton gowns designed to hide the contours of the figure, and wearing head scarves that left only the hands and face exposed, these women were the focus for a startlingly incoherent lecture on Muslim ideology by a frenzied Muhammad Ali.

Not, one might say, entirely unexpected behaviour from a man who had attached himself so securely to the Muslim movement that he had been prepared to make the ultimate statement of reinvention and actually change his name. However, his actions take on an entirely different complexion when we realise that Ali, by then married to Belinda Boyd (having divorced his first wife, Sonji Roi, when she refused to discard her Western clothing in favour of her husband's preferred attire) was involved at the time in an extra-marital affair with the decidedly un-Muslimesque Veronica Porche (amazingly, while in the Philippines in 1975 for his third fight with Joe Frazier, Ali would actually introduce Veronica to president Ferdinand Marcos as his wife). Although Miss Porche would go on to become Ali's third wife, such extra-curricular canoodlings were in direct contravention of the guidelines set down by the Nation of Islam.

The breaking of rules, however, was a distinctive and important feature of the Muhammad Ali mystique. After all, are we not talking about the man who literally rewrote the boxing rulebook? Was Ali not the fighter who eschewed boxing's conventions and chose to dance around the ring with arms dangling and chin exposed rather than adopt the forward guard employed by tradition?

Similarly, was he not the self-styled poet whose charm and intelligence reduced us all to tears of laughter while simultaneously being classified 'not up to current standards' by the US draft board, after an aptitude test in 1966 which revealed Ali's IQ to be only 78.

It is for reasons such as these that we, perhaps, should not be surprised if Ali's interpretation of the doctrine of Elijah Muhammad was occasionally subject to a little surreptitious adjustment. Indeed, it would appear that Ali was actively encouraged to do so. The media coverage that was ensured by his involvement in the Muslim movement was apparently sufficient to enable its leaders to turn a blind eye to even the most fundamental of Ali's behavioural transgressions. The Muslim decree which expressly forbids one man to commit violence on another could, it appears, be conveniently overlooked when you had Ali as a frontman.

Yet despite everything, I– we – cannot stop loving him. I/we cannot help but shield our eyes in the radiant glow of the man's achievements. Ali may have been the man who proclaimed that the white man was the 'Devil' while surrounding himself with a coterie of pale-faced acolytes; he may also have been the pacifist who was prepared to sacrifice both career and personal liberty for a principle while continuing to earn a living in the most brutal and deadly of occupations; he may have been the womaniser who refused to view his women as equals; and he may have been the spokesman of a generation whose words were all too often not his own, but somehow none of these things seem to matter.

Except, of course, that they do.

The luxury of time has permitted me to conclude that in order to enjoy the vicarious friendship of Muhammad Ali you have to be prepared to compromise; you have to be able to turn away from his more baser indiscretions. In the end, you must come to realise that even one such as he, so perfect in so many respects, was not, in fact, perfect.

It's a similar predicament that one faces when one finds oneself in a situation in which a friend or work colleague suddenly comes out with a racist or sexist statement that appears totally at odds with the person you had imagined them to be. On such occasions you have to very quickly decide how you are going to react. There are, I believe, two basic alternatives: you can either do the right thing and tell the other person that you find their comments offensive and would they mind very much not repeating them again. Or you can do the more cowardly thing and pretend that you haven't heard them call a black man a 'nigger' or smile uncomfortably and attempt to change the subject. In my case – if I am honest – I can tell you that on those instances in which I have found myself in such a circumstance I have been known to offer both reactions –

I have been both righteous and a coward. Yet not forgetting more obvious considerations such as how much bigger and how much stronger the offending person is than you, the deciding factor in such an dilemma is usually not solely determined by whatever value you place on your moral being, it is more to do with how much you are prepared to put up with in order to remain in the company of the offending person.

In the case of Muhammad Ali I am willing and able to put up with everything that he is prepared to throw at me. If I was, for example, to pick up a newspaper tomorrow morning and discover that Ali is a mass murderer with a propensity for fucking teddy bears I doubt that the news would in any way dim my blind, dumb admiration for the man. He's inside me, I'm afraid. When I talk about him and I talk about his deeds, I'm talking about that little part of me I mentioned earlier. The one that is a subconscious contributor to Ali's many achievements. The little piece that is lodged under my flesh like shrapnel. And however much it itches and threatens to come to the surface, I know that it will never leave me.

Fourth Rule Of Boxing: Boxing Has No Respect For Its Icons

It is, of course, one of life's greatest ironies that the man who had done so much to transform the public perceptions of what boxing is all about should wind up becoming the sport's most damning indictment. I'm talking now about the third – and possibly final – incarnation of Muhammad Ali. An image that many of us feel an overwhelming urge to turn away from whenever the media chooses to confront us with it.

Even though most of you will already know the story of Ali's decline into ill health it is still worth repeating the facts, if only to remind ourselves, once again, of those occasions when even the most articulate of boxing's defenders find themselves utterly unable to justify the sport's inclusion in modern society.

According to Ali's official biographer, Thomas Hauser, the knowledge that the boxer's physical well-being was not what it should have been was an open secret almost a decade prior to his humiliation at the gloves of Larry Holmes. That he was permitted to resume his career in the aftermath of a medical examination by Dr Frank Howard of the Department of Neurology at the Mayo Clinic in Rochester, Minnesota, is nothing short of scandalous. Far from giving the boxer a clean bill of health, Dr Howard noted at the time, 'I saw Muhammad Ali for a neurological evaluation on 7-23-80. He was concerned about some comments that he might have brain damage, because following a filmed TV interview in London, it was commented that he staggered and that his speech was slurred. The patient attributes this to excessive fatigue from an all-night flight to London, and claims that he has always had some mild slurring of the speech for the past ten to 12 years... Other than the occasional tingling of hands in the morning when he awakens which clears promptly with movement of the hands, he denied any neurological symptoms. On neurological examination, he seems to have a mild ataxic dysarthria. The remainder of his examination is normal except that he does not quite hop with the agility that one might anticipate and on finger to nose testing there is a slight degree of missing the target.

'A CT scan of the head was performed and showed only a congenital variation in the form of a small cavum septum pellucidum ([a hole in the membrane separating ventricles that can be enlarged by concussive blows to the head]... On extensive psychometric testing, he showed a minimal decrease in memory that was more pronounced when he was fatigued but all other intellectual functions appeared to be intact.'

Yet we should not be at all surprised when boxing allows its finest asset to be fed as sacrificial lamb to the latest flame. That Ali, prior to his humiliation at the hands of Larry Holmes, had difficult touching his nose with his finger and was unable to even hop satisfactorily – let alone dance – is unimportant. Boxing, after all, has been treating its icons in this manner since its very beginnings.

Consider the case of Aaron Pryor, for example. Remembered for a pair of classic battles in the early 1980s with Alexis

Arguello, Pryor was already a hopeless cocaine addict when he retired in 1985. Coming back four years later when the money had inevitably run out, Pryor was controversially allowed to box on in certain American states with the unfortunate disadvantage of being blind in one eye.

Equally tragic is boxing's treatment of Wilfredo Benitez, the brilliantly precocious Puerto Rican who won the first of three world titles at different weights at the tender age of 17. By his mid-20s Benitez was a broke, physically sick has-been, back home with his parents living in squalor and earning the occasional $200 here and there so that mediocre fighters could have the privilege of seeing his famous name on their career records.

Finally, there is the lesson provided by Jerry Quarry: this former world heavyweight title challenger fought many of the top heavyweights of the 1970s, including the likes of Joe Frazier and Muhammad Ali. After being allowed to launch an ill-fated comeback in the early 1980s he is cared for these days by his family. Unable to function at the most basic physical level, Quarry cannot even comb his hair without assistance. The list, unfortunately, is endless.

This is not to suggest, however, that boxing's overlords do not attempt to prevent their sport's figureheads from destroying both reputation and legend by climbing into the ring to become somebody else's punch bag. Indeed, copious amounts of money, time and effort are annually expended in a genuine and ongoing attempt to make the sport safer. The establishment is, however, fighting a losing battle: it is, after all, pitting its wits against the very essence of boxing itself. And boxing, as has been proven on so many separate occasions, is never happier than when its heroes are exposing their mortality to the full mercy of the bitter elements.

5

The Ankle Tap

S TRICTLY speaking, it was not the first time I had been sacked. In fact, the person with the dubious distinction of having put an end to my debut appearance in the paid ranks was a one-legged local newsagent who went by the name of Mr Lomas. One winter's morning back in 1975 he had shown absolute ruthlessness when he handed me my cards as punishment for oversleeping and arriving two hours late for my paper round on my first morning in the job. 'Nobody got their papers, you daft bugger!' he had yelled as he bustled me out of his shop. 'They all went undelivered!' I was 13 at the time and, in truth, somewhat relieved to have managed to spare myself the inconvenience of rising at 6.30am every morning in order to spend several hours inserting copies of *The Sun* through people's letterboxes, in return for what amounted to a little more than a handful of loose change. This time, however, it was different.

I should have realised I was overstepping the mark when Smokin' Joe (not the boxer, but a 65-year-old wine waiter with nicotine stains on his lower lip, chronic lung cancer and a sonorous turn of phrase that could have earned him a living doing voice-overs for the Mr Kipling adverts) passed me in the corridor and offered me a response to a question that it had never been my intention to ask. 'You're a cheeky little cunt!' he angrily proclaimed with a disdainful shake of the head. Although I wouldn't have agreed at the time, I have to say now that old Joe probably had a bit of a point.

Despite my initial reluctance to commence supplementing my salary by illicit means, I had turned out to be something of a natural: in only a few short months I had risen from a position of raw novice to reach the very top of the thieving rankings table. It was a meteoric assent. A quickfire journey which allowed me to return home every night with a sackful of stolen booty that would have put the Maxwell dynasty to shame. In addition to a wallet overflowing with crisp portraits of Queen Elizabeth II, I had also been able to accrue an impressive collection of exotic alcoholic beverages – my bedroom was beginning to resemble the bar at the Copacabana.

I had been concealing that night's prize – a bottle of brandy – under my purple waiter's jacket when Smokin' Joe had spotted the tell-tale bulge and been inspired to deliver his damning assessment of my merits. He had probably been working at the Grand Hotel since before the Coronation and with the benefit of hindsight it is easy to understand his displeasure at my antics. Like the rest of his colleagues, Joe had been happily feathering his nest from the pockets of the upper classes for as long as he could recall. He was not impressed that I was taking more than my fair share and quite rightly recognised that my recklessness could very well put an end to his perks.

Up until then the hotel management had tended to turn a blind eye to the wine waiters' illegal practices. They were prepared to tolerate the odd missing bottle of wine as long as it didn't happen too often, and probably appreciated that some of their waiting staff needed these little extras in order to eke out even a semi-decent living. I, however, had other ideas. I had become a slave to opportunity; if there was anything liquid and in a bottle lying unattended in the hotel it would be in my pocket. If there was any possible chance of relieving an unsuspecting customer of a pound note I would grab it with both hands. It wasn't greed that compelled me to go that extra yard; in fact there was no single motivating factor to explain my transformation into Thatcherite Artful Dodger. In truth, like many of us who have found themselves taking home a few pencils or paper clips from the office, it didn't even occur to me that I was actually stealing. It was just something that I did.

In an attempt to redress the balance I must stress that these days I'm not in the habit of nicking booze and ripping off the blue-blooded. It helps, of course, that I'm no longer employed as a wine waiter, thus lessening the opportunity for me to indulge in those particular vices, but there are other reasons. In my current occupation the only objects that I'm likely to steal are other peoples' words. And frankly, Scarlet, I don't give a damn about that.

So they sacked me. One evening as I was leaving the hotel I was stopped by a uniformed security guard and led away into a back office. There, we were joined by Gerry the banqueting manager who, in conspiratorial tone, asked me to open the canvas haversack that I was carrying. It was obvious that somebody in the hotel had turned informer and taken it upon themselves to draw the management's attention to the bulging packages that I often had difficulty dragging out of the hotel. As the two men looked on I did as requested and, in a moment frozen in time, could scarcely withhold my glee as my inquisitors' mouths drooped open when they saw that the bag was empty.

No, I hadn't had a tip-off. For some reason something inside me that night had prevented my fingers from going about their usual business. Call it luck or call it sixth sense, whatever it was had somehow managed to dissuade me from pulling on the Lincoln Greens of Robin Hood. However, it was then that I did something totally inexplicable: instead of catching my breath and taking a moment or so to contemplate my lucky escape I decided to labour the point.

I stared back at my accusers and quickly moulded my features into what I considered to be a fairly reasonable impersonation of someone who has been mortally sinned against. Then I raised my teenage hackles and, in a display of petulance that eerily anticipated the David Beckham ankle tap that would one day put him out of the World Cup in disgrace, I demanded to see The Hotel Manager.

The significance of this request is not to be underestimated. Gaining an audience with The Hotel Manager of the Grand Hotel, although far less pleasurable, was about as probable as waking up on Blackpool Sands to find yourself being given the kiss of life by the entire cast of *Baywatch* (excluding David Hasselhoff). The Hotel Manager was an important man. Far too important to waste his time listening to a thieving-teenage-wine-waiter-intent-on-pushing-his-luck-after-narrowly-avoiding-being-caught-with-his-hand-in-the-till. Nevertheless, see him I did.

Gerry, the banqueting manager, stood behind me with hunched shoulders as I marched into The Hotel Manager's office and gave a performance worthy of Olivier in *Richard III* (I'm referring, of course, to Kevin Olivier in the lesser-known Orpington Town Hall autumn 1987 presentation of the Shakespeare classic). 'This is unacceptable behaviour!' I told with trembling lip the Grand Hotel's equivalent of J.R. Ewing. 'How dare your staff accuse me of stealing? Why, the very thought!' The man sitting before me gave a weary shake of his head and through clenched teeth mumbled a few words of apology. Then he shot a stony look at the other man and ushered me out of his office, assuring me that a similar incident would never happen again.

As we stood together in the lift I could sense that Gerry was so angry that it was all he could do to prevent himself from punching me. He knew that I knew that he knew that tonight's empty haversack had been an aberration. Moreover, I knew that he knew that I knew that in overplaying the role of innocent victim I had crossed the line between what was acceptable behaviour and what amounted to blatant insolence. We were both aware that it would probably be some time before I would be donning my purple waiter's suit again.

The sacking itself was a curiously muted affair. Instead, of doing what I had seen them do on TV or in the movies: i.e. issuing an angry ten-minute lecture and perhaps throwing a chair or two in the soon-to-be-unemployed employee's general direction, the banqueting manager merely gave a shrug of his shoulders and said, 'I don't think we'll be needing you for a while.'

For a few days I clung to the unlikely notion that his words were merely intended as a sort of slap on the wrist. After a short suspension, I imagined, I would receive a telephone call asking me to come back and resume twisting corkscrews, telling me all is forgiven – just don't be so bloody cheeky in future and for Christ's sake keep your thieving fingers to yourself! But the call never came. And I suppose, some 20 years after the night that I behaved like a complete prat, I might as well get used to the fact that it never will.

Nevertheless, I learned a valuable lesson from first experience of being sacked in the world of grown-ups. A lesson, it has to be said, that has held me in good stead ever since. I discovered that on those occasions when you've been accused of stealing at work and have been lucky enough to survive a search of your belongings because you didn't feel like stealing anything tonight, don't piss off your immediate boss by moaning about it to his immediate boss. It's a sure-fire way of losing your job.

The benefits of having a regular schoolboy income of several hundred pounds a week as opposed to having a regular schoolboy income of precisely nothing were also made clear to me within a surprisingly short period of time. Like the soap actor who decides to leave The Street and hit Hollywood, the sound of the telephone's ringing became almost deafening in its silence. Overnight, all the new friends who had flocked in my general direction when I was standing at the bar with bulging wallet seemed rather less enamoured of my magnetic personality. Unlike that aforementioned soap star, however, there was no pantomime circuit awaiting to allow me the opportunity to lick my ego. Even my mother, when I sheepishly broached the idea of her restoring the pound or so of pocket money that had been supplied to me in the days before my misadventures in the architectural and hotel industries, seemed understandably less than sympathetic to my plight. I had lost my title: I was no longer Prince of Thieves. My teenage hangers-on quickly found somebody else to hang-on to and my life turned full circle. From fighting the main event I was now back in the six-rounders.

It would be nice to able to reveal to you that this experience proved to be a pivotal moment in my life; of how, in the same way that the young Cassius Clay had laid the foundations of his legend after someone had stolen his bicycle, I was inspired to turn my first real taste of adversity into dazzling triumph. But the truth of the matter is a rather more mundane: I simply found another job. Once again I paid a visit to the local Job Centre and flicked through the cards and got the lady behind the desk to ring for an interview and went to the interview and got a job working in another drawing office.

My become-a-famous-artist scheme was turning out to be rather more difficult to achieve than I had imagined.

Fifth Rule Of Boxing: All Boxers Lose

As always there are exceptions. The already mentioned Rocky Marciano, for example, managed to make it through 49 fights without even a single blemish on his career record; while Britain's Terry Marsh was able to retire in 1987 as unbeaten IBF light-welterweight champion, having resisted the urge to lose on no less than 27 separate occasions (in fairness, it must be admitted that Marsh's record did include one draw). Nevertheless, it is an accepted fact that at one point in a boxer's career he is going to bump into someone who will give him an abject lesson in what it is like to come second. It's a pity really, I suppose. In a more ideal world – a fairer world – no boxer would ever lose. They could have a bit of a box, exchange a few jabs, cuddle for a while on the ropes and both men would be declared unanimous winners. Unfortunately, however, the world that such men choose to inhabit prefers a conclusion; programming directors at Sky would, after all, very quickly tire of things if every fight that they broadcast was a draw.

THE ANKLE TAP

Whereas once I would have half-believed such shenanigans, these days I can only shake my head and laugh at the antics of people like the current WBO featherweight champion Naseem Hamed. As he circumnavigates the globe telling anybody who will listen of his invincibility, I can only hope that buried away somewhere in the deepest recesses of his ego there is a part of that talented young millionaire which is aware that he is talking utter nonsense. All boxers lose – and, regrettably, it is only a matter of time before the self-styled Prince will have this truism bludgeoned into him.

Just as it was a lightly-regarded journeyman who shattered Mike Tyson's aura of invincibility, Naseem Hamed's eventual conqueror will probably hail from the most unexpected of quarters. Just as the great Mexican Julio Cesar Chavez found his march towards one hundred fights without loss halted in a routine defence against America's Frankie Randall, Naseem Hamed's hour of reckoning will come at the moment when he least expects it. And just as boxing legends such as Ali, Louis, Leonard, Robinson, Hagler and Hearns all had to prove that they had the ability to learn from their mistakes, so will Naseem Hamed one day be forced to realise that he is only flesh and blood.

In many ways, however, a loss can be the making of a boxer. Some maintain that truly 'great' boxers never really demonstrate their greatness until they have shown themselves able to lose. It is how they react to the loss that is important. Some fighters will instantly hit an irreversible decline, their ambitions dulled by their realisation of their own fallibility. Others will grow, returning to the scene of their previous disaster to face their conquerors and find a way to turn negative into positive. It is often said that a boxer never thinks that he is going to lose when he enters the ring, but even if this is merely evidence of trench mentality or a misguided sense of destiny, a boxer is always aware that in order to win, somebody else must lose. Boxers lose because it is in their nature to do so. They lose because the act of winning and the act of losing are mutually inclusive.

6

Middle-Aged Madness

We slip back in time slightly for a sad storyette:

It is the summer of 1976. The long, hot, scorching summer of 1976. It is the dawn of punk and the inauguration of an upsurge in safety pin sales totally unanticipated by market forces. As we sit swatting flies, rock legends Chicago, Pussycat and Dennis Roussos take turns perching cheerfully at the top of the music charts; but all the talk among those yet to buy their first razor is of the Sex Pistols: the snarling, spitting pop combo from north London shortly to be responsible for a whole generation of bad hair days. There is a wind of change in the air; the sense that something is happening, that something is spiralling out of control, the feeling that nothing will ever be the same again. And there is a man. A 36-year-old man who, for the purpose of this sorry tale, we will refer to as my father.

Even now, the only thing I have to say about that afternoon is: What could he have been thinking? Just what exactly was going through his head?! The more charitable among you might be prepared to put his peculiar behaviour down to some form of mid-life crisis but I'm not so sure. All I know is that with just one – albeit woefully – misjudged action my father managed to wipe away a sizeable portion of any respect that I held for him and become, from my 14-year-old perspective, quite possibly the least cool man on the planet.

And what was his crime?

I'll tell you what his crime was but first allow me to backtrack slightly and attempt to provide you with a brief pen picture of the person who committed this heinous violation of good taste. Bear with me for the odd paragraph or two and try to let me put you in the shoes of such a man:

Let's see… You're on the wrong side of 30. You have a wife and three kids. You have a mortgage, a second-hand car and a steady if not particularly well paid job at a local factory. You have a garage – an allotment even – and on weekends you usually go to the pub and meet up with the family to play cards. Very nice, some might say – nothing too unusual but very nice all the same.

Then one day you hear a noise on the radio. A noise that shocks you to your very core. At first it doesn't even sound like music because it is totally unlike any kind of music you have ever heard before. Screeching, anarchic guitars are wielded like machine guns against drab convention; the singer – if you can call him that – makes no attempt to sing but instead hurls himself at the microphone like some kind of demented daemon. Try as you might you cannot get this sound out of your head; it seems to follow you around wherever you go. Prodding you, nudging you, forcing you to remember a feeling buried deep in the pit of your memory.

Then you see pictures of the originators of this cacophony of chaos: underfed, anaemic teenagers dressed in mutilated clothing, spitting both defiance and warm phlegm in the direction of anyone who happens to wander by. And no matter how much you try to ignore these images they will not go away. Despite yourself, you find yourself being drawn towards whatever it is that is occurring. Finally, when you can bear it no more, you take a long, lingering look in the mirror at the person you have become and realise that it all could be slipping away from you. So what do you do? How do you react to the realisation that your youth is being eroded away by mediocrity and routine?

Well, what my father did – according to all available evidence – was to go for a total change of image. Something that would perhaps bring him more in line with what people were wearing at that pivotal moment in sociological history. Nothing too drastic, mind you. Nothing too OTT. Just enough to let everyone know that he had not yet achieved middle-age; that he could be as hip as the next man when he set his mind to it.

%% %% %% %%

It was Saturday afternoon. My sister and I were sitting in the living room watching TV when my father arrived bearing the package that contained the physical manifestation of an inner struggle that had obviously been going on for some time. 'I've got something to show you,' he breathlessly informed us.

Looking distinctly nervous, my father began to peel away the brown paper that covered this mysterious object. Whatever it was, I noted, it was oblong in shape.

In many ways it is a great pity that my father had chosen to keep to himself the details of whatever had caused him to take such a radical step. Surely if the punk revolution was having such an effect on his senses it would have been far better to share this torment with someone else – someone, say, like myself. For one thing (having read up on the subject) I would probably have been able to advise him on the most suitable locations for the insertion of safety pins; likewise, I may also have been able to offer my opinions as to the most effective means of making one's hair point northwards (soap, actually, not hairspray or gel). More importantly, however, with a little rumour-mongering the occasion of the unveiling of my father's new alter ego could quite possibly have evolved into a seminal family event – a *Wonder Years* moment, no less. A moment etched into celluloid time, such as the occasion in which that little American kid on the programme stole his first kiss, or when his dog died – a moment of extraordinary revelation to be accompanied by several paragraphs of schmaltzy, heartfelt self-awareness, delivered in an apple pie American accent: one of those rare episodes that can bind a family together.

Either that or it would have been even more buttock-clenchingly amusing.

The brown paper fell away and my father slowly began to open the box that he was hugging to his chest like a new-born puppy. What could it contain? What was inside the cardboard receptacle that held the key to the wardrobe of this unprecedented act of reinvention? Were we about to see my father discard the hosiery of establishment and step into the leathers and zips of the New Age? Would he soon be sporting a stud through his nose and a pair of bondage trousers? Just what had he bought?

The box fell open to reveal a pair of very large, very black, platform shoes.

My sister and I began to laugh as the expression on my father's face quickly moved from one of anxious anticipation to a grimace of confusion and, finally, to one of excruciating embarrassment. Then, as our eyes pleaded with him to put an end to this act of couturial suicide, he removed his normal shoes and stubbornly pushed his feet into their modernistic replacements.

These were no ordinary platform shoes. With eight-inch heels forged from the purest moulded plastic, they filled the room with their dreadful presence. It was as if someone had scraped away the silver from the shoes that Elton John had worn in *Tommy* and then sold them to my dad. Already a tall man, his head now brushed the ceiling as he tottered before us and waited for our reaction.

We laughed some more.

%. %. %. %.

Being today more or less the same age that my father was when he purchased his tribute to the Glitter Band, it is tempting to claim some form of empathy with his ill-conceived attempt at a makeover. But I simply cannot. Naturally, having myself evolved into someone who teenagers now refer to as 'middle-aged', I am not immune to the same sort of pangs, insecurities and gaping chasms in one's knowledge of youth culture that led my father up the path of insanity. However, even though I am nowadays often forced to lie through my teeth when anyone mentions a pop group that happens to be in the top ten, I still cling to the conviction that, if and when my hormones demand that I make such a transformation, I would likely make a better attempt at becoming someone else than my father did. I would not, for instance, replace my current attire with the tartan kilts and crimson lip gloss of Steve Strange and his band of New Romantics from the early 1980s. Nor, for that matter, would I grow what remains of my hair and slip my portly frame into the tight jeans and willowy blouses of Deep Purple circa 1973. I am more sensible than that. At least I hope I am.

Actually, in the end he turned out to be more sensible than that. In fact, the attachment between those shoes and my father was over before the wedding vows had even been spoken. The sum total of their relationship was confined to that Saturday afternoon and that room – and our mocking laughter. Those shoes very quickly took on the status of a one-night stand: stealthily discarded and given rented accommodation among the mothballs and copies of *Reader's Digest* at the bottom of the wardrobe. He wore them once and only once.

There is, unfortunately, an aftermath to this brief meander down memory's back alley. Perhaps even a lesson to be learned somewhere along the way. It's what can happen when the sentimental among us allow our misguided perceptions of what constitutes fair play to take precedence over less ethereal qualities such as good sense and reality. It's the reward I got for attempting to soften the blow by making it known to my father that those shoes, after all, weren't as bad as our laughter that day had implied. My intention had been borne of genuine feelings of sympathy concerning his predicament; my desire had been only to make him feel a little better about himself, to restore some of the self-confidence that he had lost as a result of his aborted stylistic metamorphosis. It was the wrong thing to do.

Never being less than a thrifty sort of person, my father took my words of encouragement to be some kind of hidden signal. Extraordinarily, he somehow managed to reach the conclusion that I, in fact, had suddenly and mysteriously developed an overpowering urge for those shoes to become part of my personal property. So he gave them to me!

The actual exchange of goods was presented to me as a fait accompli; being a constituent of a household in which the less senior members rarely possessed more than one pair of shoes (and one pair of plimsolls or daps as they are known in Bristol, pumps in Burnley), which were replaced only when they were worn out, my father waited until my current pair were literally on their last legs before furnishing me with the items of footwear that would soon become my life's greatest burden. Thus in one easy movement that was both cunning, cost-effective and seamless in its execution, my father hoisted the remnants of his afternoon of middle-aged madness on to my shoulders. Or rather, he provided the shoes for me to step into. Instead of reinventing himself, he reinvented me.

So I spent the summer of 1976 a pimple-faced relic from a bygone age. The prisoner of a pair of shoes that proved an instant conversation stopper wherever I hobbled. Eight-inch heels that steadfastly refused to succumb to my numerous attempts to destroy them on the way home from school so that they would have to be replaced. A chick magnet whose poles had been irrevocably reversed. Unscuffable, unburnable and with an apparently unlimited lifespan, those shoes enabled me to experience the summer of punk from a vantage point many metres above my contemporaries.

Sixth Rule Of Boxing: Boxers Very Seldom Know Who They Are

Like rather more muscular distant cousins of Noel Edmunds, professional boxers are curiously immune to the changing tides of fashion. This is not say that they are prone to wandering around with beards or fluffy jumpers capable of inducing epileptic seizures, it's simply that, in common with their illustrious relative, they seem to have happily settled upon an image that carefully side-steps any of the stylistic conventions of modern society. Impervious to developing trends, steadfastly refusing to corrupt their self-imposed image with any of the condiments of culture, boxers have been successfully erecting their own particular kind of time capsule since the days of Jim Corbett. Indeed, if one were to photograph almost any modern boxer at random and add a touch of sepia to the development process, it is likely that he would not look out of place in any era. Mike Tyson? Put him in black and white and he could easily be presented as Marciano's next opponent. Nigel Benn? Throw away the Kodachrome and it would not be difficult to imagine him exchanging blows with Emile Griffith back in the 1960s. Joe Bugner? Remove the boxing gloves and it would take no great leap of the imagination to picture him comparing girths with John L. Sullivan.

There are, of course, many good reasons why boxers tend to look like they do. The close-cropped hair that they often favour is, for instance, an obvious functional device; it being far easier to avoid being punched in the face without the constant need to sweep a floppy fringe away from the eyes. Likewise, the sculpted frame that the majority of boxers are apt to carry is an obvious requirement of their trade in much the same way that an inflated belly is an expected attribute of a professional darts player. In the defence of prize fighters it would, however, be prudent to concede that there is only so much that can be done with the standard uniform: a gum shield, a couple of rolls of bandages, a pair of gloves, a pair of shorts, a jock strap, some socks and a pair of boots offer limited scope for experimentation.

There have, nevertheless, been countless attempts by boxers to add a touch of glamour to their apparel. Muhammad Ali, for instance, hung a pair of swinging tassels from the tops of his socks in his quest for individuality; similarly, the great 'Sugar' Ray Robinson often allied his dazzling ring skills with a pair of sparkling sequinned shorts. In more recent times we even have seen the likes of Jorgé Paez and Hector Camacho enter the ring dressed in a bizarre variety of leopard skin skirt or Roman gladiatorial costume. While America's Roy Jones opts to wear a dressing gown that resembles a dinner suit with matching bow tie, which is theatrically removed at the appropriate moment. Once the bell sounds, however, such trimmings quickly become forgotten as a boxer's priorities inevitably shift away from sartorial matters.

This is not to suggest that your average boxer is not capable of holding his own with the fashion-conscious when he is absent from the ring environment. Indeed, the garish manner in which boxers often choose to dress when they are in public is more than just a combination of social ineptitude and an apparent attempt to compensate for the Spartan nature of their working attire. Yet perhaps the real reason that professional boxers demonstrate such indifference to their appearance is because their minds are usually elsewhere; indeed, they are far too busy rearranging the contents of their skulls to be overly concerned with the external.

Over the course of a fighter's career he will become many different people: with each and every fight will come the opportunity for reinvention; the chance to reject the person he was just the day before yesterday, to redefine priorities and re-adjust attitudes to life. The arrogant braggart that is often characteristic of a boxer's early years will, for example, quickly give way to a more reflective and melancholic demeanour if the fighter in question has been unfortunate enough to suffer a defeat. Likewise, the quiet boxer with the mediocre record who scores an upset victory over a top line fighter will magically transform himself into an arrogant world beater, insisting that he has been telling us all along of his greatness.

A boxer's identity, however, is governed by more than simply winning or losing. It is not for nothing that he will often refer to himself in the third person at the conclusion of a fight; when he does this he is not referring to the team of cuts men, trainers and spit bucket carriers that share his corner, he is alluding to a mythical 'other' person. This 'other' person is a multi-layered creature, capable of sweeping personality changes, wildly inconsistent opinions and bewildering switches of allegiance. When a boxer loses he will often lay the blame for his defeat on this psychological doppelgänger; when he wins he will often contend that it is because he has somehow managed to tame his alter-ego – to hold this imaginary being in check.

Boxers change their personalities with the same frequency that most of us like to change our shirts. Sometimes – as in the case of George Foreman – they will turn from killer into cuddly toy. On other occasions – as in the case of 'Sugar' Ray Leonard – they will turn from idol to anti-hero. Boxers reinvent themselves in an effort to scale a peak that is constantly moving away from them. They become somebody else because to remain the same person is to accept responsibility for their own success or failure. For this reason, although one fighter may look very much like another, when you talk to him you can never be entirely sure who it is you are talking to; because boxers, like pop stars, politicians and schizophrenics, very seldom know who they are.

7

Naked Ambitions

AS it turned out my father had been right all along – it was where they splashed paint all over the walls and went to orgies. At least that's how it appeared to me when a middle-aged man with a beard led us all into a room with a high ceiling and told us to take a good look at her. It was my first day at art college. My first afternoon. The year was 1981, the location the rather grandly named Bath Academy of Art and I was about to catch my first glimpse of a completely naked woman.

Okay. I'm going to try and be honest with you for the next five or ten minutes. Even though a fairly large chunk of my ego would enjoy regaling you with stories of my precocious sexual adventures, and even though another fairly large chunk of my ego is aware that there are probably going to be people who know me reading this paragraph, I'm going to resist the urge to falsify records and instead attempt to come clean. I do this with confidence partially bolstered by the memory of countless drunken confessions from both friends and non-friends, and in the knowledge that when compelled to talk about the first time that they 'did it' with a girl, all men are liars.

The naked woman in question's name was Linda. She was in her early 20s with long black hair and the face of a young Kate Bush. She emerged from behind a screen wearing a floral patterned dressing gown and strolled confidently into the centre of the room. There were about 30 of us looking on: a rough mix of young women and young men from a broad range of backgrounds but all with a similar set of aspirations. Future Damien Hirsts, future Vivienne Westoods, future David Hockneys, future Tony Harts. Linda's eyes sought out the man with the beard and he nodded to her as if transmitting a prearranged signal. Then she loosened her gown and let it fall to the floor.

'Take a good look at her,' proclaimed Mr Beardy. 'Form a circle and walk around her. Look at her breasts, look at her buttocks, look at the colour of her flesh. Smell her... Sense her. Take in her very essence.'

For anyone out there who has never been compelled to sit in front of a naked woman and attempt to draw her, I feel it is my duty to report that this activity is not quite so appealing as it might first appear. Despite the fact that the majority of heterosexual men spend inordinate portions of their lives attempting to reduce women to such a state of undress, when you are holding, as it were, a pencil in your hand all established behavioural practices corresponding to what a man is supposed to do in the presence of a naked woman have to be very quickly redrawn. For one thing, the overwhelming urge in such a situation is to not look at the person you are supposed to be drawing. An obvious disadvantage for a budding famous artist, which may go some way to explaining why the vast majority of people I have shared a life drawing class with seem to end up with a drawing that bears scant resemblance to the naked human being posing in front of them. Of more importance, however, is the fact that no matter how much one attempts to dress up the artistic and moral ethics of the relationship between artist and model, their interaction is inevitably sexual in nature.

Speaking purely for the male fraternity, this is not to say that a trip to the life drawing class will automatically summon up a raging erection of John Holmesian proportions. Quite the contrary, in fact. Indeed, the majority of life models are either,

a) skinny blokes with long stringy hair (all down their back, as they say, not on their head), or b) middle-aged housewives in the throes of a deeply submerged mid-life crisis that appears to be resolving itself by compelling the sufferer to tear off all her clothes and allow a roomful of strangers to peer into the deepest crevices of her rolling flesh. By definition such people have usually long since given up any hope of becoming a gladiator and seem content in providing a cautionary lesson to us all in the debilitating effects of both time and a high cholesterol diet. Their unadorned body language cries out to you: Take a good look at me because this is you in ten or 15 years. Personally, I have lost count of the number of occasions that I have set up an easel and readied myself to go to work only to find myself confronted with an apparition that is eight parts Hattie Jacques and two parts Mandy Dingle. Not that I'm sizeist. At least, I'd like to think I'm not. It's just that when you've been secretly preparing yourself to spend the next hour or so running your pencil around the lithe contours of Elle McPherson, it's always something of a disappointment when Mrs Bridges from *Upstairs Downstairs* steps out on to the podium. Very few life models, it has to be said, ever look anything like Linda did that day.

I was 19 when the bearded man decided to show me what Linda looked like without any underwear, and no matter how much I attempted to cleanse my mind of inappropriate thoughts, no matter how many random images of fried eggs... of dog turds... of Amy Turtle... that I attempted to conjure up as hormonal anaesthetic, I could not seem to escape the fact that I was standing next to a girl with no underwear on. In terms of past sexual encounters, you have to understand, total nudity was something of a quantum leap for me. I may have had a few girlfriends by then, and I may from time to time have found myself overwhelmed by that strange condition we've all suffered from which seems to transfer all responsibility for your actions into your fingertips, but total nudity had conspired to be completely out of bounds for me. If you wanted total nudity the closest you could get to it was if you watched a French movie or sat through an episode of *I, Caligula* or something. This, thankfully, was a predicament that I appeared to share with a substantial proportion of the male inhabitants of that room, who, like me, shuffled uncomfortably around Linda with eyes screwed firmly to the floor.

Of course, now that I'm older, allegedly wiser and have in the past spent far too many long hours sketching the nipples of a varied assortment of strangers, it is tempting to proclaim the image of the virgin teenager and his encounter with the voluptuous model as just another of life's many rites of passage. Indeed, I can honesty tell you that with time the curious ritual of nameless woman presenting me with her nameless sexual organs eventually became almost routine. Honestly, but not quite honestly. For in truth, like many men I have talked to who have shared this experience, it was a situation that I was never entirely comfortable with.

We can all draw some solace from the understanding that even the most famous of famous artists seem to have encountered similar feelings of discontent. This can be demonstrated by the fact a surprisingly large percentage of famous artists evidently found it impossible to concentrate on their brushwork in the face of all that bare flesh. Which is possibly why people such as Picasso, Modigliani, Gauguin, van Gogh, Schiele, Klimt and Renoir, to name but a few, all ended up bedding their models on a daily basis.

Of course, the more worthy among us will stress that the act of picking up a pencil or paint brush and using it to draw or paint a naked woman sitting in front of you is entirely devoid of any sexual implications. They will talk about form and space and perspective and light and shade; and they will be appalled at the suggestion that one of the art world's finest and longest-established traditions could possibly possess any more sexual tension than a visit to Dot Cotton's laundrette. But in my experience these people are usually running the life drawing classes; and too many of them seem to pay far too much attention to the chalk lines that they trace around the model's body when it is time for her to take a break.

※ ※ ※ ※

Although I am still unable to understand exactly what point Mr Beardy was trying to make that afternoon, in many ways a naked woman seemed just reward for all the effort, hard work – and lies – that it had been necessary for me to produce in order to edge my way through the back door of an actual art college. And if looking at naked women was part of what it took for my become-a-famous-artist master plan to succeed, it was something I was certainly prepared to put up with.

My decision to apply for the foundation course at the art college in Bath had been based on one important feature: in contrast to practically every other art institution in the country, Bath was the only place which insisted that potential students undertake a traditional drawing test as part of the admission procedure. Elsewhere, the ability to actually draw had long since been deemed a redundant characteristic by those whose job it was to choose who was going to be the next David Hockney. The art college in Bath, however, clung stubbornly to tradition; perhaps it was because the college was situated within a pair of beautiful five-storey Georgian town houses that had been converted into one building. Or perhaps it was because the whole city of Bath was literally oozing with yellow sand-stoned history; whatever the reason, the art college governors were keen to ensure that any student entering their building had a reasonable idea of how to sharpen a pencil.

On the face of it, taking a drawing test suited my purposes almost perfectly. This was not because, like the young Mike Tyson I mentioned earlier, I was finally beginning to believe my own publicity – indeed, the prospect of taking such a test filled me with fear and dread – it was just that putting myself through that harrowing procedure represented the only real chance I had of becoming a famous artist.

My summer in the purple polyester suit may have been financially lucrative but it had been at the expense of my long-term ambitions. Instead of taking drawing classes I had been too concerned with taking money out of the wallets of the rich. Instead of assembling the bulging portfolio of sketches and paintings that was a fundamental requirement of the art college interview procedure I had been too busy assembling my private collection of exotic alcoholic beverages. And instead of getting myself the A Level I had been told was essential to my quest for famous artistdom, I had gained myself a well-deserved 'F'.

I took the drawing test one morning in June. Getting the coach to Bath from Bristol, I arrived at the college and was handed an apple, a mirror, some pieces of paper and a pencil. I sat down at a desk, drew the apple, sketched a self-portrait, ate the apple and then committed perjury by telling my interview panel that I had passed my A Level in art, and that the reason I had not brought a portfolio with me because I had lost it on a train to Leeds (please don't ask me why I chose, of all places, Leeds, as the setting for this particular untruth). Then I was asked who my artistic influences were by another man with a beard. I mumbled something about Cezanne and was given a sheet of lined paper and a biro and instructed to write a short essay about one of the many wild explosions of colour that were hanging framed on the wall opposite my chair. I believe it may have gone something like this, 'This painting displays the obvious influence of Matisse in his Fauvist period. Its violent use of colour and dangerous compositional elements confront the viewer with a dazzling melange of bollocks. Breathtaking diagonals and sparkling bullshit combine to make bollocks. Bollocks... Bullshit... Bollocks.'

At least that's what I think it might have said.

A few weeks later I got a letter from the college telling me that they liked the drawing of the apple and the page of pretentious mumbo-jumbo I had presented to them – would I like to come and spend a year or so doing some more? With drugs, orgies and paint splashing beckoning I quickly left home and looked forward to phase two of Operation Famous Artist.

※ ※ ※ ※

As well as taking a wide-eyed look at my first fully undressed woman, several other things happened to me within a very short time of my embarking upon my new career in Bath as a fully-fledged apprentice famous artist. First of all, I began smoking roll-ups: painfully thin cylinders of tobacco that never quite managed to stay alight for more than a few seconds and would often lose you the skin on your lower lip. I decided to start doing this because I had noticed several of the other students smoking painfully thin roll-ups in the college refectory and it looked like the sort of thing that art students ought to be doing. Secondly (also for the same reason), I began wearing baggy woollen jumpers and severe looking black jackets that I procured for myself at the local Oxfam. Thirdly, and more significantly, I threw away a good portion of my record collection.

Even though a similar act of peculiar cultural reinvention has recently been discussed at length in Giles Smith's excellent paean to the pimpled generation, *Lost in Music*, I feel obliged to provide you with a few brief facts relating to my decision to dump some of the music that I had grown up with and up until very recently had quite enjoyed listening to. Among those titles that bit the dust was my entire Queen collection (starting with *Queen 1* and ending with *Jazz*); *Out of the Blue* by ELO, as well as a three-record box set of their early albums that had been given to me as a birthday present; several Beatles albums including *The White Album* and *Sgt Pepper*; *Who Do We Think We Are*, *Stargazer* and *Deep Purple in Rock*; *Grave New World* by the Strawbs; and *Love Gun* by Kiss. All of these records were surreptitiously placed inside carrier bags so that nobody could see that I was throwing them away and deposited at the bottom of the dustbin prior to my leaving home for college in Bath.

I sometimes wonder about the reaction of the dustman who may have discovered this bundle of musical faux pas – was he by some divine coincidence a Queen, ELO, Kiss, Deep Purple and Strawbs fan who for some reason hadn't got around to purchasing any of the aforementioned items and therefore able to whoop with delight at his unexpected good fortune? Or did he display the contents of those carrier bags to his colleagues in disgust, taking careful note of the street number of the house from which they had originated for the purpose of future blackmail letters?

What remained was, I thought, a fairly good estimation of what art students circa 1981 were supposed to be listening to in between smoking painfully thin roll-ups and painting their latest masterpieces. Surviving album titles, in no particular order, included: *The Scream* by Siouxsie and the Banshees; *Unknown Pleasures* and *Closer* by Joy Division; *London Calling* and *Sandinista!* by The Clash; *Gentlemen Take Polaroids* by Japan; and *Orchestral Manoeuvres in the Dark* by Orchestral Manoeuvres in the Dark, an album considered cool at the time by virtue of its cut-out grid cover design by Pete Saville. Gloomy stuff.

The motivation for this cruel culling was, I think, obvious. Quite frankly, there was simply no way that I was going to let any of my new art school chums poke their way through my record collection and discover that I still owned a copy of *The Black Eyed Boy* by Paper Lace or *January* by Pilot. Thus, even though I was aware that I was about to become a member of an institution that both encouraged and demanded originality from its adherents, I was just not prepared to be that original.

Also out of the window, I'm afraid to say, went boxing, which, among my new peers was considered as socially acceptable as owning a signed copy of *Combine Harvester* by the Wurzels. Actually, my decision to disown boxing was not solely based on social acceptability. For one thing (although I know for a fact that this suggestion will have boxing aficionados ringing their hands together in protest) British boxing was going through something of a fallow period at the time. Although there were a few homegrown fighters of genuine merit around in the early 1980s such as Maurice Hope, Mark Kaylor, Herol Graham and Colin Jones, in general the quality of boxer plying his trade in this county left rather a lot to be desired.

Who, save for the most committed of boxing anorak will remember, for example, Gordon Ferris's titanic struggle with Billy Aird for the British heavyweight crown in March 1981? Similarly, does anyone out there really feel a warm glow coming over them when we recall British middleweight champion Roy Gumbs's trio of title defences against the likes of Eddie Burke, Glen McEwan and Howard Mills? Not me for sure.

Another reason that I waved a temporary farewell to boxing was because I didn't have a TV. Having obtained a legal separation from the large colour television set in my parents' living room, it was now impossible to watch any boxing that may have been broadcast even if I had wanted to. Of more importance, however, was the fact that my evenings were no longer my own. For in addition to spending my days smoking painfully thin roll-ups and painting masterpieces, I would now be spending my nights working behind the counter of the local Kentucky Fried Chicken.

Boxing, however, was already working on a plan to counter this.

※ ※ ※ ※

Sad fact: when I was a youth one of my most eagerly anticipated occasional treats was to be supplied with two pieces of Kentucky Fried Chicken and chips by my parents after they had been for a night out. This didn't happen all the time, mind you; it was most likely to occur on the first Saturday of the month when my father was still flush from having just collected his paycheque. Tragic as it might appear, those sleek crimson boxes, embossed with an image of a smiling Colonel Sanders, remain one of my happiest childhood memories. With their natty little sachets of salt and pepper, snazzy plastic forks and lemon scented clean-up wipes, these streamlined works of culinary free association were many light years away from what the great British take-away buying public were used to. In terms of presentation, the Colonel's little box of tricks rated a Torville and Dean-esque maximum 6.0 when compared to the

4.8 given to the soggy newsprint that was traditionally used to wrap our fish and chips in this country.

In my defence, however, I seem to remember that I was not alone in my appreciation of one of the first American franchises to invade our culture. Indeed, one of my closest friends at school was such a devotee of the Colonel that he would often save up several weeks' worth of pocket money so that he could enjoy the privilege of cycling down the Gloucester Road in Bristol and purchasing his very own Colonel's Special. Such enthusiasm seems odd now but among the people I hung around back in the days before Kentucky Fried Chicken became KFC, the concept of fast food was so new as to be almost revolutionary.

However, whatever fond memories I may have held for those bygone suppers quickly evaporated away into a sea of sweat and grease when I discarded my baggy blue sweater and severe looking black jackets in favour of the more colourful red-and-white-striped pinnies that were the standard attire of anyone unfortunate enough to be in the Colonel's employ. And if I was feeling cool and self-satisfied because I had finally managed to wheedle myself a place at art college, this attitude was quickly put into perspective whenever any of fellow art student's happened to call in for a Colonel's Special and found me wearing a paper hat which bore the legend 'It's finger lickin' good!'

Of course, it was purely a question of economics that precipitated the creation of my late night alter-ego. For various reasons my local council had decided that I was ineligible for a student grant; nothing unusual in itself but nevertheless a potentially catastrophic position for me to find myself in. In simple terms, I needed to earn some money and, as the only real qualifications I had at the time involved counting bricks and serving drinks, I chose a job that was vaguely related to the latter talent. Thus, by day I was a young Picasso, sucking on pencil-thin roll-ups and squirting oil paint on to pieces of sized cloth before having deep and meaningful conversations on the merits of these incoherent squiggles, and by night I was serving pieces of dead chicken coated in the Colonel's Special Recipe to boozed-up punters.

This, I am afraid, is why you will rarely find me queuing at the local KFC these days. It's also the reason why, whenever I think of the former British welterweight champion Dave 'Boy' Green, I am invariably overpowered by a long-forgotten aroma of congealed fat that instantly transports me back in time and finds me standing behind a red counter wearing a stripy apron and that fucking awful paper hat.

By accident or otherwise, it turned out that the manager of the Kentucky – who was called Po and hailed from Thailand – was also a boxing fanatic. As well as being an expert kick-boxer (a useful deterrent on those all too numerous occasions when customers would take one look at him and attempt to demonstrate their over-developed sense of humour by ordering 'thlee plieces of Kentucky flied chicken and ships') Po's knowledge of the fight game was almost encyclopaedic. For this reason, while my fellow paint splashers remained blissfully unaware of my peculiar and unfashionable penchant for watching people punch each other in the face, I was secretly able to follow the latter part of the career of Dave 'Boy' Green, otherwise known as the 'Fen Tiger', on the radio, up to my elbows in flour and herbs and filth, with the diminutive figure of Po cheering wildly by my side in fluent Thai.

I suppose it would be wrong of me to expect all but the most passionate boxing fan to have anything more than even the dimmest recollection of Green. For your information, Green was a light-welterweight – later a welterweight – from Chatteris, near Peterborough, who also happened to be one of the clumsiest boxers that I have ever seen attempt to throw a punch. He did not so much box as batter his opponents into submission, using a combination of fists, elbows and forehead to make whatever point it was he was trying to make. When his fights were televised, Green – who, by coincidence was another of those boxers whose home-made portrait had adorned the walls of my bedroom as a teenager – left observers in little doubt that what they were witnessing on screen was more than a just sporting contest. His actions, his movements and the look on his face seemed to belong to a man who was willing to die rather than risk defeat. However, while his fights were far from pretty they were compelling occasions – even on the radio.

Of course, by this time Green's days as a boxer were well and truly numbered: a year earlier he had travelled to America to fight the brilliant 'Sugar' Ray Leonard and had been totally outclassed before being poleaxed in round four by an uppercut that could have knocked out a buffalo. But that did not seem to matter to the part of my personality that was itching to escape from the artistic facade that I had erected around myself. Nor did it seem to matter to Po, who, with fists flailing, was usually more concerned with providing a frantic physical enactment of what he was hearing on the radio to be bothered with insignificant details such as whether or not the boxer he was allegedly supporting was actually winning the fight. When Po listened to fighters on the radio he was back in Thailand as a boy; either that or he was in the ring himself throwing his own punches at his own opponents. And he was happy. So, for that matter, was I: for as long as I was standing next to somebody who shared even a limited understanding of the ties that bound me to boxing, the Colonel and his Special Recipe seemed many miles away.

Seventh Rule Of Boxing: Inside Every Boxer Is A Fat Man

Inside every superbly conditioned, heavily muscled, beautifully sculpted professional boxer there is a fat man waiting patiently to escape. This, for those of us who stand on the scales each morning and wonder where it all went wrong, is one of boxing's more palatable ironies, and another reminder that what happens between the ropes is so often an illusion.

Although this number is subject to change, modern boxing has a total of thirteen established weight divisions. These range from the heavyweight division, in which there is no limit to a fighter's mass; to middleweight – with a weight limit of 160lb, traditionally considered the sport's most compelling division; down to flyweight, which insists that its competitors weigh no more than 112lb. Interestingly, there have been attempts to institute further weight categories below the flyweight limit: these include strawweight and paperweight, divisions which come and go according to the somewhat limited availability of fighters possessing the physical characteristics of an 11-year-old.

Boxers usually compete at a poundage that is well below their normal 'walk around' weight. To achieve this weight loss, many are forced to commit themselves to what amounts to a starvation diet. In the days leading up to a fight, some will have no option but to exist on minimal rations. Britain's four-time world champion Duke McKenzie, for instance, admitted to living only on water and biscuits in order to make the 108lb limit when he was campaigning at flyweight during the 1980s; while South Korean light-flyweight great Jung-Koo Chang allegedly trained for his fights on a liquid diet dressed in a plastic sweat suit in order to force his body to perspire at an accelerated rate.

The ability to lose weight is every bit as important an attribute in a boxer's personal armoury as his capacity to give and accept a punch. A boxer who possesses sufficient self control, or is blessed with a natural predisposition for not gaining weight, will be at a distinct advantage to an opponent who struggles to fight off the pounds. He will be stronger, faster and have greater powers of endurance; he will also have the confidence of knowing that he has entered the ring at the peak of his ability.

Often, it is only a defeat that will persuade a boxer to try his luck in a higher weight division. Even though he may have been putting his health at risk in a futile attempt to outsmart Mother Nature, it is not until he meets an opponent who is able to exploit the battle he has been having with the scales that a fighter will finally admit defeat. He has, however, good reason to be wary of moving up in weight, for now he will be fighting people who are naturally bigger and stronger than he is; fighters who stand taller and punch harder than the people he has grown accustomed to.

Truly great fighters have shown the ability to remain outstanding while boxing in more than one weight category. 'Sugar' Ray Robinson, for example, was not only the welterweight division's finest practitioner, but was also one of the premium middleweights of the modern era (Robinson even made a valiant attempt to gain the light-heavyweight title before succumbing to exhaustion and dehydration). His namesake, 'Sugar' Ray Leonard, managed to be several stages better than his illustrious predecessor: in a career full of false retirements and fleeting comebacks, Leonard won world titles at welterweight, light-middleweight, middleweight, super-middleweight and light-heavyweight. Leonard's great rival Thomas Hearns, now in his 40s and still fighting, is also the possessor of five championship belts in separate weight divisions; currently operating at cruiserweight, and almost 50lb heavier than in his heyday, Hearns is chasing another title shot that could make him the most decorated boxer in history.

When a boxer finishes his career, his body will often exact a harsh revenge for all the years of self-denial. It is not just Muhammad Ali who has been forced to suffer the ridicule of the press because of an over enthusiastic appetite: distinguished fellow bingers include the likes of George Foreman; Larry Holmes; James Toney; Michael Moorer; Roberto Duran, Buster Mathis Senior and Junior, Tony Tubbs and Tim Witherspoon to give you but the tip of the ice cream. All of these boxers have fought at the highest level and all have been able to demonstrate that, at the dinner table their bellies have as equal a propensity for over inflation as their egos.

Sometimes the difference in appearance between a boxer and his later incarnation can be startling. Often – as in the example of James 'Buster' Douglas, who, after losing his heavyweight title to Evander Holyfield added more than 60lb to his body weight – a retired boxer will bear no resemblance whatsoever to his former self. This is all part of the mirage that boxing erects around itself, and a physical demonstration that what goes on inside the ring is but a fleeting glimpse of a world that is in constant flux. For this reason, should you ever feel the desire to watch boxers ply their trade, be aware that what you are seeing is only temporary. Those superbly conditioned, heavily muscled, beautifully sculpted bodies that I mentioned earlier are all part of the lie; for you can be sure that one day their owners will look just as old and just as withered and just as fat as you or I.

8

The greatest loss

SOMETIMES I forget it's there. In fact, as time goes by I find myself almost believing the words of people like my mother, who once told me that it would mean nothing to me when I got older. But then something will happen to remind me of it: someone in the office will suddenly stutter in mid-conversation and I will find their eyes covertly creeping up my forehead in that familiar way; someone in the pub will present me with a childish and usually completely unsolicited reminder of my condition; someone in the street will nudge their companion as I wander by.

It was a lovely summer's day and I was in my third term at the art college when I first noticed that something was not quite right. Even now I can remember that day with almost supernatural clarity. I was soaking in the bath at the time, using, of all things, Head and Shoulders to wash my hair. And then some of it fell out.

It wasn't a huge quantity. Maybe a dozen or so hairs mixed in with the bubbles that clung to my fingers. Just enough to make me raise an eyebrow and conclude that it was perhaps time to change my brand of shampoo. Then some more fell out. And some more. I began to get a little panicky.

Losing one's hair is something that no-one is ever prepared for. And no matter what sufferers of this age-old affliction will tell you, it is something that no-one ever quite manages to come to terms with. It is no consolation whatsoever when sympathisers tell you that it is a natural thing, that it doesn't really matter, that it makes you look sexier. Such sympathisers invariable possess a flourishing head of hair or are female and cannot even began to understand the complex mental processes that are facilitated by the loss of the eight-inch-square thatch of dead cells and keratin that constitutes such a defining feature of the human species.

Strangely enough, I have to confess that my initial reaction to the discovery of what was soon to become a mass exodus of hair from the top of my head was curiously nonchalant. On a visit to my parents I even drew the attention of my father to my retreating hairline and jauntily – perhaps even proudly – proclaimed that I was 'receding'. It was a term that I associated with Hollywood heartthrobs such as Cary Grant or Bogie, a symbol of maleness, of the attainment of adulthood. I had heard people refer to these actors as 'receding' and it didn't seem to in any way compromise their desirability or acceptability. Quite the opposite, in fact.

I remained unconcerned by growing events for some time. Even when I was one day reading a newspaper and noticed that a neat line of hairs had formed along its crease before I had even reached page five. Yet despite the fact that any attempt to comb my diminishing locks would produce a confetti-like shower of expired hair that would float gracefully off in the breeze, I viewed my strange predicament more with curiosity than dread. Until the day, that is, when somebody else noticed it.

The person in question was called Guiseppe; if he had a surname I am not sure that he ever used it. He was the barber I had been going to since I was about 12 and our relationship had by then developed to the point that he was even able to remember my name whenever I paid him one of my thrice-yearly visits. One afternoon – it may have been a Saturday if I remember rightly – I found myself covered in towels in his familiar chair as, before the eyes and ears of a shopful of customers fidgeting in their seats for their turn, Guiseppe ran his fingers through my hair and declared in an Italian accent that was considerably more credible than the following phonetic attempt: 'Heya, youa losin' your haira… Youa goin' bald!'

As my mouth hung open and the blood rushed to my cheeks, I could swear that I heard a ripple of laughter from the shop's other occupants. Bald? Me? Bald? I thought to myself with mind racing. What does he mean I'm going bald?

It was the first time that I had ever found myself associated with the dreaded 'B' word and by no means the last. It was also the first time that I was to encounter the unique form of embarrassment that such a statement will generate. And it was the last time that I would be brave enough to set foot in a barber's shop for ten years.

My uncle Alf was the next person to focus upon my expanding forehead. One Sunday afternoon in my father's local his face wrinkled up and he knowingly informed me: 'Hey, do you know you're going bald?' And then suddenly the floodgates opened. It was as if everyone in the world seemed to be telling me all at once: family members… complete strangers… friends… television presenters; it was as if there was some kind of conspiracy solely designed to make me feel uncomfortable.

And yet it was not as if I didn't have hair on my head. I had not overnight turned into Yul Brynner. Sure, my hair obviously looked thinner than it had a year or so ago, and yes, my temples were becoming more clearly defined by the day. Yet if I combed what remained a little differently than usual the hair loss was practically unnoticeable, or so I thought. But then the conspiracy would kick in once more: girls that I knew would come up behind me and place a hand on the thinning patch at the back of my head and giggle; at a wedding a cousin I hadn't seen for a while approached me and stuck his thumb up like Paul McCartney and smiled: 'receding nicely!' Worse still, people no longer thought I was Robin Cousins.

Little known fact: Whilst walking through the centre of Bristol one day sometime in my mid-teens I was suddenly accosted by two teenage girls. Pushing slips of paper towards me they demanded my autograph and seemed most disappointed to discover that my signature was spelled differently to Robin Cousins'. This was to be no isolated incident. By the time that it had happened three or four times I began actually signing his name; it was not, I might add, that I had any particular desire to be Robin Cousins, it was just easier than having to prove to people that I wasn't.

Robin Cousins, I feel it fair to explain to younger readers, was an Olympic silver medal figure skater who came from Bristol. Along with Kevin Mabbutt (the Bristol City striker and elder brother of Spurs stalwart Gary) and Acker Bilk, Cousins was one of the city's biggest and most recognisable celebrities at the time. Although by no means a dead ringer for Cousins, it is not too difficult to appreciate how people might have thought I was he. We were both approximately the same height; we had similar haircuts, the sort of long straight fringe favoured by the Osmond brothers (Robin still has his); and our facial features were not too unalike. In all honesty, it was not altogether unflattering to be compared to Robin Cousins, my only possible cause for complaint was his nose – surely mine was not so big as his?

Nowadays I look like Alexei Sayle. Although I can see no earthly physical connection between the stout, shaven-sculled comedian and myself, sheer weight of numbers forces me to accept that I must resemble him (I can hear the pages flutter as you turn to the inside back flap of this book and take a look at the picture of the podgy looking guy responsible for the sentence you are reading – '…hmmmm,' I hear you say. 'I see what you mean…'). I was 24 years of age when I mysteriously mutated from Robin into Alexei. It was in the middle of a summer job when the director of the company I was working for, a man notorious for his cruel wit, cheerfully advised me that I looked like 'Alexei Sayle on a diet'. Now that I am 12 years older and my waistline is eight inches fuller the bit about the diet is rarely mentioned.

If I had a hair for every time somebody has come up and informed me: 'Hey, do you know that you look like Alexei

Sayle?' I am sure that I would have no problem in passing an audition for the job of ancillary guitarist with ZZ Top. I have simply lost count of the number of times that this has happened and I am still completely unable to perceive any apparent resemblance between us. I have even met Alexei on two separate occasions and remained totally unimpressed by our alleged physical similarities. (Actually, when I say met I mean that I once walked past him on the Tottenham Court Road when he was looking into the window of Argos with someone whom I took to be his mum, and once when he rode past on a bicycle when I was sitting at the table of a West End pub with some workmates (one of whom took it upon himself to loudly proclaim in a voice that Alexei was fully intended to hear: 'Look – there's Ian!').)

Which brings us, of course, to the other side of the coin. It may be unlikely but it is nevertheless entirely possible that Alexei himself is getting well and truly fed up of people approaching him at parties and saying: 'Hey, did you know you look just like Ian Probert?' If this is indeed the case, I can draw no solace from the statement he once made when he appeared as a guest on a television chat show: 'People are always coming up to me and saying that I look like someone they know,' he said. 'And they always turn out to be really ugly.'

※ ※ ※ ※

By my mid-twenties the hair situation was getting out of control. 'If you recede any more it'll meet the middle,' a friend from college helpfully pointed out. And he was right. In the classic manner, the bald patch at the back of my head was expanding like ink on blotting paper; whilst, in an unwarranted act of compliance, my temples seemed determined to head northwards to greet it. From above, my hairline looked a little like the bat-signal. It was then that I decided to do something about my predicament. One day I booked an appointment with the doctor, who turned to be in his mid-thirties and sporting – predictably – a ridiculously thick head of curly hair. He took some blood and asked me to return in a week's time, when he was able to cheerfully inform me that I was 'sickeningly healthy'.

'So why is my hair falling out?' I asked.

'Oh,' he replied. 'It's because you're going bald.'

Then he reached up to a bookshelf and pulled out a medical encyclopaedia that contained a selection of photographs of people in varying states of hairlessness. Pointing out an image depicting a man suffering from an advanced form of Bobby Charltonitus, the doctor genuinely seemed to have my best interests at heart when he offered me the heart-warming prediction: 'This is what you'll look like by the time you're 30.'

Thanks doc.

From then on my attitude towards anyone who happened to mention the 'B' word grew increasingly aggressive and spiteful in nature. I found myself practising what I considered to be witty retorts intended to transfer the burden of shame to the other person whenever the subject of my lack of hair came up. To the female friend of a girlfriend who greeted me on first meeting with: 'Oh, I was expecting someone a little more hirsute,' I responded: 'Yes, and I was expecting someone a little less corpulent.' To another girl who tactfully informed me that I had a hairstyle that resembled a shaving brush came the reply: 'True, but you're ugly and I could buy a wig.' (Actually, this retort was a rehearsed adaptation of the well-known Winston Churchill quote in which he told the unfortunate woman who had regaled him for being drunk: 'Yes, and you're ugly but in the morning I'll be sober.') Hardly state-of-the-art comedic put-downs, I readily admit – in fact, I'm sure that my twin brother Alexei could do a whole lot better than my meagre efforts – but, as anyone who has experienced the sensation of waking up in the summer to find the skin at the top of one's head peeling away from sunburn will understand, every little helps.

This is not to say that having one's hair fall out does not hold certain advantages. It has been well over a decade, for example, since I have found it necessary to purchase a comb, in doing so easing the strain on both pocket and environment. (If I'm honest with you the main reason for this is that the last time I went into a newsagent's to buy one, the bloke behind the counter took one look at me and laughed: 'Don't waste your money, son!') Similarly, my shampoo consumption is many times inferior to that of someone who possesses hair, thereby conserving worldwide shampoo reserves. Finally, in common with the rest of the balding fraternity, I am an absolute whiz at spotting anyone who happens to be wearing a wig; it is as if I have developed some kind of inner radar specifically designed, as it were, for surreptitiously identifying the syrupticious. Using this sensory enhancement I was able to recognise, for example, that Ted Danson from *Cheers* wore a toupee throughout the series' seven-year run long before anyone else had noticed; that Paul Daniels was resting a squirrel on his head many years before that fact was ever alluded to by the *Spitting Image* team; and that a well-known television presenter whose surname is shared by a famous Hollywood family of thespians currently uses a form of black spray paint to conceal the gaps in his hairline (discretion and the predatory reputation of the team of libel lawyers that he employs prevents me from naming names).

I will forgive you if by now you have reached the conclusion that my hair loss has obviously become something of an obsession for me. You would not be the first person to have made such a deduction. But you are wrong because I know that I am not alone in my reactions to this plight. Although it is rare for a bald man to stoop to the lengths of some of the fellow suffers I have encountered, (one or two people I have met having been desperate enough to undergo a scalp reduction operation, an expensive and indescribably painful process originally devised by Josef Mengale which involves the surgical removal of a strip of flesh from the bald bit at the top of the head so that the hair on the sides can be stretched up and sort of stitched together, allegedly endowing the patient with a seamless new head of hair), there is not a single bald-headed person alive who would not sell his mother to white slave traders if there was a remote chance that he could get his hair back. Indeed, many of us spend time, money we cannot afford and an inordinate amount of effort attempting to do just that.

※ ※ ※ ※

It was another baldie – also named Ian – who was to be instrumental in ensuring that boxing continued to tighten its grip on my life as I strode purposelessly towards Famous Artistdom. As well as being a closet boxing fan, he was also an art student; we were able to strike up the peculiar kind of relationship that only the hairless will understand. I had originally made his acquaintance in a bar, when he had slipped up behind me and whispered into my ear: 'I see you're going too.' To most of you, an abstract comment of this nature could have meant anything, but I was only too aware of what this person was talking about. Already dipping into my library of contrived caustic responses, I turned to face the newcomer and was relieved to discover that his hairline had also seen better days; in fact, it was considerably worse off than mine.

From then on we became staunch allies and shared many long and beery conversations that stretched off into the night on the pros and cons of bald patches. We discovered that the neuroses that had been building up inside us both were identical; we felt strangely liberated to find that we were not alone in our anguish. Primary among our shared concerns was, of course, the effect our diminishing hairlines would have on our chances of success with the opposite sex. Whilst neither of us, it has to be said, could have been exactly considered Tom Cruise lookalikes (or even, by then, Robin Cousins lookalikes), we both felt scalded by the gross injustice of being forced to compete for female attention with people who had the luxury of being able to fashion their hair into the latest style. And it was no consolation whatsoever that some of those people chose to adopt the style that had been pioneered by the lead singer of A Flock Of Seagulls or Limahl from Kajagoogoo. The fact of the matter was that they had hair and we didn't, a disability on the dancefloor somewhat akin to starting the final of the Olympic 100 metres minus a foot.

(Don't be fooled by newspaper polls which would have you believe that women find Sean Connery to be the sexiest man in the world. Whilst it is true that a small percentage of females genuinely appear to be speaking the truth when they tell you that they find bald men attractive, there are far too many who consider baldness to be a physical attribute on a par with leprosy. If Sean Connery is indeed the sexiest man alive he has reached this lofty position despite his lack of hair not because of it. Of course, it doesn't exactly hurt that Sean Connery is a multi-millionaire and used to be James Bond.)

Of course, when two balding art students named Ian tired of fretting about their hairlines there was always the other thing to talk about: the one which involved ropes and bells and gum shields. Please don't get the idea that I spent my formative years interacting only with boxing fans whilst somehow managing to avoid striking up a conversation with anyone who didn't know the difference between a left hook and a right jab. Of course, this was not the case. In fact, the vast majority of people that I came across as I endeavoured to achieve Famous Artist status – like almost everyone else on the planet – were not remotely interested in watching semi-naked men punch each other about the body and head. However, although I had from time to time demonstrated a fairly passable ability to exist quite happily alongside non-boxing folk, it was usually with people who shared my fascination for the sport that I ended up spending the most time.

Ian was the first person I ever met who subscribed to boxing magazines: piles of them, filled to the brim with photographs and records of all the current fighters. His knowledge of boxing was far superior to my own, as was his passion for the sport. It was in Ian's student bed-sit, for example, that I first saw a picture of Mike Tyson, the boxer who was being tipped for greatness by the American boxing magazine *The Ring* and who looked to me at first glance to be, well, just strange. Ian was also the possessor of a large colour television (an unheard of luxury among students) on which we were able to watch with the dedication of true disciples as one of the most exciting eras in modern boxing unfolded.

Looking back at boxing's state of affairs in the period that to me began in 1980 with the ribald execution of Muhammad Ali and climaxed with a night of unimaginable excitement in Manchester in 1990 when Chris Eubank battled his rival Nigel Benn to a standstill, it is difficult to appreciate how simple, how straightforward, things were back then. Although you will hear many old-timers reminisce with aching hearts about the great days of the seventies when Ali, Frazier, Foreman, Monzon, Napoles, Foster and Duran to name but a few were carving out their legends, to me it is the eighties that mean the most.

In superstars like 'Sugar' Ray Leonard, Thomas Hearns, Marvin Hagler and Roberto Duran, boxing possessed standard bearers for the decade who were more than capable of emulating the achievements of their illustrious predecessors. Indeed, the rivalry between these fighters – beginning at welterweight and moving all the way up to super-middleweight – propelled the fight business one step closer to soap opera, and in doing so created a new kind of boxing event, which the money men dubbed the 'Superfight'.

The boxers who were usually deemed suitable for participation in a superfight were exceptional creatures. Not only did they have to be willing to demonstrate a public disdain for one another, they also had to come complete with a list of ring accomplishments that could have been taken from the pages of a Marvel comic book or, at the very least, a Rocky movie. To become a superhero of boxing it was fairly essential to have won world titles at as many different weights as theoretically possible; to be a champion at the weight in which nature had intended you to compete simply wasn't good enough any more (thus, when Leonard and Hearns stepped into the ring in 1989 for their long-awaited rematch, the fighters' combined tally of world championships of one sort or another amounted to 12 separate titles). Still, the public lapped it up.

Who could blame them? Certainly not me and certainly not my new buddy Ian. We were both happy and thrilled to be able to sip beer and witness that quartet of fighters indulge in some of the most exciting ring encounters in living memory. And if you ever grew tired of watching the big boys in action there were always plenty of lesser lights to grab your attention on the flickering television screen. In the lower divisions there was Julio Cesar Chavez, Hector Camacho, Azumah Nelson and Aaron Pryor ready and willing to show all-comers how it should be done; at welterweight there was Marlon Starling and the slick and stylish Don Curry – not to mention his eventual conqueror, the hard-hitting Lloyd Honeyghan; waiting in the wings at middleweight was Mike McCallum, Michael Nunn and the brooding James Toney; at cruiserweight was a considerably slimmer (and hairier!) than we know him now Evander Holyfield; and at heavyweight, of course, would emerge the biggest name in boxing per se – 'Iron' Mike Tyson.

Yet even though the decade was graced with an array of talent that was the equal, in my opinion, of any previous era, it was during those years that boxing fell victim to a terminal sickness that still affects it to this day. It seems hard to believe now that at the beginning of the eighties there were only two governing bodies vying for the right to call their premier practitioners a world champion (a cause of great concern to boxing aficionados at the time, but nothing, as you will learn, in comparison to the jumbled mess that the people who run boxing have since made of the sport). Nowadays, as well as the WBC, WBA and IBF, there are innumerable self-appointed governing bodies including the marginally more legitimate WBO, and back room Johnny-come-latelys such as the WBU. What this plethora of acronyms has managed to create is a situation in which nobody is quite sure who is champion of what. It has enabled fighters who would once have struggled to progress beyond the eight-rounders to strap a belt around their waists and proclaim themselves the best in the world.

And it has robbed boxing of any last vestige of the fallacy that what occurs inside the ring might have anything to do with sport.

Although boxing's remarkable ability to help fill the pockets of its deal makers with hard cash had certainly not gone unnoticed in the past, it was during the eighties that the moneymen began to operate on a truly global basis. It was only then that boxing began to strip itself of its prime assets and starve itself of oxygen at root level. The likes of Leonard, Hearns and Tyson may have proven that when it came to generating dollars boxing had no equal; but in doing so, the growth of their fame was sufficient to ensure that others of their ilk had far to travel if they were ever to escape the shadow cast by these sporting superstars. In short, boxing began to sell itself short: all of its energies were devoted to its established stars whilst its future talent was left to sink into a swamp of obscurity. Boxing abandoned its breeding grounds and concentrated on eating its fruits.

We weren't aware of this at the time, of course; just as we are not aware now of the repercussions of boxing's continued crawl towards self-parody. We just wanted to see what would happen when Marvin Hagler got hit on the chin by Thomas Hearns; or whether Michael Spinks would dance Mike Tyson a merry dance. We just wanted to see some boxers do some boxing.

Eighth Rule of Boxing: The best boxer is the prettiest boxer

It will seem obvious to you but I'll tell you all the same. There is an easy method to determine whether a boxer is a good fighter or a bad fighter. It has nothing to do with statistics or measurements or fat-to-muscle ratio. Likewise, it has little to do with push-ups or how many miles a fighter runs each day. It's simply this:

The next time you happen to be watching a fight on the television or wherever else it is that you go to watch boxing, take a look at the faces of the two men involved. If the one with the cauliflower ears and the broken nose and the heavily-scarred eyebrows looks tough to you, think again before you attempt to pick a winner. He's got those cauliflower ears and that broken nose and those heavily-scarred eyebrows because people keep hitting him in or around those places.

It's the pretty one that you should be putting your money on: the one who looks like he's just stepped down from the vicar's pulpit; the one who looks like he'd have trouble fighting off your sister – the Muhammad Alis, the 'Sugar' Ray Leonards, the Oscar de la Hoyas of this world. The reason that fighters such as these haven't got cauliflower ears, broken noses and heavily-scarred eyebrows is at the same time both simple and a happy condition that the majority of boxers will never enjoy: it's because people don't keep hitting them in or around those places.

9

Me and David Lynch

BOXING was beginning to bubble away inside me. Gradually it was getting to the point where I was at least prepared to acknowledge its existence to a few of my trendy art college buddies. But as my allegiance to the sport that had helped me through my childhood years continued to grow, so my commitment to the lifestyle of an embryonic famous artist steadily began to diminish. It was not that I'd gone off the idea of all the rewards that such an occupation promised, it was just that it was taking a lot longer to achieve than I had originally budgeted for.

At the end of 1986, weighed down by the combined ballast of countless failures, innumerable rejections and several cubic litres of wasted effort, I finally decided that I no longer wanted to become a famous artist. I admitted defeat. At the ripe old age of 24, I reached the conclusion that I'd had enough of trying to be the next David Hockney. It was just too difficult. It was time to grow up and discard such foolish dreams. Instead, I'd become a famous film director.

I don't quite know how everything managed to go belly up: as far as I was concerned I'd made all the right career moves. I'd completed a foundation course, which, according to all available evidence, was what famous artists were supposed to do before the big bucks came rolling in. I'd gotten myself a place on a degree course, which, again, was a procedure that the vast majority of famous artists seemed perfectly happy enough to put themselves through prior to getting invited to parties at Mick and Jerry's place. Surely now, it was simply a matter of daubing an appropriate number of canvases with appropriately bright arrangements of colour before an agent who happened to be down from London for the day caught a glimpse of your efforts and discovered you? But somehow this never quite managed to occur.

What had actually managed to happen was that I ended up spending most of my young adult years living in abject poverty, attempting to combine my day job as a budding famous artist with a million shitty evening and weekend jobs. It was probably all that I deserved: washing dishes in a restaurant one week, scraping the mould from pieces of bread at a motorway service station the next. Cleaning offices; landscape gardening; working in a clothes shop; selling external wall cladding over the telephone; serving behind bars; shovelling earth on building sites; sorting through mail at the Post Office at Christmas; putting the crosses on hot-cross buns in a bread factory at Easter. Yet even though I could console myself that this collection of doleful activities would make great reading when Richard Dimbleby eventually got around to writing my biography after my retrospective at the Tate, it did not seem to make the majority of these tasks appear any more enjoyable.

I suppose, in hindsight, that the real reason behind my failure to become David Hockney had something to do with the fact was that I wasn't David Hockney. Although I had – arguably, it has to be said – been the best drawler at school in Bristol, that particular attribute was simply not enough when it came to trying to earn yourself a place among the art world's elite. And I was not alone in the sense of disappointment that gripped me as I trundled through my second year at art college: to a man and woman all of my contemporaries seemed destined for careers that would have very little to do with the practice of painting masterpieces.

ME AND DAVID LYNCH

※ ※ ※ ※

By this time, it is useful to note, I was living in Exeter, or rather on the outskirts of Exeter in a little village called Starcross, semi-infamous in Victorian times because the Devil had apparently gone for a stroll there one winter's night, leaving a set of cloven hoof prints in the snow that reputedly ran up the sides of buildings and over rooftops. There was one very good reason why I had elected to migrate to the outskirts of Exeter: I had elected to migrate to the outskirts of Exeter because Exeter happened to be the only art college in the country that was willing to offer me a place on a degree course.

In the summer of 1982, filled to the brim with the euphoria of completing phase two of my become-a-famous-artist scheme, I had packed in my evening job with Colonel Sanders and done what I was supposed to do and applied to a number of art colleges in the hope of spending the next three years of my life in the land of orgies (which, strangely enough, had never materialised during my year at Bath Academy), drugs (we'll come to this later) and paint splashing. I had approached this venture with the supreme confidence of only the supremely ignorant and applied to one of the top art colleges in the country in Camberwell, London. Among my fellow students, Camberwell had a fearsome reputation: as well as being the breeding ground for some of the top artists to emerge from this country during the 1960s, its exacting entry requirements were almost legendary. Nevertheless, with a sense of destiny on my side I was not to be fazed. Although I was under no illusions as to the task I had set myself when I took the coach down to London armed with a portfolio containing drawings of people with no clothes on and a healthy selection of my incoherent daubings on canvas, actually being rejected by Camberwell was something that had never really crossed my mind.

Even when this happened I refused to be discouraged. And even when my second choice college turned me down I still managed to accept the news with little more than a shrug of the shoulders. However, when my third choice wrote me a very nice letter politely asking if I'd mind not darkening their doors for the next three years I began to grow a little concerned. There was suddenly the very real possibility that I wouldn't be going to art college at all. However, I still had one chance.

I have no idea of the mechanics of contemporary procedures for anybody who wishes to become a famous artist these days, but back in the early 1980s they went something like this: having completed a foundation course, prospective students would be permitted to select three art colleges from the 50 or 60 that are dotted around the country. If he or she failed to gain admittance into their first choice college, they would then attempt to earn themselves a place at their second choice college, which, if the student had any sense, was usually several notches below their first choice in terms of both reputation and expectations, and therefore that much easier to gain entry to. However, if the student was unfortunate or had set their sights too highly, the second choice college would occasionally refuse to grant the candidate an interview; in which case it was time to attempt to woo the third choice college, which by definition was usually tucked away in some windswept corner of the Outer Hebrides and often prepared to offer bribes to any art student who was willing to consider gracing the establishment with their presence.

If, however, the unthinkable happened, and the student somehow failed to win himself a place at their third choice college, there was one final alternative. This was ominously entitled 'The Pool' and invariably comprised a ramshackle collection of art colleges that nobody had ever heard of and which were of such limited appeal that they regularly failed to attract sufficient numbers to any courses they offered, risking closure as a result; colleges which, to paraphrase the American boxing writer, Bert Randolph Sugar, were not even household names in their own households. Thus, sometime late in 1982 I found myself clutching my trusty portfolio of drawings of naked people in a queue of some two hundred or so other unfortunates also clutching similar portfolios in deepest, darkest Gwent.

To this day my experience that afternoon has left me with a deep-seated distrust of the Welsh (even though – as you can probably guess from my surname – I have a significant proportion of Welsh blood flowing through my veins). I had grudgingly decided that Gwent would be the location for my final stab at phase three of Operation Famous Artist because when I received the standard list through the post giving me the names of any art colleges that still had places remaining Gwent happened to be the only name on it.

It was raining, I remember, when I stepped off yet another coach from Bristol and trudged through the stinging wind with a photocopied map of the twisting streets that were destined to be my home for the next three years. The sullen expression on my face was replaced by one of lukewarm despair when I eventually located the art college, which seemed to be held aloft by several tonnes of scaffolding screwed gamely into its crumbling facade. Once inside the building, I realised that my Famous Artist ambitions had probably plummeted about as low as they could possibly get.

My interview was brief and to the point. In fact, what happened was that I, along with all the other unfortunate rejects who were present that day, was instructed to open my portfolio and stand in line as two blokes with Welsh accents briefly skimmed their contents. 'No... No... No... Yes... No...' I watched in trepidation as the two men edged closer to me. 'No... No... Yes... No... No... No...' Some of my fellow candidates began to sob as this awful ritual played itself out. Finally, the two men reached my portfolio and one of them dug into the pile of drawings that it contained before shooting the other man an icy look. 'No...' he said, quickly moving on to my quivering neighbour.

※ ※ ※ ※

I took a year off and paid the local Job Centre my customary visit and got myself yet another crappy job. I won't bore you with the details, suffice to say that it involved more brick counting. I moved into a bedsit in Bristol and tried to work out where it had all gone wrong. The bedsit was located in the basement of a large Georgian house in the arty Clifton area of the city; the rent was £16 a week, for which you were given a small room that was just about big enough to fit a single bed inside; a telephone box of a kitchen – which was fitted with one of those Baby Belling things, totally unsuited to the task of warming up anything other than a small tin of baked beans; and chronic rising damp, which endowed any item of clothing that happened to remain stationary for more than a night with a healthy coating of strangely-coloured mushrooms.

The following June I made another attempt at resurrecting my famous artist scheme. This time I lowered my sights slightly, making my second choice college of a year ago my first choice, and making my third choice college of a year ago my second. When the first rejection letter appeared I finally began to sense that I was destined not to be a famous artist. This feeling was reinforced when the second rejection letter arrived. And then – to my everlasting amazement – I was offered a place at Exeter College of Art and Design.

I have no idea what the people at Exeter saw in me that all the others didn't. Perhaps it was because by the time I arrived in that city ready to sit through yet another ultimately doomed interview (by now my sixth) I had long since given up caring. A more likely source of their decision to snap me up was, however, due to the fact that one of the lecturers at Exeter was particularly keen on what we nowadays call multimedia, and during my year in the wilderness I had been busy experimenting in just that field.

Before computers and 3D special effects and digital video editing, multimedia's aspirations were somewhat less grandiose than they are today. In 1983 multimedia would invariably involve someone dressing up in black and dancing around to a soundtrack of backward tapes while one of his mates shined coloured lights on him through a mist of dry ice. There was none of this internet malarkey.

My own attempts at creating artistic works in the multimedia genre were even less ambitious than the preceding description, nevertheless they seemed to do the trick. Some months earlier during a particularly boring afternoon in the brick counting office for no real reason I had photocopied a few pictures from magazines on to acetate and for no real reason had proceeded to colour them in with felt tip pens. Then, also for no real reason, I had cut the acetate into little squares and stuck the pieces, for no real reason, into 35mm slide frames. It was these examples of prime artistic genius that eventually parked the interest of one of my interviewers.

The interview had been going as badly as usual when the person in question had noticed my collection of swirly squiggles on acetate. The people sitting across from me at the table had been leafing through my drawings of naked people and stealing the occasional glance at their watches when suddenly the atmosphere changed. 'So, you're into 4D, are you?' asked one of my inquisitors, visibly growing excited (until it was supplanted by the much more groovy buzzword, multimedia, I must point out that 4D was then the generic term for any piece of high art that involved dressing in black, dancing to backwards tapes and shining coloured lights through blankets of dry ice).

'Oh, yes!' I had gushed. 'I'm really into 4D!'

And with that my paint splashing career was back on track.

% % % %

Exeter: I'll sum up my three years in that city as briefly as possible so I can get back to the business of not writing about boxing. In the summer it was sunny. In the winter it snowed like crazy. I began my first year of the degree course by standing around a lot in corridors, back on the painfully thin roll-ups and trying to work out what I'd like to paint. Occasionally I was summoned to crits, in which groups of middle-aged and extremely affable art teachers would place comforting arms around my shoulders and tell me not to get too worried about the fact that I couldn't think of anything to paint. Then I would be rewarded with D- and E marks at the end to the term because I hadn't actually got around to deciding what I'd like to paint.

ROPE BURNS

I think the main reason for my lack of inspiration may have had something to do with the amount of effort that it had taken to earn myself a place at an actual art college: when I suddenly found myself in the position of having achieved that increasingly impossible goal nothing seemed important enough to paint any more.

In desperation I diversified: I dallied with photography for a while. And then I tried my hand as a print maker. Finally, I found myself cajoled into the 4D department by the bloke who had originally liked my swirly squiggly slides. And, as a result of this person's intervention, I decided to drop the famous artist plan in favour of the famous director scheme.

For two years I walked around with a video camera glued to my chin. Actually, that's a complete lie, as, for one thing, the college only possessed two video cameras, for which there was invariably a student waiting list as long as your arm; and for another thing, the two video cameras that the college possessed, being manufactured at some point towards the end of the Second World War, were so heavy that it took three or four people to even lift the lukewarm hissing battery packs that were required to power them. However, despite the physical effort required, making videos proved to be a whole lot easier to do than painting masterpieces. A painting – even if you were only half as expeditious as Rolf Harris – usually took a minimum of three or fours hours to complete; sometimes it could take weeks, sometimes months. Making a video, however, could be achieved in real time: all you had to do was point the camera at something and hey presto – eat your heart out Fellini.

Although it not the thing that most apprentice famous directors usually do in their idle moments, there was also another reason why I was keen to have access to a video camera, and, I'm afraid to say, the root of an obsession that I am yet to shake off completely. In 1987, when I was in my final year at art college, I decided that I would very much like to commit to videotape a recording of the historic fight that was being contested between 'Sugar' Ray Leonard, coming out of retirement after a two-year hiatus, and Marvin Hagler, the undisputed middleweight champion who, you may recall, had been responsible for Alan Minter's facial blemishes when we bumped into each other at Bristol's Grand Hotel some seven years earlier. This is not to imply that it was my intention to make the long journey to Las Vegas and, armed with one of the college's antique monstrosities, fight my way to ringside and elbow one of the television cameramen out of the way. Rather, what I intended to do was point the camera at the small black and white television set that I had in my bedroom and keep quiet during the delayed ITV transmission for an hour or so.

Why not, I hear you ask, simply plug the video recorder into the television aerial in the traditional manner and let nature take its course? A fair question, and one that deserves a fair answer. The truth of the matter is that I tried to do this on many occasions and simply could not get my head around the bundles of multi-coloured cables that spilled from the back of the college recorder!

In fact, there was a quality about the whole ludicrous filming-the-TV scheme that I can only describe as, well, charming. The plan took me back to my teenage years when the only means I had at my disposal of making a recording of a record that I had borrowed from a friend would be to carefully choose an appropriate moment when I was alone in the house and take my little battery operated cassette recorder and hold its built-in microphone against the speakers of my father's giant wood panelled radiogram and hope that a) none of other members of the family would return home unexpectedly, thus making the sound of their entrance a permanent feature of whatever it was I happened to be recording (I don't suppose that people like Paul McCartney have this sort of problem when they're cutting their latest disc, although I did wonder when he brought out his *Wings at the Speed of Sound* album in 1976 and every track seemed to be overlaid with the sound of doorbells ringing or chip pans frying); or, b) that I wouldn't have a fit of sneezing, a cramp seizure or a lack of wind control scenario.

Although I had similar concerns when I sat down on that faithful night to watch the Sugarman dance to a hotly-disputed points decision over his arch rival, my apprehension was further exacerbated by the fact that I was not alone in my room at the time. Sitting beside me was my baldie boxing disciple namesake Ian, and another art student who had caught the bug; fellow-sufferers who, like me, had hardly been able to sleep for days at the prospect of two of the world's greatest boxing exponents finally getting together to settle an argument that had been going on for years. It was an unlikely spectacle: three dangerously over-committed boxing fans sitting down to watch one of the most important fights in modern history; one sitting on the bed, the other two squatting uncomfortably on the floor, all three clutching cans of lager in their sweaty hands. And nobody allowed to make even the slightest noise.

I still have my recording of the fight that I made that night, although naturally I have since purchased a professional version that is in full colour and does not contain any self-conscious gasps of excitement at the end of an epic round nine accompanied by angry 'shushing' noises from yours truly. It was the first fight that I ever bothered to record and I watched it many times, little knowing that it was destined to share a shelf with far too many companions.

※ ※ ※ ※

This period of my life was, I think, the time when boxing really began to take a hold on my senses; however subconscious such control may have been. Although I could have no idea that one day my illicit preoccupation would contrive to furnish me with a living, I should have recognised that the signs were all there. There is, for example, the simple fact that most of my memories, some ten years after I became an ex-art student, are connected in one way or another to boxing. There was the occasion, for instance, when a girlfriend decided that she'd had just about enough of me when she found me sitting in front of my stereo at 3am openly panting with excitement at the radio transmission of the Marvin Hagler-Thomas Hearns epic.

Then there was the time that I was sacked from a dish-washing job in a restaurant because my shouts of excitement during the radio broadcast of the Lloyd Honeyghan-Maurice Blocker welterweight title fight had frightened some of the diners. There also was my habit of somehow managing to ensure that I was always within the close vicinity of a television set whenever Barry McGuigan happened to be fighting – nothing too outrageously unusual for someone who professes to be a fan of the sport of boxing, one might say – except that at the time I was still in partial denial mode; not quite prepared to admit to anyone other than those who shared my curious obsession that I was in any way interested in boxing other than in a kind of pseudo-existential sense.

And that, in a nutshell, is how I drifted through my college years: making arty videos for the purpose of impressing the people who would eventually determine the grade of my arts degree; spending my evenings mopping floors or selling something over the phone or whatever other truly soul destroying job I had happened to land myself that week; and covertly listening to or covertly watching boxing in a manner that was at once dishonest, mendacious and ultimately unsatisfactory.

Then a strange thing occurred: completely out of the blue I suddenly became very good at making arty videos. Or rather, one afternoon the perceptions of what I was doing in the course of my random video camera pointing activities altered dramatically. What happened was this:

During one of my three-monthly 'crits', which, to the uninitiated, were intended as a forum in which groups of lecturers would have an opportunity to look at a student's latest masterpiece and offer various abstract opinions, one of the group suddenly decided that he rather liked what I was doing. The fantastic piece of work in question was an end of video tape containing a number of short films I had made depicting various people dressed in black dancing around with coloured lights being shined on them. It was footage that I had shot in my bedroom one night while testing one of those college camera and consisted of nothing more than me and a girlfriend sitting down at the foot of my bed, smoking painfully-thin roll-ups, drinking copious amounts of lager and having a bit of a chat.

Don't ask me why but this became the turning point of my art college career: all I can say is that the powers that be seemed to love my sitting-in-the-bedroom-having-a-chat-with-a-girl videos. From that moment on I was treated with unimaginable respect from both tutors and fellow students. Suddenly, I was being touted as one of the college's brightest hopes. And so, understandably, I shot some more footage of me chatting in my bedroom to girls and within weeks my fame had grown to the point that one visiting lecturer even offered me work as a teacher at a London art college. Was there any merit in these badly-lit sequences of me chatting to inebriated females? I have no idea. All I knew at the time was that such cinematic masterpieces were simple to make, enjoyable to star in and guaranteed winners at the box office. I felt like the Chancey Gardner of the art world.

As a result of this unexpected stroke of good fortune I was given a mark for my degree that I patently did not deserve and told that I had a great future in motion pictures. Despite everything, phase two of Operation Famous Artist had ended up going rather well, even if I no longer had any ambition of becoming David Hockney. However, the big question now was what to do next? What opportunities – other than in the skin flick business – were there in life for someone who had fluked an arts degree by pointing video cameras at drunken women? Whist I considered this point, I got myself another crappy job – this time selling advertising over the telephone for a small company in the centre of Exeter – and spent a month or two working out what I was going to do with my remaining 50 or so years on planet Earth. In the end I decided that there was only one thing for it: I would follow in the footsteps of Hitchcock and Lean and Attenborough; I would do what these people had done prior to relocating in Hollywood and making pots of money. I would head East to London and hit the world of the movies.

Ninth Rule Of Boxing: Boxers Love To Sue

In actual fact, it isn't really boxers who like to sue (though many in their time have), it is ex-boxers who like to sue. By ex-boxers I mean managers and promoters: people who used to be boxers and now earn their living alongside people who still are boxers.

They are the ones who like to sue. I'm having to tell you this now because before we go too much further I'm going to have to start watching my back; I'm going to have start changing a few names here and there, twisting a few facts – telling a few lies of my own so that I can avoid receiving that gilt-edged invitation to the great courtroom in the sky.

Managers and promoters are prone to launching lawsuits before the eyelid has even had time to go into bat. They sue with the frequency of an habitual addict, dragging their lawyers behind them like rag dolls. They use the libel laws as a weapon; somehow managing to forget that they are only able to afford their expensive legal representation purely because of the web of lies and deceit that it is necessary from them to weave in order to perform their jobs to any reasonable standard.

There is one current British promoter (for reasons that do not need explaining, he shall remain nameless) who has made a career out of suing any newspaper or periodical that dares to besmirch his good name. Indeed, such is his success in the law courts that many publishers have declared him persona non grata. Unofficially, he is not mentioned even in passing for fear of the terrible retribution he will wreak on the proprietor's pocket.

This anonymous Mr X is, however, far from being alone in seeking the Crown's protection whenever it suits his purposes. Managers and promoters will sue anything that moves should the opening arise: rival boxers, their own boxers, other managers, other promoters, their own promoters – and especially boxing writers. Quite why boxing folk are so willing to resolve their arguments with a writ is probably more to do with tradition than for any rational reason. The world of professional soccer, for example, which is rife with public name-calling, is usually willing to let bygones by bygones without lining the pockets of the law men.

Boxing, as always, seems to prefer the elaborate gesture; in threatening to hit an outspoken rival where it hurts most – his wallet – an outraged manager or promoter is only doing what comes naturally to him. After all, he is only doing to others what has been done to him on so many occasions. Boxing calls in the law in the manner that children call in their older brothers to sort out a bully. Often, however, this elaborate gesture ends up being just that – a gesture; for when the legal wheels have been set into motion and the prospect of weeks or months in the courtroom beckons, boxing has a habit of settling its differences with a grudging snarl. Disagreements are resolved in this manner for one very important reason: in boxing a friend can become an enemy in the time that it takes to throw a left hook; likewise; an enemy can become a friend before the ink has even been allowed to dry on the latest fight contract. Boxing people may enjoy the occasional loud bark from time to time but they are far less willing to burn their diamond studded bridges.

10

The Lost Weekend and a Half

JOHN Lennon famously described it as his 'lost weekend': the period in his life that went missing when he hit the bottle in New York in 1975 and ran amok with drinking buddies Harry Nilsson and Ringo Starr swaying along by his side. I, rather less famously, call it my 'lost weekend and a half': the period in my life that went up in smoke in north London in the late 1980s.

Lennon's lasted a year, I went AWOL for two. The potions he poured down his throat were rather more expensive than mine but the end results were the same. Lennon's eventual salvation came in the shape of a diminutive Japanese woman named Yoko, mine happened to be wearing a pair of boxing gloves.

※ ※ ※ ※

A quick word of friendly advice: if you're eating your lunch while you're reading this, please put down your sandwich for a minute or two; alternatively, if you have no wish to ruin your appetite simply skip the following five or six paragraphs and come back when you're feeling stronger.

ROPE BURNS

This is the story: In early October 1987 I arrived in London ready to hit the movie business and, by means of celebration, met up with some friends in an Islington pub. Inside said pub, filled with excitement at my latest adventure, I did what anyone else in this position would probably have done: I sank a few beers, chewed a little cud, shook the odd hand or three and generally expressed the sense of optimism that was gripping me like a fever. But then London decided to bring a little reality to the proceedings.

At one point in the evening I elected to answer the call of nature. Locating the toilet facilities, I entered a cubicle and did what comes naturally. It was hardly a historic event; nevertheless, it was a landmark of sorts – a kind of symbolic marking of territory. I'll spare you the details, suffice to say that nothing out of the ordinary occurred in the time that it took me to lower my jeans, empty my bowels of the last remnants of Exeter, enjoy a quick wipe-up and then hoist my trousers back up to their rightful place. It was only when I attempted to flush away the residue of this act of absolution that London chose to provide me with a glimpse of what the city had planned for me in the coming years.

As I looked on in horror the water in the toilet bowl slowly began to rise. And, as the seconds went by, it continued to rise. We've all been in this situation before, I think; and we all know that most of the time this alarming toilet condition will usually resolve itself before any panic has been allowed to set in. This particular toilet, however, had other ideas. Not knowing what else to do I stood and looked on in horror as the waterline continued its leisurely progress to the top of its ceramic container. Then, as I hastily flung open the cubicle door and backed away from the small pool of sewage that had leaked out on to the tiled floor, I heard voices. Through the frosted glass of the square window set into the door to the men's room I could see the blurred images of two men. One was holding a cigarette in his hand and talking to his companion, his other hand rested on the door handle ready to push it open at the end of his sentence.

THE LOST WEEKEND AND A HALF

When I was a child I was sometimes taken to see a circus that was held in a large theatre in the seaside town of Blackpool. I can always remember being impressed by the finale to the show, an ingenious affair which usually involved flooding the entire lower level of the structure with water and shining coloured lights through beautiful cascading fountains. At the time this vision seemed impossibly majestic to me. Now, as I stood by impotently, my own version of that childhood spectacle began to unfold. Instead of coloured lights, however, my rendering of that fondly-remembered scene was embellished with cigarette butts, bits of bog roll and pellets of indescribable brown matter that floated on the rising scum like miniature submarines. In a matter of moments the whole room was flooded.

I don't know if London was chuckling to itself as I guilty exited this dreadful scene and carefully avoided the appalled eyes of the man with the cigarette, but I think that it might have been. Whatever the case, I was not to know that I would be spending the next two years up to my knees in filth that was every bit as stomach churning as that pool of unappetising toilet broth.

%% %% %% %%

Moving to London turned out to be a big mistake. A great big stonker of a mistake. Of course, it seemed like the right thing to do at the time but in retrospect I cannot even begin to understand my motivations for doing so. Sure, Exeter wasn't exactly Ibiza – in fact, it didn't even rate as high on the excitement scale as Southend-on-Sea – but I was relatively happy there. I had friendships that had been built up over three years; a steady job which, although mindlessly boring, was, by Exeter standards, fairly well paid, and I also had a relatively comfortable place in which to live. None of this, however, could prevent me from gathering up my possessions and stuffing them into the trusty red suitcase that had been with me since I left Bristol in my teens and heading eastwards.

ROPE BURNS

I came to conquer the city; at least, that's what a part of me would have liked to believe about my foolhardy decision to migrate. In reality, however, I was no different to any of the many thousands of young men and women who regularly converge each year on London wishing to sample the bright lights. True, I had a little money – probably about £150 tucked away in my back pocket – and I was even more fortunate in that I already had a place to live, having agreed to share a flat in Islington with members of an Exeter scouting party that had moved up to London two months before me. At least I wouldn't have to sleep on the street. In actual fact, as advantages go this gave me a considerable head-start over the majority of newcomers to the city. With somewhere to live at least you could concentrate on looking for that job in the movies, which was something that I was keen to start doing as soon as I'd unpacked.

However, The Great Cleaning War of 1987 soon wiped that away.

The origins of The Great Cleaning War of 1987 can be traced back to the autumn of that year and the decision by the other tenants of the three-bedroom flat that I was supposed to be moving into to allow an extra eight or nine people to also move into the place. The eight or nine people in question were all friends of ours from Exeter who, upon learning that we had managed to find ourselves somewhere to live in London, had also decided to try their luck in the big shitty. The original arrangement had been that they only stay for a while until they found their own accommodation and cleared off leaving the rest of us to attend our own lives. However, when a couple of weeks turned into a couple of months, and that couple of months turned into four or five, the tensions that built up inside the flat between us all became too much for anyone to bear.

The straw that broke the camel's back was the refusal by some of the flat's inhabitants to adhere to the cleaning rota that had been instituted by the more organised among us. This meant that the kitchen became a kind of battleground, overflowing with precariously placed piles of unwashed dishes that were home to a miniature ecosystem of insects and strange green and purple fungal growths that crept out of the sink like alien slime. The unnatural odours that emanated from this room were just too awful to contemplate and soon led to open warfare, with militant factions and political pressure groups being formed among all the flat's disgruntled inhabitants. When this situation quickly escalated to the point where fists were about to be thrown, I, along with an ex-girlfriend from Exeter who was a member of the underground faction that I had formed during the course of The Great Cleaning War, decided that it would best all round if we cleared off ASAP. Thus the pair of us became squatters.

It was a young drifter named Terry who actually managed to persuade us that squatting was the solution to our problems. Indeed, so persuasive was Terry that if there was such a thing as a Squatters Marketing Board, he would have been a natural as its spokesman. I don't quite remember how he had managed to slip into our lives, I can only recall that he talked a good fight. Squatting, he informed us both, was as easy as falling off a log. According to him, there were thousands of empty and neglected council flats all over London. All it would take was a little ingenuity and we could easily escape the war zone that had been making our lives a misery and enter a world totally devoid of the rent book. Furthermore, explained Terry, the whole thing was totally legal. So we gathered up our belongings and did just that.

One night Terry took us to a council estate in north London. It was called the Stanford Hill Estate and, although I did not know it, was notorious at the time as the squatters' capital of London, being home to hundreds of people who, for one reason or another, found it impossible to meet their rent demands. It was a forbidding place: built, I would estimate, in the 1950s and stained dirty brown by the heavy London air. Scarcely a breeze sailed through the rows and rows of terraced boxes that blotted out the sunshine; whatever grass that grew in what had originally been conceived as ornamental gardens was also brown in colour and kept itself hunched close to the ground, as if wary of straying too close from the relative sanctuary of the black soil. Not since a family holiday as a teenager at Butlins in Barry Island had I encountered a place that gripped me with such a deep sense of foreboding.

We climbed some stairs to the top floor of one of the many abandoned shells whose access was guarded by heavy steel doors and windows, and Terry immediately set to work. To an outsider it was certainly impressive enough to watch: although Terry carried a crowbar he never actually got around to using it. Instead of wrenching away these formidable looking metallic barriers Terry simply reached into his pocket and pulled out a bunch of keys that he had somehow managed to acquire. After a moment or two spent fiddling about trying to find the appropriate key we were inside.

The place was dark and smelt of something decidedly unhealthy as the three of us nervously explored its interior. Although it was spacious, one could hardly have described the flat as palatial, there being no electricity, no hot or cold water, no carpets, no heating, no furniture and no butler. It was, nevertheless, our new home – and we had little alternative but to make the most of it.

I spent my first night there shivering on the bare wooden floorboards covered by coats. And when Terry mysteriously disappeared from sight, leaving myself and my now incessantly complaining former girlfriend to fend for ourselves, I also spent the next three or four nights shivering on the bare wooden floorboards covered by coats. It was only then that I realised just how limited my knowledge of what it took to survive in squatter land actually was. Sure, I managed to come to terms with mastering a few of the essentials of life. With a bit of jiggling with the taps under the sink, for instance, I was able to provide us both with a trickle of cold water and a means of partially emptying a toilet bowl that had begun to resemble Quatermass's pit.

I was also able to provide the pair of us with beds; well, actually, there weren't really beds – they were rolls of foam rubber that I purchased for under a pound in a shop in Kings Cross – but they were infinitely preferable to the bare wooden floorboards that had been making sleep an impossibility. When it came to things like turning on the electricity supply, however, I was a total waste of space. Although up until this point in my life I had actually been rather good when it came to less challenging electricity supply-related pastimes such as flicking on light switches, televisions and stereos, I simply did not have a clue as to how one went about furnishing a whole flat with a healthy supply of electricity, especially when every electrical fitting in the flat had been smashed by, I assumed, over-zealous members of the council's housing department, who were obviously keen to dissuade people like me from making the place my home.

To my own amazement, a couple of days after this enforced relocation I somehow managed to get myself together enough to do what I had originally come to London to do. You will be forgiven if my original purpose for hitting the capital city has slipped your mind, because, frankly, by then it had long since slipped mine. One morning, however, I gathered up my senses and several copies of my videos containing shaky sequences of me chatting to drunken women, which now seemed to belong to another lifetime and took the bus down to Soho, where I walked around and paid visits to all the film production companies I could find. No one was more surprised than I when before the day was out I had landed myself a job in the movies.

Well, actually it wasn't really a job in the movies: in fact, I would be helping to make television commercials. Nevertheless, it was my first real success since I had arrived in London. Well, in truth it couldn't really be described as that much of a success, for although I would be helping to make television commercials I would not actually find myself within touching distance of anything that remotely resembled a camera; I would apparently be doing other things. A little more depressing was the fact that although I had landed myself a job making television commercials, I was informed that I wouldn't actually receive any money for my efforts. Not, I am sure you will agree, one of the greatest career moves than one would ever wish to undertake, but at time I felt quite elated with my good fortune.

In fact, I only managed to help make two commercials: one was for Farley's Rusks – my job being to hold screaming babies in between takes and allow them to vomit liquified Farley's Rusks on to my best trousers. The other was working with those fucking chimps in the PG Tips commercials, making cups of tea for the camera crew and being scratched and spat at by the entire anthropoid cast. Still it was glamorous.

On my third scheduled shoot, however, I made a mistake that was to put a premature end to my burgeoning movie career: after explaining that I was by now absolutely flat broke and unable to even afford the bus fare into Soho the next morning, I meekly asked if there was any possibility of being paid a little money for my tea-making efforts. The director of the shoot, a rather charming country gentleman-type who must have been 80 if he was a day, greeted my request with a shake of the head and a doleful smile. 'Sorry, old chap but we don't actually pay our runners,' I was informed. 'In fact, some of them actually pay us for the privilege of working here.'

※ ※ ※ ※

Back in retirement, I soon found myself in an ocean of red, blue, green and purple hair. A week or so after his mysterious disappearance Terry had returned to the squat and, after expressing his amazement that we had been existing all this time without electricity, hot water, heating or cooking facilities, gave us some grim news. According to him the word on the street was that the Stanford Hill Estate was about to become the subject of a mass-eviction notice. What this actually meant, Terry revealed to us, was that at some point in the next month or so the estate was going to be invaded by hundreds of riot police wearing plastic visors and carrying truncheons and tear gas canisters. There they would use whatever force was necessary to ensure that the squatter menace was eradicated so that decent families could take the place of these social parasites. Barely three weeks after escaping the psychological battle zone of The Great Cleaning War, I now found myself slap bang in the middle of a real one.

The squatters, however, were not prepared to give up their territory without a fight. With admirable courage and organisation a series of planning meetings were quickly arranged, during which counter measures were plotted. The chairman of these meetings was invariably a young Welshman with a shaven head and a stud through his nose who spoke with an intelligence and intensity that reminded me of Neil Kinnocks's rousing speeches during the 1980 miners' strike. His words certainly found an appreciative audience, most of whom young and most of whom in possession of what appeared to be the required squatter uniform, which involved multi-coloured hair, dog on string and various metallic appendages inserted through various pieces of the anatomy. Although the majority of these people could only have been a couple of years younger than me, I felt like I belonged to a different generation and knew that they could sense it, too.

Nevertheless, I was determined that I would play my part in the proceedings. This meant getting up very early in the morning and joining the squatter patrols that kept a constant vigil around the perimeter of the council estate. The theory was that at the first sign of trouble an alarm would be raised and a squatter's army would immediately emerge from every building in the complex. Armed with Molotov cocktails, knives, pieces of wood and whatever else they could lay their hands on they would then engage the enemy and fight them to a thrilling finish.

The patrol was maintained with religious fervour for more than a fortnight, but if we were kept on our toes by the police helicopters that constantly circled the estate, it was not too long before our self-righteous enthusiasm began to wane. By now it was winter and freezing enough to invite the onset of hypothermia if one were foolhardy enough to remain outdoors for more than an hour at a time. Furthermore, it must be remembered that the people manning the patrols were squatters, who by their very nature were totally unused to the discipline of regularly rising early in the morning and, therefore, completely unsuited to the task. With each passing day the number of patrol members dwindled until finally, there was no more than a handful of people who were prepared to leave their beds and brave the bitter cold.

There was also the fact that people were now beginning to doubt Terry's words. In the course of further squatter meetings, voices were angrily raised and Terry was asked to reveal the source of the mass eviction rumour, which he refused to do. As well as this, other rumours were also beginning to circulate; principle among these was the story that the police had, in fact, got wind of the squatters' defence strategy and had decided that they really couldn't be bothered to get into a skirmish with a group of people with nose studs and would rather stay at home in bed themselves. There was also the theory that the police had found themselves a 'mole', who was keeping them constantly up to date with the squatters' plans. The whole thing was beginning to get a little too much like the meetings held between Napoleon and Snowball that George Orwell describes in *Animal Farm*.

Then it happened.

They came early one morning, five or six dozen vans filled to the brim with riot police and snarling dogs. By now, the lookout patrol could have comprised no more than three or four people; nevertheless, an alarm of sorts was raised. This took the form of patrol members frantically running from flat to flat and shouting through the letterbox, 'They're here! Get up! They're here!'

However, as it turned out there was no army ready to pick up their weapons of war and repel the invaders. Most of the squatters chose to remain buried beneath their bedclothes, somehow hoping that the forces of establishment would grow bored of the whole thing and go away and leave them alone. Much to the dismay of the television crews that had turned up to record the battle, the majority of the squatters were unwilling to risk cracked skulls, instead they poured their pets and possessions into cardboard boxes and went off in search of somewhere else to live. Within a day the estate was cleared. The only sign that there had been any sort of battle came from the black smoke of an abandoned car that someone had decided it would be a good idea to put a match to.

%% %% %% %%

Even though I was a relative newcomer to pros and cons of the squatting genre, it did not take me long to locate alternative rent-free accommodation. Minus the incessantly complaining ex-girlfriend, who, when all the excitement was over moved back to the safety of Exeter, I found myself another squat, this time back in Islington. This one was something of an improvement over its predecessor. This one was like a real flat: it had hot and cold water, electricity and even a couple of beds. I was joined in my new home by two Exeter ex-pats who, like me, were refugees of The Great Cleaning War. Any relief at escaping the nightmare of Stanford Hill quickly evaporated, however, whenever I chose to reflect on what I planned to do with my life. Like my famous artist plan before it, the famous director plan seemed to have well and truly ground to a halt.

Tenth Rule Of Boxing: Boxers Like To Fall Out

It is not for nothing that a manager will often refer to his fighters as being part of his 'stable'. Indeed, the horse analogy is a good one; for it can be claimed that a boxer's career follows a very similar path to the one trodden by our four-legged friends. Like a potential Gold Cup winner, a boxer is taught how to win by his trainer. And like that prize-winning stallion, there are prizes aplenty to be claimed by his handlers should the boxer manage to reach the top.

Although a boxer's professional contract will tell you otherwise, throughout the course of his career he will belong to someone else. His livelihood and his life will be in the hands of a manager and a promoter who have it in their power to control the boxer's destiny.

In all too many cases, however, the relationship between these three men is not a healthy one; more master and servant than employee and employer. Which is why, more often than not, boxers and their managers will eventually end up falling out.

A boxer turning professional has very little choice but to sign up with an established manager. But even though he many be well aware of the manager's dubious credentials, the advantages of hooking up with someone with the experience of operating in the fight business will usually far outweigh any reservations that the boxer might have. As well as finance, an established manager will also be able to provide those all important contacts: he will know other managers, he will possibly have long-standing connections with promoters, and, more importantly, he will be able to get his man's face on a television screen.

Interestingly, a boxer's relationship with his manager tends to follow a well-established pattern. During the early part of his career, the manager will often adopt the guise of a surrogate father, placing a paternal arm around his young ward's shoulders at the end of an undercard fight and grinning at the camera like a second-hand car salesman. Curiously, the boxer will often respond to this gesture in kind; peering up at his manager with sheep dog eyes as a television interviewer pokes a microphone into his unspoiled face.

Once a fighter has enjoyed a little success, however, this loving vision soon begins to fade. By now the boxer will be beginning to feel more confident about his abilities; already he will be looking at his stablemates' purses and wondering why theirs are always so much fuller than his. This change in attitude will sometimes manifest itself in a visible distancing between himself and his manager. On public occasions the boxer will make it his body language's business to ensure that everyone present is aware that things are changing. Nevertheless, despite such rumblings of discontent this reluctant partnership will somehow manage to persist.

However, should a fighter win a title – especially a world title – the relationship will alter dramatically. Many professional boxing contracts contain a clause which compels a fighter to commit to his existing manager for a further three fights in the event that he wins a title; and though some might argue that such a clause is reasonable in preventing a manager's investment from running off and fighting for somebody else, this piece of legal sleight of hand is but one of many reasons why a boxer will now view his manager with extreme distrust. Sooner or later the fighter will go public with his grievances. He will criticise his manager, his manager will criticise him, lawyers will be telephoned.

In general, however, boxers tend to stick with their managers until the moment that they lose. Although they may have spent several years grumbling about their guardians to friends, family and newspaper reporters it is usually only when somebody has beaten them that they choose to do anything about their grievances. At this point, the manager will be discarded and the legal battles will commence. In addition to suffering this gesture of public abandonment, the manager will also now officially become The Excuse. He will be the reason why the boxer lost his last fight; it will be the manager, not the man who threw the punches, who is to blame.

I could give you a long list of boxers who have lost a fight and then dumped on their managers soon afterwards but I'm not wealthy enough to try. I could also give you a fairly extensive roll-call of those fighters who tried to make it in the pro game without an established manager, but it's not worth bothering with as I know you'll never have heard of them. What I can say, however, is in boxing don't be too surprised when a match made in heaven fails to ignite. Because even though one would have never thought it possible, for example, that a youthful Barry McGuigan would eventually part company with his mentor, Barney Eastwood (McGuigan even released a dreadful record in homage to his manager entitled *Thank You Very Much Mr Eastwood*); and even though it would once have been unthinkable that Herol 'Bomber' Graham could ever leave the side of the man who had practically raised him from child, Brendan Ingle, both of these fighters did so. And they are far from alone.

※ ※ ※ ※

Because there is a part of me which would like to believe that I am not one of those journalists who would sink his sixth pint at the bar in the middle of writing tomorrow's latest pissed Gazza story, I feel duty bound to attempt to provide you with an explanation for my decision to spend the large part of two years living with people who financed their lifestyles by selling drugs. What, I hear you say, has this got to do with the business of not writing about boxing? Not much, it has to be admitted. Not much at all. Other than to say that, as well as in the company of countless other people from countless other walks of life, it has been my pleasure on occasion to sit down with a boxer and indulge in the consumption of chemicals that cannot be purchased at the local chemists.

Before we go any further let me tell you that my decision to live with people who sold drugs was not a conscious one: indeed, in view of the circumstances I could quite justifiably claim that I had very little say in the matter. Even so, it would be wrong of me to expect you to believe that I was totally blameless in my choice of accommodation – I could, after all, have made alternative arrangements if I was really so appalled by the way that my flatmates made their money. For this reason, on those occasions when I have found myself in the midst of a horde of reporters baying for the blood of a sportsman or celebrity who has been caught on the bottle or putting white powder up his or her nose, I have elected to remain as un-vocal in my condemnations as discretion permits.

To talk about drugs places one's fate at the disposal of a wide variety of potential audiences. On the one hand there are the pious and the ill-informed, who will advocate that the recreational use of any substance which society deems to be illegal is an activity to be placed on a par with paedophilia;

these are people like your mum and dad – like my mum and dad – individuals for whom no amount of rational argument will ever succeed in altering their opinions. Their conceptions of drug taking are drawn from the popular media and strewn with images of a screaming Gene Hackman in *The French Connection* or spaced-out juvenile delinquents from films like *Trainspotting*.

Then there are the casual drug users: young businessmen in smart suits with credit cards and girlfriends named Zoë who drink cocktails. You see these people on Friday nights in Soho brasseries, creeping off into a cubicle to snort a crafty line that has come to them via a friend of a friend of a friend; these people would probably not even describe themselves as drug users, and if the legalisation of drugs was put to a public vote many of them would find themselves placing their crosses in the 'NO' column.

Finally, there are the committed drug users: people with mobile phones and serious expressions that you might meet occasionally at a party; or, at the other end of the social spectrum, people that you see outside tube stations with plastic cups and cardboard placards asking for money. To these people the consumption of drugs is such a large part of their lives that they would doubtless take one look at the words on this page and wonder what on Earth my hang-up was. These three extreme personality profiles offer, I believe, a fairly reasonable representation of the range of reactions one can expect when the subject of drugs is put up for debate.

※ ※ ※ ※

It was an older friend named Jon who gave me my first taste of an illegal substance. I was in the third year at school and he was in the fifth when one afternoon we sat in a field and he produced a pouch of Old Holborn, a roll of cigarette papers and what looked to me like a pile of dead leaves. As I watched in fascination, Jon pulled out three cigarette papers and stuck them together in the shape of an 'L'; then he carefully mixed together a portion of the tobacco with some of the dead leaves; finally, with a bit of jiggery pokery, he eventually managed to roll the mixture into something that resembled a kind of badly-made Caucasian cigar. After jamming a small rectangle of cardboard into one end, Jon then produced a Zippo lighter and, accompanied by my scarcely concealed gasps of excitement, set fire to the other. With his creation safely locked between his teeth, Jon lay his back on his back and stared at the sky. I felt suddenly very adult as I watched the streams of thick smoke gush from his mouth and nostrils. Then he handed it to me.

The giant roll-up smelled vaguely of cow dung as I raised it to my lips and prepared to make what was undeniably the most decadent action of my whole life. Compared to sagging off school or copying somebody else's answers in class this was a whole different ball game. Yet even though this was the first time I had ever held such a contraption in my hands, I still had a reasonable idea of the effects that one could expect from it. I had read, for example, how The Beatles had apparently suffered uncontrollable giggling fits when they had been given their first badly-made Caucasian cigar in 1965 by Bob Dylan. And, in films like *Yellow Submarine* and records like *Revolver*, I had seen and heard the magical results of this chemical alliance. The dead leaves had turned The Beatles all groovy and colourful and surreal. I wondered if they were about to do the same to me.

The smoke burned my throat as I tried to inhale. As well as smelling like cow dung it seemed to taste of what I imagined cow dung might taste like. 'Puff harder!' urged my companion as I proceeded to suck for all I was worth. 'Try to hold it in as long as possible.'

I tried to hold it in as long as possible but it was not easy. Nor, for that matter, was it particularly pleasant. In fact, as pleasant experiences went, this one was definitely somewhere in the lower reaches of the Northern Premier League. Furthermore, all the effort and unpleasantness that was required to participate in the ritual clearly outweighed its rewards. There was no dazzling explosion of light and there was nothing to giggle about in particular. Nothing seemed to happen at all.

I passed the disagreeable object back to my mentor and watched as he once again placed it in his mouth. Jon certainly appeared to be enjoying himself. His eyes had gone all dreamy and his voice all sing-song. Judging from his appearance he seemed to be getting his money's worth. Perhaps I was doing something wrong.

I tried again. When the fragile cylinder was passed back to me I closed my eyes and sucked in as much smoke as my young lungs could possibly hold. After the inevitable coughing fit had subsided, however, I still felt no effect. My eyes did not open up on another world. Nor did I feel myself gripped by any overwhelming sense of spiritual self-awareness. If this was what it was all about you could keep it as far as I was concerned.

Meanwhile, Jon's behaviour continued to grow more eccentric by the second. Now he was pointing at nearby objects and muttering things about their colour and using words that were not usually part of his vocabulary, or rather were part of his vocabulary but never, to my knowledge, previously used in the context that he was using them now – words like 'man' and 'far out' (really!). And so, having no desire to spoil the moment, I did – I believe – what many people have probably done at least once in their life: I pretended to be stoned. I rolled over on to my back and did a little sky watching myself; I followed the example set by my older and incalculably more experienced friend and found myself also enthusing about the amazing colours that he was seeing.

It would be many years later before Jon would finally confess to me that he, too, had been lying. The dead leaves had also left his senses completely untouched; as far as we knew it could have been cow dung that we had been smoking that day.

※ ※ ※ ※

What you may ask, had happened in the intervening 15 or so years to separate this spluttering teenage sceptic from the man who would one day sit at table with a boxer who was the British champion in his weight division and smoke a rather more authentic pile of those dead leaves? The answer to this question, depending on which of the personality profiles I mentioned earlier you might belong to, is, all at the same time, nothing much or rather a lot.

I promised you a while ago that I would give you all the gory details relating to the drug-taking bit of the warning that my father had flashed at me all those years ago when I had originally announced my intention to become an art student. Well here goes. The tragic fact of the matter is, rather like the spliff Jon passed me in the field that day, that the whole thing turned out to be something of a damp squib. Just as there were no orgies, and just as the paint splashing part of my father's prediction had ended up being a pursuit that was entirely optional, drug taking at the art college was far from compulsory. Sure, there were drugs around. From time to time, for example, one of my more daring colleagues would go to elaborate lengths to accidentally give you a glimpse of the small lump of brown stuff wrapped in clingfilm that he was carrying in his pocket. Some would even go so far as to set a light to a bit of it. In general, however, drugs were conspicuous by their absence.

As a matter of fact, you had more chance of getting high at the Kentucky Fried Chicken where I worked, wherein my manager and fellow boxing fan Po would attempt to fight off the tedium of his job with an endless supply of Thai Sticks that his family regularly posted to him.

Drugs kept their distance from me, which was fortunate really because had they been more readily available I know for certain that my student finances would have prevented me from ever stocking up on dead leaves. Drugs kept their distance from me even as I entered my mid-20s. And, were it not for the fact that I ending up squatting in London for the best part of two years, I dare say they'd have kept their distance from me to this day. I suppose the real reason that drugs refused to become a part of my life is because I didn't particularly like them. Even though I had tried my best not to be too put off by my experience in that field with Jon and the cow dung, I could never see what all the fuss was about. Whenever somebody happened to pass me a spliff at a party or wherever I would gamely give it another go; but nothing much ever seemed to happen when I did. As a mind transforming agent alcohol was far more reliable – and far cheaper according to what I'd been told. And it wasn't just the dead leaves that left me unmoved. I tried other things, too. But while swallowing little bits of paper, drinking mushroom tea or dabbing white powder on to your gums were all sort of fun to do when somebody else had gone to the trouble of procuring or preparing these substances, I never felt driven to repeat the experience of my own volition. Perhaps there was only enough room for one drug in my life; and that place had already been taken by you-know-what.

%% %% %% %%

I was already into my third squat when this situation suddenly changed dramatically. By now I was living in a council estate in Hackney with three other squatters who I knew only vaguely. They were all former neighbours of mine and we had ended up cohabiting after we were evicted from our respective abodes on the same morning. As far as I could tell they were all like me: unemployed and on the dole. However, I soon noticed that, unlike me, they did not seem to have the same money problems that were currently blighting my life. The fridge always seemed to contain a healthy supply of lager and, more significantly, none of my flatmates came knocking on my bedroom door asking for a sub when it was giro day. They were by no means rich: it was not as if they were all driving around in Ferraris, but they certainly had more money than I did. I wondered perhaps if the government was overpaying them.

I found the solution to this mystery a week or so after I moved into the flat. The regular stream of visitors that came calling were, I discovered, in no way a reflection of my enigmatic flatmates' astonishing popularity, personable enough fellows though they all were; it was more to do with the enormous lump of brown hashish that I discovered sitting on the bed when I walked into one of their bedrooms unannounced one evening.

They sold drugs for a living. Speed, cocaine, hash, and anything else that there was a demand for. At their level it wasn't the most brilliantly paid job in the world but it was how they made their money. I had little knowledge of their background but sensed that at that stage in their lives it was what all three were probably best qualified to do. So now, from famous artist to famous director, I was cabin boy to a trio of small-time candymen.

As I said before, I could have moved on if this situation really left me so morally outraged. It would have been a bit of a hassle but I could have climbed aboard Keith Joseph's bicycle and found myself somewhere else to break into. I could have gone home to Bristol, or I could have moved back to Exeter. But I didn't. Instead I carried on living with these people. And when the time came for me to vacate the flat I ended up moving in with some different people who also sold drugs for a living. After a while, whatever guilty overtures that my upbringing had been threatening to make began to fade into the background. How my flatmates chose to make their money didn't really concern me. They were all nice enough fellows, and what they were doing didn't seem to be hurting anyone – quite the opposite, in fact, judging from the expressions on the faces of some of their clientele.

※ ※ ※ ※

Although anyone in boxing will probably be able to guess the identities of the boxers who ended up sitting across from me some years later at that aforementioned table with lips wrapped around a rather more accomplished version of one of those badly-made Caucasian cigars, I'm not going to name any names. It's me, after all, who's doing the confessing and it would be unfair to drag somebody else into this addled narrative purely to provide a little surface colour. Suffice to say that the majority of boxers who joined me in my attempts to get groovy and colourful and surreal were all extremely successful in their chosen field. They were not has-beens; they were all highly accomplished fighters – some, as I said before, were even title holders.

Of course, by this time I was living a very different life to the one that I have been recently describing, and the dead leaves had finally begun to have some effect on my senses. This, I suppose, is what happens when you live with drug dealers for any amount of time: sheer ease of availability eventually ends up breaking down any reservations you might have. At least it did with me.

This is not to suggest that by the time I'd finished my stint as a north London squatter I'd managed to turn into a drug-crazed dope fiend who prowled the streets looking for another fix. Quite the contrary, in fact; for even though I was by then finally able to see what all the fuss was about, drugs – in the form of hash or cocaine or anything else that my flatmates offered to donate to me – would always remain something that I could either take or leave. Indeed, I can honestly say that I have never been compelled to steal or lie or cheat in order to procure drugs; nor, for that matter, have I ever suffered withdrawal symptoms from any type of illegal substance (although, this is certainly not the case with cigarettes). In fact, should the anti-drug lobby ever decide to use me as a case study I would probably end up being the worst possible deterrent for the evils of drug taking.

Birds do it, bees do it, and even, though it would surprise me at the time, boxers apparently do it. Lawyers do it, dustmen do it and doctors do it. Sometimes people who earn a living by not writing about boxing do it.

11

The Lost Weekend and a Half: Part Two

I SHOULD have guessed that things had reached breaking point when a young man with a beard like Catweazle appeared in the living room and asked if I would mind jacking him up. He was fairly self-sufficient in most respects. He could do the majority of this exercise with his teeth and feet: he could assemble his works, he could put a match to the spoon and transfer its boiling contents into the hypodermic. It was only when it came to the act of actually inserting the needle into a vein that he found himself rueing the day he had lost his fingers.

I'm not sure that I was ever given the name of this tragic person. I'm not entirely sure that I even wanted to know it. Yet if I close my eyes I can remember the contours of his face as if it was yesterday. For your information, his digits were no longer in his possession because he had somehow managed to burn all ten of them off when – bombed out of his head on heroin – he had set fire to his squat. Curiously, his fingers were the only parts of his body that were damaged in the blaze. Apart from that he was unblemished. If he kept his hands in his pockets you would never have known that you were talking to a person who could quite justifiably have laid claim to the title of World's Most Unsuccessful Hitchhiker.

He had come to the squat to buy drugs from the people I was living with in what was now my fourth or fifth rent-free flat. He was just one of many shabbily dressed waifs and strays who shuffled in and out of the place at all hours of the day and night. For me, though, his unexpected arrival was a turning point of sorts. It was an indication that the lack of control that had been impregnating my life for far too long had now reached its nadir. It also signalled the beginning of the end of my lost weekend and a half.

It had now been two years since I had arrived in London ready to set – forgive me when I say this – the world on fire. Two years that had become a stoned, drunken blur punctuated only by days and nights of hunger and untold hours spent sitting in front of the television set. Although I had occasionally managed to get hold of a little casual work here and there, I had not held down a real job in the accepted sense of the term for more than six years. I had become a prisoner of the sort of routine that only those who know what it is like to try to exist on state benefits for any amount of time will understand.

By this stage my life was ruled by the fortnightly cycle of waiting for my dole cheque to arrive so that I could pay back all the people I had borrowed money from in the interim. Then I would take what remained out of the £72 that the government graciously thrust into my coffers every 14 days and celebrate my good fortune by going out for a drink. By the next morning I would be lucky if I had more than £20 left to last me until the next giro and through a steaming hangover would carefully plan another two weeks of survival, allotting myself one or two pounds a day to buy food and other essentials.

Looking for a job by this point was almost entirely out of the question. For one thing I now had nothing left in my wardrobe that could even vaguely be described as an interview suit, my clothing being a collection of tattered jeans and ragged T-shirts that were all well past reasonable retirement age. This meant, of course, that even if I was ever fortunate enough to find myself in the position of attending an interview for a job that I felt capable of doing, my appearance would have provided the ultimate deterrent for any potential employers. More importantly, however, whatever self-confidence I might once have had was now shot to pieces and in terminal decline. Indeed, were it not for the sudden reappearance of boxing I have no idea what would have become of me.

Boxing came back into my life at a time when I really needed it most. It arrived via a fellow squatter, who was himself something of a boxing nut. His name was Jim and like me he had plenty of spare time on his hands. Jim hailed from Ireland and was an alcoholic. When he wasn't drinking copious quantities of frothy light brown liquid he was cutting up huge bricks of hashish and making a reasonable living by selling bits to people who rolled them up in pieces of paper and set fire to them. When he wasn't cutting up huge bricks of hashish, he was talking about boxing, dreaming about boxing, watching boxing, or reading about boxing in one of the many magazines he subscribed to. Naturally, we became soulmates.

Jim was not your normal run-of-the-mill squatter. He came well prepared. Instead of the usual collection of cardboard boxes that were a constant companion to others of his ilk, Jim had been known to hire removal vans to transport his impressive array of possessions. Jim owned his own furniture; he even had a video recorder, which was state of the art and undoubtedly of dubious origin; more importantly, Jim had amassed a limited library of videos of people hitting each. Had he only been female, he'd have been perfect for me. Inevitably, we spent far too many hours watching this collection: McCallum versus Curry; Hearns versus Roldan; Leonard versus Lalonde; Ali versus Foreman. In the end, the pair of us could almost recite their accompanying commentaries word-for-word.

By this time I had lost count of the number of times that I had received the dreaded letter from the council, asking me if I would mind very much picking up my belongings and clearing off somewhere else. In fact, if I say so myself, I had become something of an expert in squatters' protocol. The letter usually dropped on to your mat some two or three months after you had moved into a property; it gave you six weeks to vacate the premises before the men in the blue boiler suits came to kick the door in and seal the place up with steel doors and windows. Before this happened it was usually not that difficult to find alternative accommodation. Sometimes you would have to crack open a new place yourself: this was often done with the assistance of a crowbar or heavy boot or even, if the indigenous squatting community was sufficiently well organised, via a set of keys similar to the one that Jerry had used to gain access to the squat in Stanford Hill almost two years earlier. Once inside your new home there were the standard things to attend to: minor details such as turning on the water, the gas and the electricity supply (an activity which I had by now finally mastered). Alternatively, there was always a chance that someone would hear of your ill-fortune on the squatters' grapevine and be able to offer you a room in an existing squat.

This is how I ended up sharing a flat with Jim and two other Irish friends of his, who were also rather too keen on the bottle for their own good and financed this propensity in the purveyance of various narcotic substances, including speed and cocaine.

In truth, my memories of the five or six months that I shared with Jim and his two friends is at best hazy. I can remember that I drank a lot of alcohol and smoked a lot of Jim's hashish. I can remember that the day did not start for me until sometime after 2pm and usually did not end until five or six in the morning. I can remember watching a hell of a lot of television and never quite managing to rid myself of the empty feeling inside my stomach. And I can remember being so short of money that on several occasions I lived on nothing but a diet of boiled potatoes for days on end.

So how, you may be wondering, did I allow myself to be sucked into such a depressing scenario? There was certainly no denying that in comparison to the majority of people with whom I was now cohabiting my upbringing had been privileged. I was from a family with middle-class aspirations, I was educated – I had a fucking degree, for Christ's sake – and yet here I was quite happily drinking and smoking my life away, all aspirations of famous directordom long abandoned. Believe me, I have attempted to find an answer to this question on many occasions and I simply cannot.

Of course, there are peripheral explanations for my behaviour: cynics like my father, for instance, would probably put a lot of my predicament down to nothing more than simple laziness, and they would be partially right, for there is no doubt that the acquisition of even the lowliest paid of jobs would have been enough to totally transform my circumstances. Indeed, many of my fellow squatters had even offered to get me work on building sites or wherever else the source of their income happened to be at the time – but somehow I was never interested.

Other reasons may have something to do with depression; except that I don't really believe that I was ever depressed in a way that I would personally define depression: although it wasn't fun to have pockets that were consistently empty, there was certainly no shortage of laughter around. The only marginal solution that I have to offer is that I felt trapped: trapped by the routine of day-to-day survival, too concerned with the present tense to be bothered about what might happen in the future.

This, I believe, is a situation that is all too easy for all too many people to fall into.

However, if the man with no fingers had demonstrated to me that it was about time that I gave myself a good shaking, there was yet one more act required to be played out before I would finally get around to doing something that might actually improve my living conditions. This happened one night in September of that year, when I was arrested and placed in a Kings Cross cell.

The arrest came as an indirect result of yet another eviction notice being shunted into my general direction. Accompanied by Jim and his two compatriots, my response to the familiar letter from the council had been to go on the bender to end all benders.

It had started off early in the evening at a local pub and continued late into the night back at the squat, where bottle after bottle of Newcastle Brown Ale was greedily consumed. The atmosphere in the place had been gloomy: all four of us were becoming drained by the continual pressure of moving from place to place like gypsies. Then, at some point in the proceedings I did something foolish: by now completely drunk, I decided it would be a good idea if I discarded the bottle opener that we had been using to gain access to our cheap booze and instead use my teeth for that purpose. With the others looking on I raised a bottle to my mouth, bit into its metal top and gave a short twist of my head. The sound of laughter filled the room and an awful clicking sound could be heard as a piece of one of my teeth fell out on to the carpet.

Through my drunken haze this seemed to me like the final insult. Even though I had somehow been prepared to put up with the catalogue of failures that I'd managed to compile since I had first got it into my head to become a famous artist some nine years earlier there was something about the fact that I had now fallen so far that I was not even able to open a bottle of beer without some form of miniature disaster befalling me that was just too much for me to take. With a yelp of pain I punched the wall in both anger and anguish.

People who know about my connections with boxing occasionally ask for my opinions as to what was I thought was happening on the evening that Mike Tyson ended up biting off a chunk of Evander Holyfield's ear in the third round of their controversial rematch. I have a feeling that I will never come closer to understanding the set of conditions that conspired to turn Tyson into a temporary cannibal than I did on the night that I lost half a tooth trying to open a bottle of Newcastle Brown Ale. In the same way that Tyson had found himself forced to face up to the fact that the one consistent factor in his turbulent life – his ability to be better inside a boxing ring than anybody else on the planet – was now being laid to waste by a man who stood for everything that Tyson was not, I was finally compelled to confront the fact that I had failed at everything I had ever tried to do. It sounds melodramatic, I know. And yet my reactions to a childish gesture that had culminated in a mouthful of salty blood and a gaping hole where one of my incisors used to be, were strikingly similar to the way in which Tyson had found himself reacting on the occasion when he realised that destiny had turned against him. Like Tyson, I closed my eyes and struck out. Although using my teeth was out of the question, I struck out with my fists and feet at whatever was around me. I kicked the furniture in the flat, I used my elbows to gouge holes in the wooden door panels, I hurled the unopened bottle I was holding against the wall. Like Tyson, a red mist descended over my eyes and I lost control.

Unfortunately, however, my three companions were just as drunk and just as disillusioned and just as desperate as I. Instead of grabbing hold of my flailing fists and attempting to calm me down, they looked on with growing interest and finally decided that what I was doing seemed like fun. Do you recall that scene in the Monty Python movie *Life of Brian*, the one in which a group of Israelites are gathered for a stoning and cannot wait for the action to begin? First one stone is thrown and then another, until eventually a barrage of rocks are hurled in the direction of the unfortunate victim; finally, a dozen or so men are seen carrying an enormous boulder, which is then dropped on to the unhappy stonee. This was what it was like in the squat that night: holes were punched in doors, furniture was mangled and crushed, windows were smashed, and television screens were booted in and thrown through third-storey windows. With the four of us running through the flat laughing maniacally and atomising everything that lay in our path, this orgy of destruction went on uninterrupted for hours.

By the time that we had finally begun to grow tired of our frenetic exertions nothing in the place remained intact: every item of crockery, every plate, cup, saucer and ashtray now lay in broken pieces. On the pavement outside the flat rested the remains of a television, a stereo and an old fridge. Everything that could be broken had been broken. There was nothing left to sit on, nothing left to sleep on and nothing left to even shit into. And one wonders why the council don't like squatters.

However, even as the echoes of our combined primal scream were fading away there was an urgent hammering on what remained of the front door. Then said door remains were forced open and all at once the room was full of men and women in black uniforms wearing crash helmets. A pair of handcuffs was hurriedly placed around my wrists and along with the rest of the wrecking crew I was bundled into the back of a police van.

My belt, my shoelaces and the contents of my pockets were taken from me and I was placed on my own in a police cell. It was thankfully the first and only time that I would sample the delights of such a place. Inside, there was a single bed with a blanket and no pillow (presumably to prevent the cell's occupant from smothering himself), a toilet with no seat (presumably to prevent the cell's occupant from defecating in even the mildest of comfort) and several small novelettes worth of anti-police graffiti scrawled over the cold stone walls (presumably placed there by my predecessors and not, as had briefly occurred to me, by congenial police officers hoping to make their captives feel a bit more at home).

I lay on the bed and tried to rest. Strangely enough, I felt vaguely at peace as I waited to see what would happen next. However, as the hours ticked by and the alcohol started to drain from my system I began to grow more concerned. As far as I knew there were drugs in the flat; although none of them belonged to me it was unlikely that the police were going to believe that I, of all the flat's four inhabitants, was the only person who didn't happen to be selling them for a living.

My captors left me and my fears to fester for more than three hours before I finally heard the sound of a key turning in a lock and was asked to accompany a portly looking sergeant into an office. Behind a desk sat an irritated looking man in another black uniform, who, I guessed from his posture, must have been in charge. He was not a young man and eyed me with the look of a person who had just been raised from his bed.

'I've let your mates go,' he said sternly, lowering his gaze to a slip of paper that was lying on the desk before him and scribbling something on it in biro. 'You, however, are another thing altogether.'

This was an unexpected turn of events; you could almost hear the beer soaked gears turn in my head as I struggled to make sense of his comment. It took only a moment or so for me to reach a dreadful conclusion: there could be no possible explanation for his words other than the fact that my fellow squatters had turned traitor; I had no idea how they had managed to do this but somehow they must have convinced the person sitting opposite me that it was I who was responsible for the drugs that the police search had to have uncovered in the wrecked squat. As far as he was concerned I was Mr Big.

'Ever seen this before?' asked the man, thrusting a small slip of paper towards me.

'No,' I said honestly.

'Are you sure?' asked the man.

I took a closer look at what he was holding and realised that the markings on the piece of paper seemed familiar. It appeared to be a giro cheque.

'This was found on the floor of what, I'm told, used to be your bedroom,' said the other man.

The it came back to me.

A few weeks earlier I had found a giro cheque on the street. It was, I remembered, made out to someone I'd never heard of for the sum of precisely £1.75. Even though that amount represented a day's food rations I had never been inspired to do anything with it. I had simply put the giro on a table and forgotten all about it. I told the police officer the story.

'Don't you realise that's stealing?' he said angrily.

I was given a lecture as I sat wondering how on earth the police could have searched the squat and missed the plastic bags full of white substances that were sure to be hidden under one or another of my flatmates' beds. Did their sniffer dogs all have colds? Then I was told that I was in luck this time but if I ever stole anything again I would be in trouble. I apologised and was given a caution for my crime.

'And get that fucking mess cleared up,' my captor advised as I prepared to exit my temporary prison. 'I don't know how you people can live like that!'

I arrived home several hours later, crippled by an acute toothache and nursing a hangover that simply defied description. The flat looked like it had been decorated by Stevie Wonder. My three flatmates were all lying in the rubble sleeping off their own hangovers. I went into the wreckage of the bathroom and examined my broken tooth in a shard of equally incomplete mirror that only the night before had been securely attached to the wall. Then I did something inexplicable.

You will remember how I droned on several hours ago about my general lack of enthusiasm concerning that enforced physical transformation from Robin Cousins into Alexei Sayle. There was, you may be pleased to learn, a reason for my inane bleatings. It was to save myself the trouble of having to do it at this exciting point in the proceedings, and it was by some means an explanation for doing what I was about to do.

As I stared at my smashed tooth I also found myself staring at the rest of my sorry figure. It was not a particularly appealing sight: a 26-year-old squatter with yellow eyes and a comical smile which looked as if someone had blotted out one of his teeth with a felt tip pen. Skinny and under-fed due to the practically non-existent diet that I was forced to adhere to, and possessing a haircut that resembled Jim Bowen on a bad day.

I don't know what made me do it. Certainly if I had any idea of what was about to happen to me in the coming weeks I would have made more of an effort to remain as presentable as possible. All I can say, as I covered my cranium with shaving foam and set about it mercilessly with a disposable razor is that it seemed sensible at the time. It took about five minutes to complete the task. The sides of my head, which were as thick as they had always been, gave me a little trouble but removing what remained of Robin Cousins's hair from the top of my head was as easy as skimming the skin off a bowl of custard.

There is a train of thought which suggests that such an extreme act of depilation has the effect of imbuing its perpetrator with hitherto un-hinted at levels of attractiveness. Indeed, when you look at people like Telly Savalas, Yul Brynner and even Evander Holyfield, one might say that lack of hair in their case was a positive advantage. With me, however, it was a different story. Minus my sparse locks I did not suddenly mutate into some kind of sex god; to my dismay I bore more than a passing resemblance to that bleached alien in the faked Roswell autopsy video that got fans of *The X-Files* all excited a few years ago.

By the end of the day I had purchased a black cap, which I refused to remove when I wasn't lying in bed. I looked, as my mother pointed out to me on a visit home, 'like a refugee from a concentration camp'. And yet, perhaps, there was a reason, after all, for my self-mutilation. Although I was not to know it, before the year was out I would be keeping company with people who were many light years away from the people I was currently sharing my life with. And when the trainers, managers, promoters and boxers whom I attempted to interview took one look at the pathetic spectacle standing before them, who can blame them if they felt a little sorry for him?

※ ※ ※ ※

Fed up of walking on broken glass I moved again. I found another abandoned flat and, with Jerry and his collection of videos and boxing magazines safely beside me, broke inside. The flat was part of the same estate from which we had just been evicted; inside, it was an almost carbon-copy of the one that we had recently wrecked. We decided we'd be more careful with the furniture in future. There was, however, one fundamental difference between the flat that we had just left and its undamaged replacement. It had nothing to do with the fact that the carpet was not covered with smashed crockery and shards of splintered wood; nor did it have anything to do with the fact that the front door was still on its hinges and that the toilet bowl was not in several pieces. This flat came with a typewriter: a great big rusty old thing that the previous occupant had left behind. I started tinkering with it and wondered vaguely how much it was worth.

※ ※ ※ ※

Having nothing else better to do with my time as I waited for the next eviction letter to arrive, I decided to try my hand at typing something with a view to attempting to persuade someone, somewhere, to purchase the results of my efforts. I really have no idea as to the source of this farfetched scheme, but at that point in my life it seemed like the right thing for somebody with a lot of time on his hands who had just found an old typewriter to be doing. It was, I guess, only natural that the first thing I would decide to write about on my new toy would be boxing.

Because I thought there might be money in it I had toyed for a while with the idea of writing soft pornography and sending it to *Penthouse* (somewhere, at the bottom of an old suitcase, I still have several laughable attempts that I made in that genre) but my heart wasn't in it. It had to be boxing; it was, after all, the subject which, deep down, I realised that I probably knew most about. In the midst of all my failed attempts to become someone I never could be – it had been something that I just couldn't seem to completely let go of.

I burrowed through Jim's pile of boxing magazines and tried to work out how the professionals did it. I pondered for a while as to what the subject of my debut effort as a boxing writer might be. In the end I chose Frank Bruno. Bruno, it has to be said, was something of an obvious choice. At the time he was only a month or so away from a doomed ring confrontation in Las Vegas with the ferocious and then-unbeaten heavyweight champion Mike Tyson. He was everybody's favourite and, I figured, a subject who provided me with my best chance of ever having anything published.

I got hold of Britain's only boxing publication, *Boxing News*, and counted the length of one of its features. Then I sat down behind my inherited typewriter and wrote 2,000 words about Frank Bruno. Then I read the 2,000 words I had written about Frank Bruno and screwed the pages into little balls and threw them into the bin. Then I sat down behind my inherited typewriter and wrote another 2,000 words about Frank Bruno. Eventually, by a process of slow osmosis I was able to make those 2,000 words read like they had not been written by somebody with the mental age of a seven-year-old. Then I stuck my words in an envelope with a covering letter and sat down and waited.

Three weeks later, to my everlasting astonishment, my article appeared on 21 October 1988 in the centre spread of *Boxing News*. Entitled, 'Mighty Tyson must forgive and forget' it had my name underneath the headline in bold capitals. I danced in triumph, not daring to believe that I may have at last found something I was halfway decent at. I wrote another article and *Boxing News* published it again. I was paid £50 for each of these efforts. A fortune.

Then, all at once my fortunes seemed to change. During my regular Christmas stint at the Post Office I met someone who was looking for a flatmate. She was a student who lived in a small council flat in Finsbury Park and didn't seem remotely concerned by the state of my clothing or the fact that I'd demolished one of the last places that I lived in. I moved in with her and bade a welcome and relieved farewell to the world of squatting. My lost weekend and a half was over at last. There was, however, now rent to be paid, a minor detail that I had not had to concern myself with for the past couple of years. It was time, I decided, to get myself another shitty job. Before I did so, however, I'd try to make a bit more money by writing some more boxing articles. Perhaps I'd even try to meet a real boxer and write about him.

Tenth Rule Of Boxing: Boxers Are Not Angels

I think it's asking rather a lot of a person to expect him to be able to ride roughshod over some of society's most fundamental values with complete impunity, and at the same time behave like a vestal virgin. This is why one should never be surprised when a boxer takes it upon himself to revert to character when he is outside the ropes. By definition, a fighter's predominant means of communication is violence; it is the language in which he is most fluent – who can blame him if he sometimes finds himself using the wrong words?

The boxer who misbehaves outside the ring is unfortunately one of the sport's most recognisable clichés. The boxer who drinks too much, who womanises, who snorts cocaine, who smashes up hotel rooms or gets involved in public brawls is far more likely to grab the headlines than the boxer who sits at home doing a jigsaw puzzle. This is one of the reasons why boxers are often perceived by the public as ignorant thugs who just happen to be good at fighting, when in reality the majority of boxers possess a refined form of intelligence that only those who study the sport can even begin to understand. Indeed, I can honestly say that I have never met an unintelligent boxer; although I have come across many who would doubtless struggle with quantum mechanics, and I have also met some who would even have difficulty reciting their six times table, I have never been in the presence of a fighter who could in any way be described as stupid. Boxers are decision makers: they are trained to reach a conclusion at speeds that would be impossible for the likes of you and I. Moreover, the decisions they are compelled to make are so often life transforming. When you are sharing a ring with someone who has the capacity to kill you, there are far more important things to think about than how many sugars you take in your tea.

When a boxer makes a decision he must usually commit to it instantly and immediately prepare to suffer the consequences of his actions. This can happen outside as well as inside the ring and unfortunately the repercussions in both situations can be every bit as catastrophic. It is tempting at this point to offer Mike Tyson as a prime example of a boxer who has lived to regret some of the decisions he has made in his short life. You could ask him why, for example, he decided to bite off a chunk of another man's ear when the eyes of the world were staring over his shoulder; you could enquire as to what exactly was going through his mind when he took that one drink too many and drove his car into a tree one evening back in 1989; or you could demand to know the reason why he threw away three years of his life when he took that girl to that hotel room and did what he did to her. But that, I feel, would be picking on him.

Instead, I can focus my gaze almost at random upon boxers such as Hector Camacho, Michael Nunn, Michael Moorer, Trevor Berbick, Riddick Bowe, Leon Spinks, Carlos Monzon, James Toney, Mitch Green, Tyrell Biggs, Don Curry and Sonny Liston; people you may or may not have heard of, but all guilty in one way or another of crossing the line. People who happen to share Mike Tyson's unhappy propensity for making decisions that end up being the wrong ones.

Yet while a boxer is not be congratulated for his behavioural transgressions, he does at least deserve a little sympathy on those occasions when he slips over the edge. He has, after all, been taught that in order to succeed in his line of work it is compulsory that he break the law. The violent and – in any other walk of life other than on the battlefield – quite illegal spectacle of one man committing physical violence on another may be kept separate from the law-abiding public by a set of ropes or a television screen, but a boxer can be forgiven if he sometimes forgets where he is. Boxers are not angels: they are people who punch each other for a living; for this reason one should not be too startled if from time to time they end up taking a little of their work home with them.

12

Strange Town

MICHAEL Watson stood in front of the enormous mirror and looked at himself. Dressed in a pair of crisp white shorts and a loose T-shirt adorned with a necklace of sweat, he regarded his reflection as if he were seeing it for the very first time. Occasionally he would throw a short jab at the image before him or puff out his cheeks to expose his teeth in a kind of comic book snarl that I would come to know well. And now and then he would steal a glance at my reflection, checking out the worried looking young man sitting self-consciously on a wooden bench in the background. Then, with his face refusing to betray any emotion, his eyes would return to himself.

This curious ritual carried on uninterrupted for more than ten minutes. Watson and the mirror. The mirror and Watson. Watson dancing on the balls of his feet and aiming punches at his own reflection. Watson ducking the blows of an imaginary opponent in some imaginary world title fight. Watson launching uppercuts and sweeping hooks into the empty air. Watson standing still as a statue. Watson inspecting the goods. Watson looking at himself.

Michael Watson was only a week or so away from his next fight. He was boxing an American stepping stone named James Shavers on the undercard to the Gary Mason-Trevor Hughroy

Currie British heavyweight title fight at the Royal Albert Hall and was not expected to lose. In fact, he was scarcely expected to even break sweat. This, however, did not deter the 24-year-old from taking a lingering look at the results of months of hard labour: hour after hour spent working in the gym; endless mornings running through the streets of Islington while others slept; night after night lying in his bed dreaming starstruck dreams. This was Michael Watson's ultimate creation: the body, the bulging muscles polished by his own sweat, the glistening torso, the athletic tree-trunk legs. This was the physical manifestation of his self-image. And soon it would go to work.

It was the first time I had ever visited a boxing gym, and yet gaining access to such a place had proven to be a surprisingly straightforward procedure. It had taken only two telephone calls: one to the editor of *Boxing News*, who, after being reminded that I had contributed two articles to his publication, kindly supplied me with a contact number for Michael Watson; and one to the boxer's trainer, Eric Seccombe. In response to my request for an interview with his ward, Seccombe had replied, 'Michael's training at the gym tomorrow afternoon – why don't you come down then?'

The gym was located among the leather jackets and cheap tourist baubles of London's Carnaby Street. It was hidden away in the basement of one of the shops and I had to walk up and down the street several times before I spotted the small hand-written sign that was propped up against a door. Access was facilitated by the use of an entry phone that was guarded by the practised growl of the gym's owner, who took a moment or so to consider my somewhat unconvincing claim that I was a reporter with *Boxing News* before he agreed to let me in.

Inside, the gym conformed to almost every stereotypical Hollywood cliché of what a boxing gym is supposed to look like. It was dark and dingy, with a well trodden boxing ring at one end of an oblong room and a variety of weights and hanging punchbags filling the remainder of the interior. At the centre of the ring two black heavyweights were half-heartedly swinging punches at one another as a handful of tired old men with pug noses looked on. The pervading aroma was a mixture of sweat and cigarette smoke. Here and there the face of an old time fighter peered out of a yellowing poster, celebrating the triumphs and failures of another era. And, as if to reinforce the illusion that I had just stepped on to the set of *Rocky IV*, there was a man sitting on a chair in the corner of the room holding a spit bucket.

I stood in silence for several minutes, taking in the sights and sounds, wondering what to do next; focusing alternately on the large, balding man who was bellowing instructions at the fighters and the solitary figure dancing with a skipping rope at the far end of the room. Then without warning a bell sounded and all at once everything in the gym stopped: the heavyweights nodded wryly to each other and let their fists fall to their sides, the fat man ceased his shouting and slumped into a chair, and the man with the skipping rope slowly wound down his movements. Then out of the corner of my eye I saw a small figure edge towards me.

'You the reporter who wants to meet Michael?' said a voice.

※ ※ ※ ※

I had decided to try and meet Michael Watson simply because it was something that I thought I'd be able to do. Spurred on by the glory of the two articles that had been published in *Boxing News* I had determined that my third effort would be a little more ambitious. I would attempt to interview a real boxer.

Watson, I must explain, had first caught the eye of the boxing fraternity a year or so earlier when, after being drafted in as a late replacement for the exciting British middleweight Tony Sibson, he had looked more than capable in taking the step up in class to stop the world rated American puncher 'Dangerous' Don Lee in five rounds. It had been a curiously ambiguous performance, however; for although Watson had dealt with the more experienced man with unexpected aplomb, he had somehow not looked good in doing so. Despite the fact that the punches he had thrown at the American had been both accurate and hurtful, they were not the eye-catching blows that boxing fans demanded. For this reason the press were yet to be inspired to turn him into a star.

I had watched that fight on a black and white television set in yet another Islington squat, and had been interested to learn that Watson lived in the same district of London as I. He was also about the same age as me, I later discovered, and I guessed that of all the reasonably well known British boxers on the scene at that time, Watson would more likely be willing to speak to someone with only two published articles to his name than, say, Lloyd Honeyghan or Frank Bruno.

And that was the way it turned out. During our initial telephone conversation Eric Seccombe revealed to me that only one other journalist had bothered to get in touch with Michael Watson since the Don Lee fight. Seccombe was more than happy for me to do an article on his fighter; as a matter of fact it was all I could do to dissuade him from coming round to my flat with Watson and doing it right there and then.

The trainer had been waiting for me for almost half an hour at the Carnaby Street gym when I arrived. I was wearing an old pair of blue jeans and that black cap to hide my shaven Roswell alien head and Seccombe assumed at first that I was courier, there to pick up a package or something. 'You don't look like a boxing writer,' he said after we had made our introductions.

'What do they look like?' I had replied.

Eric Seccombe was a short man in his early 50s who, as well as being the trainer of Michael Watson, was also a London cabby. Although his frame had filled out over the years, Seccombe had once enjoyed a moderately successful career in the amateurs, boxing at bantamweight. In spite of the increased bulk, however, his movements were still quick and graceful. He had been training Michael Watson since the boxer was a boy and had been there to help his charge make the transition from the unpaid ranks, where Watson had claimed the London middleweight title, to professional contender. Seccombe's love for Watson was all too easily apparent, as was his pride in the man whom he treated like a son.

'Michael's just doing some final exercises,' said Seccombe pointing into the corner of the gym at the man who had been skipping rope. 'If you wait a few minutes I'll bring him over.'

I sat down on a wooden bench by the doorway to the gym and tried not to stare at Watson, who by now had taken up his position in front of the mirror that spanned the whole length of one side of the gym. I could not help feeling like an interloper. I wondered how long it would be before Watson and his trainer realised that I was not who I claimed to be. I wondered how they would react when they discovered that, instead of the seasoned *Boxing News* reporter they had been expecting from my description over the telephone, what they had got was a recently retired north London squatter who had had been writing about boxing for little more than a couple of months. And I could not help but ask myself what I was doing on the set of *Rocky IV*.

What was I doing in the midst of real professional boxers and real professional trainers and real professional spit bucket carriers?

Watson walked slowly over to me followed closely by Seccombe. He seemed wary. His hair was cut short and he wore a thin moustache above his mouth. He did not smile but offered me his hand. 'You that reporter?' he inquired, already, it seemed to me, sensing from my appearance that he was being asked to be party to some kind of inelegant charade.

I gulped a little and came partially clean. I told Watson my name and admitted that I was new to this role. I told him that I written only a half-dozen or so articles on boxing and that he would, in fact, be the first boxer that I had ever interviewed. Watson's face drooped slightly and he turned towards his trainer in disappointment.

Seccombe peered at me over his glasses and thought for a moment. I could feel my cheeks redden. They were on to me: it had taken only minutes for them to realise that I was more boxing fan than boxing scribe. Any moment now I would be asked to leave. But then something unexpected happened. As I struggled to keep my composure, the diminutive trainer brought a hand up to my shoulder and his face broke into a smile. 'Never mind,' he said, patting me on the shoulder. 'You're on the way up and Michael's on the way up – let's see if we can't help each other out.'

We pushed our way through the crowds of tourists and walked to a nearby café, where I hurriedly took notes as I sipped at the coffee they had bought for me. Now that I was actually in the position of interviewing a living, breathing boxer, I didn't really know what to say to him.

All the questions I had been carefully rehearsing refused to come out of my dry lips. Instead, I was happy to let Watson do the talking.

With Seccombe grinning indulgently at his fighter, Watson told me of his plans for world domination. Of how he intended to clean up the middleweight division and become its leading exponent. Of how he would unify the various titles and retire still young and unblemished. Of how he would become the best middleweight in the world. It was, I was later to realise, standard stuff for any young boxer to be saying when confronted with the reporter's notebook. It was a litany that was scheduled to be repeated to me on many different occasions and by many different fighters.

Then Watson's attention turned to more immediate matters. 'But there's one person I've got to meet in the ring before all this happens,' he announced.

'Who's that?' I asked.

'Nigel Benn,' he replied.

'Yeah, Nigel Benn,' echoed Seccombe. 'Up until now he's just been fighting light-middleweights. Wait and see what happens when he meets someone with Michael's strength.'

'He'll be in serious trouble,' agreed Watson.

Seccombe leaned towards my seat and tapped his nose knowingly. 'Benn's frightened of Michael,' he said, lowering his voice. 'Tell him, Michael.'

For this first time that afternoon a smile appeared on Watson's handsome face. 'Yeah, he's scared of me,' he agreed self-consciously.

'Tell him, Michael,' urged Seccombe once more.

Watson cleared his throat awkwardly. 'I went down to a club one night and Benn was there with all his mates,' revealed the boxer. 'When he saw me he turned away from me and wouldn't look me in the eye. He was scared.'

※ ※ ※ ※

In many ways Nigel Benn was the exact mirror opposite of Michael Watson. He was from east London and a West Ham supporter, Watson was from north London and an Arsenal fan. Benn was the ex-soldier whose inherent violence never quite managed to settle beneath the surface, and Watson was the quiet family man who went to church. Benn was the knockout specialist whose image dominated both the front and back pages of the nationals, and Watson was the thoughtful craftsman, world-rated due to his victory over Don Lee but ignored by all but the most ardent boxing fan. Benn was high-profile and Watson was practically anonymous.

Watson was already three years into his boxing career when Nigel Benn had exploded on to the scene in 1987. Never going beyond round seven, in 20 fights Benn had managed to knock out every one of his opponents. He was excitement on a stick; a reckless fighter whose disregard for the quality of his opposition frequently placed him in danger of coming unstuck.

In a memorable 1988 defence of his Commonwealth middleweight title against Anthony Logan, Benn had swayed on the precipice of disaster before his great equaliser had found its mark at the end of round two. This mixture of vulnerability and concussive power meant that Benn was big business. While Michael Watson continued to fight on the undercards, Benn was already a headline fighter. There was rarely an empty seat in the house when Nigel Benn was fighting.

There had been talk in the boxing press for some time about the possibility of getting Benn and Watson in the ring together. On the face of it, this match-up seemed a natural. It had all the ingredients of a truly compelling encounter: good against bad, power versus fortitude, north London against east; everybody knew that a Benn-Watson fight would be a tremendous money-spinner. There was, however, one fairly major obstacle standing in the way.

Michael was managed by Mickey Duff, at the time the dominant force in British boxing. Like many fight managers, Duff was himself a former boxer and had been one of the sport's leading money men for more than three decades. An articulate and aggressive speaker, Duff possessed an impressive CV: since he had entered into management in the early 50s after finding himself 'at the wrong end of the right business', he had led a number of British fighters to world titles. Although now in his early 60s, Duff's stable of boxers was still one of the most impressive in the country. As well as Michael Watson, Duff was also currently responsible for directing the careers of other top fighters including Frank Bruno, Gary Mason, Lloyd Honeyghan, Kirkland Laing and John Mugabi. However, there were signs that his empire was crumbling.

The first chink in Mickey Duff's armour had appeared back in 1985 when a *Sunday Times* exposé had revealed that, along with fight managers and promoters Terry Lawless, Jarvis Astaire and Mike Barrett, Duff had formed a secret cartel. Although not illegal, this alliance had effected a pooling of resources and profits, a situation that to many represented a clear conflict of interests. In view of the fact that a boxing manager's traditional role was to ensure that his fighter's purse was as large as possible, and that a promoter's modus operandi inevitably involved him endeavouring to pay featured fighters as little as possible, the feeling was that it could not be to a boxer's benefit if his manager happened to be Terry Lawless and his promoter happened to be Mickey Duff.

When the news broke, an inquiry was immediately ordered by the British Boxing Board of Control. After lengthy interviews with all participants the board eventually exonerated Duff and his allies, stating, 'But for the aggressive participation of these people, boxing would not be in the healthy state that it's in today.' For Duff's rivals, however, this acquittal only served to deepen their resentment. Duff was the man whose stranglehold over the BBC's coverage of domestic boxing prevented them from getting a share of the lucrative fees that television offered. Duff was the person who all the best young boxing talent still flocked towards. And now, thought some, he was the man who appeared to have the Board in his pocket.

Yet just as the younger Duff had found himself forced into battle three decades earlier with boxing's established overlord Jack Solomons now it was his turn to lock swords with the younger generation. Chief among his rivals was the maverick promoter Frank Warren, who was currently reaping the rewards of a contract with ITV of a similar nature to the one that Mickey Duff enjoyed with the BBC. Warren's shows were featured regularly on programmes such as *Fight Night* and *The Big Fight Live*, the tidy sum that the promoter earned from this happy situation had enabled him to lay the foundations of a power base that would one day see him take control of British boxing.

Far less powerful but much more threatening was Warren's former press agent Ambrose Mendy. Mendy brought glamour to the business and promised the dawning of a New Age of boxing. Articulate, elegant and always dressed in the latest designer gear, Mendy was seen by many in boxing as the Antichrist. There was good reason for this analogy, for as well as threatening to transform the sport into a more brutal version of professional wrestling, Mendy was also black. Moreover, Mendy was black and proud to be black in a white man's business in which the Negro had traditionally played a subservient role.

It was not long before Mendy's cellphone began receiving eager calls from boxers all over the country. Principle among those anxious to place themselves in the manicured fingers of Ambrose Mendy was Nigel Benn, who was prepared to visit the courtroom in order to invalidate a managerial contract that he held with Frank Warren. With Benn as his figurehead, Mendy's fame was assured. His acceptance by boxing's ruling classes, however, was not. Mendy, it transpired, had a prison record – he had done time for a variety of petty crimes. It was ostensibly for this reason that the BBBoC declined Mendy's application for a manager's licence, thus preventing him from being able to stand in his fighter's corner when he was working. The boxing establishment's commendable if rather uncharacteristic desire to see its sport disassociated from any hint of criminality also had other repercussions for Ambrose Mendy: chief among these was the fact that it was forbidden for him to put his name to any legal contracts that involved a boxer. Ostensibly, it was for this reason that Duff refused to sit down with Mendy at the negotiating table and set a date for Michael Watson to fight Nigel Benn.

While the rest of the country licked their lips at the prospect of Benn climbing into the ring with Watson, Duff was busy refusing to have anything to do with Mendy. This meant that both boxers had little choice but to carry on fighting meaningless fights in the hope that they could eventually be manoeuvred into a world title shot. This situation was far more of a cross to bear for Watson, who could only watch as his rival continued to grab the headlines with his exciting knock-outs, and part of the reason why, to my great surprise, he telephoned me a couple of days after our interview with a suggestion.

'How's the article going?' he asked.

'Almost finished,' I lied, a little annoyed that there was nobody else present in the flat to bear witness to the fact that a real, live boxer had actually telephoned me.

Being not quite sure what to do with them, I had left the pile of jumbled notes I had taken during our meeting stranded on the kitchen table. 'I've been thinking, Ian,' Watson explained (now we were on first-name terms!). 'Why don't you sell the story about me and Nigel Benn in the club to the *Daily Mirror* or something?'

Why didn't I sell the story about Watson and Benn to the *Daily Mirror*? I have to confess that the thought hadn't occurred to me (how could it have?) but in principle it sounded like a good idea. However, quite how one went about doing this I really hadn't a clue.

'What should I do?' I asked. 'Just ring up a newspaper and offer it to them?'

'Why don't you try?' said Watson.

I decided to attempt to use a little common sense. I took a walk down to the local newsagents and I bought myself a copy of *The Sun* and the *Daily Mirror*. I took them home and ran my eyes over their sports pages until I located an article about boxing. Then I got a number for the *Daily Mirror* from directory enquiries and called them. I asked to speak to Ron Wills, whose name was attached to a story about Frank Bruno in that morning's paper. He answered.

'Hello,' I said nervously. 'I'm a freelance boxing reporter and I've got a story about Nigel Benn.'

I explained the background to my world exclusive and Wills appeared less than impressed. After a long silence he told me, 'Okay then, send over the quotes over and I'll take a look at them.'

Wills gave me another number to call. It was answered by a bored-sounding voice, to whom I breathlessly read out a selection of quotes from Michael Watson on the subject of his cowardly rival which I had rescued from the kitchen table. I heard the click-click-click of a keyboard as the person on the other end of the line duly recorded my words for posterity.

'That it then?' the bored sounding voice said when I had finished speaking.

Ron Wills called me back half an hour or so later. 'I've just seen the quotes,' he said coldly. 'Not up to much are they?'

I tried to think of some response but all that came out was a kind of spluttering noise.

'Listen,' Wills continued. 'You're new to this game, aren't you.'

'Fairly,' I agreed.

'Well let me tell you that stories like this are ten a penny – I'll give you £50 for it.'

Fifty pounds. It was what I had been paid by *Boxing News* for a whole 2,000-word essay. Not bad going for an morning's work. Not bad at all. However, there was something in the tone of the boxing writer's voice that deterred me from instantly agreeing to his offer. 'I'll call you back,' I said cautiously.

I telephoned Michael Watson and told him what I had been offered for the story. He seemed disappointed. The thought that his utterances were considered to be worth only £50 apparently did absolutely nothing for his ego. 'Call *The Sun*,' he advised. 'See if they'll give you a bit more.'

I rang *The Sun*, this time asking to speak to Colin Hart, its chief boxing writer. Hart, however, was out of the country at the time and I was instead put through to the sports editor. I gave him the same spiel: I told him about Watson and Benn and the club and was once more requested to send over the quotes. Then I was passed over to another bored sounding voice sitting behind a typewriter and again I dictated Watson's words.

The phone rang 20 minutes later. 'Great stuff,' enthused the sports editor. 'We'll give you £250 for it.'

An even better morning's work.

I was feeling more than pleased with myself when the telephone rang for a third time. For doing next to nothing I had just earned a small fortune. In the Christmas job I had only recently finished at the Post Office it would have taken me a week – plus overtime – to have earned such an amount. 'I've been thinking,' said the voice of the *Mirror*'s Ron Wills. 'Perhaps we can offer you a hundred for those quotes.'

I cut him short before he could continue. 'I've already sold the story to someone else,' I revealed.

'Can I ask who?' demanded Wills.

'*The Sun*,' I replied.

Without saying anything more he put the phone down on me.

%% %% %% %%

My story, imaginatively entitled 'Benn Running Scared', appeared in *The Sun* the very next morning. Although I could scarcely contain my excitement at hitting the heady heights of tabloid journalism, I was nevertheless disappointed to discover that my newsprint debut had not managed to make the back page. Nor, for that matter, had it been able to find a home on the penultimate page. In fact, the story had just about managed to crawl on to the racing section, some four or five pages from the back, where it lay buried among the day's betting forecasts. More immediately irritating was the fact that they had also spelled my name wrong. Instead of 'Benn Running Scared – by Ian Probert', the headline read, 'Benn Running Scared – by Colin Hart'.

Actually, I was perhaps a little fortunate that *The Sun*'s senior boxing correspondent had erroneously elected to accept responsibility for my words that morning. For somewhere deep in east London, an infuriated Nigel Benn sat behind his copy of *The Sun* seething with rage. It may not have been at that precise moment that the self-styled Dark Destroyer decided that he had to get Michael Watson into the ring with him at all costs, but it must have been at some point around that time. In any case, the very next day a story detailing Benn's hatred of Watson appeared on the back page of *The Sun*. Apparently Benn did not appreciate being called a coward and could not wait to make Watson and the author of that article suffer for their insults.

※ ※ ※ ※

That same morning Michael Watson telephoned me again. He had seen Benn's response to his story in the paper and was elated. It may not have been his picture on the back page but it might just have well been. Thanks to Benn his profile had been raised considerably. Watson was about to go off to the gym and had called to tell me that his mother had just received a call from the *Sunday Sport*, who wished to follow up on the two fighters' burgeoning war of words. Why didn't I call them and offer them some more quotes? Why not indeed?

I called their sports desk and a northern accent answered the telephone.

I went through the Benn/Watson/Club routine for a third time and optimistically told them that Watson was prepared to say anything they wanted him to about Nigel Benn.

'You a boxing writer?' said the voice.

I thought for a moment before formulating my response. In the accepted sense of the term I supposed I could call myself a boxing writer. After all, I'd had two articles published in a boxing magazine and if you were prepared to excuse the mis-spelling, I even had my name beneath an article in today's *Sun*.

'Yes,' I said finally.

'Do you want a job?'

Eleventh Rule Of Boxing: Boxing Writers Are A Rummy Bunch

Summer 1974:

In a bizarre twist that had ASFC officials hastily consulting the rule book, yesterday evening's eagerly anticipated match-up between reigning ASFC lightweight champion Gary 'The Runner' Peacock and Ian 'Odd Accent' Probert ended in disarray when the elder sister of Burnley's unheralded challenger burst into the ring to break up the action. It was a farcical climax to a contest that had promised so much.

'I just didn't see her coming,' said After School Fights Council president David Flood, 12. 'She came out of nowhere and I couldn't do anything about it.' Flood was speaking at a hastily convened press conference held in a corner of the Lockleaze adventure playground. He seemed visibly shaken as he chain-sucked wine gums in an effort to calm his nerves. Also present were the two fighters, who were both claiming victory and apparently eager to settle their differences as soon as a date could be set.

Yet it had all been so different less than five minutes earlier when the crowds of onlookers had gathered outside the school gates to witness the end product of two weeks of bad blood between the two protagonists. The atmosphere had been almost carnival as, accompanied by swelling entourages, the fighters had briskly stepped up to face each other. Indeed, such had been their eagerness to commencing exchanging blows that the formality of the national anthems was mutually waived so that the action could begin forthwith.

Peacock was wearing a black jacket with a red school badge as he cautiously circled his opponent, while the slightly smaller Probert had opted to wear a black jacket with a red school badge. Both were also wearing stripy ties, although the knot in the champion's was slightly larger than his opponent's and, from the sound that his shoes made as he stomped about on the pavement, he was wearing Blakeys. But if there was any psychological advantage to be had from this disparity in size and noise making potential, it certainly did not seem to concern Probert who, even before a punch had been thrown, was demanding that the champion remove his glasses.

The action – what there was of it – was frenetic and fast paced. The first attack came from the challenger, who lunged towards his rival with a howl of rage and threw a volley of punches in his general direction. The blows, however, were merely arm punches and hit the empty air like slightly undersized unexploded bombs, giving Peacock the opportunity to launch a counter attack which Probert cleverly parried. There was a gasp from the crowd and suddenly Peacock was down for the first time in his career. He did not appear dazed, however, climbing quickly to his feet and managing to avoid several kicks that his opponent aimed at his ribs.

Now Probert had the champion in a neck hold, squeezing the breath from his lungs. Incredibly, with only four seconds on the clock Peacock was in danger of losing his unbeaten record. With the champion's face turning red from his exertions it looked like the AFSC lightweight crown was about to change hands. The startled crowd could only watch in amazement as Probert grabbed a handful of Peacock's hair and demanded to know if the champion had had enough.

Before he could answer, however, there was pandemonium at ringside as a larger figure dressed in a white blouse and grey pleated skirt stepped into view. While the referee and other officials looked on impotently, the newcomer was quickly between the two fighters. In each hand she held one of their ears.

'I thought she'd already gone home,' said a despondent Probert afterwards. 'I had no idea she was going to do that!'

Probert's opponent, however, was less than charitable, 'He was losing so he got his sister to break it up,' said Peacock to hoots of appreciation from his followers. 'The fight was fixed – next time we'll do it somewhere else, somewhere where his sister can't get to us.'

※ ※ ※ ※

It is the job of a boxing writer to try and add a little dignity and order to a ritual that is so often steeped in chaos. It is his function to use words to dress up the inherent barbarism contained in the sport and attempt to persuade the reader that the ceremony being described has little to do with two men beating each other up for the privilege of finding out who is the strongest. All the more surprising, then, that some of the finest writers in history have at one time or another taken it upon themselves to undertake this responsibility.

From William Hazlitt, who wrote of the skirmish between one Bill Neate and somebody called Thomas 'The Gas Man' Hickman back in the 19th century to recent Booker Prize nominee Tim Mo, noted exponents of literature have shown an unceasing fascination for boxing. Ernest Hemingway, Oscar Wilde, Lord Byron, Norman Mailer, Joyce Carol Oates, John Milton, Arthur Conan Doyle, George Bernard Shaw, Budd Schulberg, even Homer – who covered boxing back in 1184BC when he wrote of the monumental battle between Epeus and Euryalus: these are just some of the eminent wordsmiths who have been drawn to pugilism.

Over the years, a plethora of explanations have been offered up to attempt to account for reasons why people with surely the most tranquil and contemplative of occupations continue to be fascinated by one of the most violent and reckless. American writer Budd Schulberg contends that boxing is a microcosm of life, 'an intensification of the life forces we struggle to understand'; while, as well as seeing the sport as a 'dazzlingly explicit display of masochism' Joyce Carol Oates suggests that boxing exhibits a 'theoretical anxiety' that lies at the heart of its seductiveness for the writer.

Personally, I've never been entirely sure about and – as you have probably guessed by now – entirely happy with my motivations for wanting to write about boxers. But while it would be a scandalous overstatement to suggest that any of my abstract musings have come even close to encapsulating the essence of the sport in the manner that any of these aforementioned literateurs have been able to, it is an activity that for me is almost addictive in its allure.

To the observer, boxing appears to run the full gamut of human emotions; in its motley collection of winners, losers, liars, cheats and Samaritans, the sport presents a shrink-wrapped ready meal of the complete range of the human condition. For someone who believes they have something to say about the nature of the way in which we live our lives, boxing as source material is worth a hundred Greek tragedies and a thousand Shakespearean epics. Perhaps the more pertinent question should be how someone who calls himself a writer could not be interested in writing about boxing.

Part Two

Me and

Muhammad Ali

13

Incident in a Nightclub

OF course, now that I've been in the 'business' (on and off) for the best part of a decade I realise how very lucky I was. I recognise that under normal circumstances managing to land yourself a plum job on a national newspaper (for, whatever its credentials, and however dubious the nature of its ethics, that is what the *Sunday Sport* purported to be) is usually rather more difficult to achieve than it was for me. And I know that were it not for a quite unprecedented mixture of coincidence and pure dumb luck, there is every likelihood that I would still be daydreaming my life away in a London squat, ten years older with a decade's worth of wrinkles and lost hair; just another statistic of a society that so often fails to function at even the most basic of levels. Either that, or I may have ended up going back home to my mum.

As it turned out, the call that I placed to the *Sunday Sport* that day could not have been more opportune. It came only a week or so after the whole sports desk had resigned in protest at the paper's decision to run a world exclusive (complete with photographic evidence) outlining the story of how a flying saucer had happened to land in the centre circle at Old

Trafford. Naturally, I had no knowledge of this mass exodus at the time. I was also not to know that since then the *Sunday Sport* had been putting out feelers and trying without success to find replacements for its errant sports desk for some time. They were getting fairly desperate and I was available.

To me it seemed both natural – and to some extent almost pre-ordained – that the path which had led me to dump the life that my parents had chosen for me all those years ago, to become a failed famous artist, failed famous director and end up living on potatoes would finally culminate in boxing. It had, after all, been there, simmering away inside me all of that time. Sometimes temporarily discarded, sometimes blatantly betrayed but all too often simply too much of a part of me to be able to successfully ignore indefinitely. In some ways it was a relief that I at last seemed to be acknowledging what was really important to me. There was also the fact that here at last was an opportunity to begin making something that resembled a regular income. It had, after all, been more than six years since I could count myself lucky enough to be in such a position.

However, before I could begin my new career as a gutter pressman there were one or two minor details to be ironed out. More lying, I'm afraid. Chief among these minor details was the small matter of my having no other contacts in boxing apart from Michael Watson and his trainer Eric, a fact that I had been at great pains to avoid revealing when this subject had been broached both on the telephone and during a subsequent face to face meeting with my prospective employers. This was by no means a small problem. And even though the people at the *Sport* seemed impressed when I explained with fingers appropriately crossed that 'me and Michael Watson were like "that"' and I could obtain for them an exclusive with the boxer any time they liked, I felt sure they would pretty soon get bored of things by the time that a Watson exclusive had appeared in their back pages for the third week in row. It was, therefore, fairly imperative that I got to meet a few more boxers.

I gained an opportunity to do this only three or four days after I first made that call to the *Sport*. In their infinite wisdom my prospective employers must have decided to set me a few tests before they committed themselves to granting me the status of full-time staff member. You could scarcely have blamed them: with my shaven head and ramshackle clothes that had obviously seen better days I bore scant resemblance to the battle-hardened professional boxing writer that I claimed to be.

One morning I got a call from the newspaper's sports editor, who asked me if I was available to take a trip down to a hotel in the East End, where a press conference promoting Nigel Benn's next fight was due to take place. He cagily explained that the paper wasn't prepared to offer me any money for doing this but hinted strongly that any fruitful compliance on my part would be ultimately rewarded. I put on my black peaked cap and bought a tube ticket to London Bridge.

The press conference was being held at a place called the Tower Bridge Hotel, a large, modern-looking building which was already surrounded by a posse of men carrying cameras by the time that I arrived. During the train journey my mind had been racing as I considered what lay imminently ahead. It was not the notion of being in attendance at a Benn press conference, involving the participation – presumably – of a real, live Nigel Benn, that was worrying me the most; it was more the fact of what might happen if I turned up to the place and was refused admittance. According to my limited experience of what was supposed to occur at such occasions – which, I have to admit, was mainly gleaned from the movies – a proper journalist had to be the member of a union, and as such had to be carrying an NUJ card before he could be granted access to the press room (flashing a press card at the appropriate moment certainly appeared to come as second nature to Dustin Hoffman and Robert Redford in *All The President's Men*). Visions of my turning up at the hotel and being unceremoniously exposed as an impostor refused to leave my mind.

As it turned out my fears were ungrounded; and having since attended countless press conferences held for the benefit of countless boxers it is difficult to understand what I was getting all flustered about. As I approached the hotel no one seemed to care who I was: there were no guards waiting to challenge me; not a soul could be bothered to ask me which paper I was from; in fact, nobody gave me so much as a second glance as I shuffled into a large banqueting room and took a seat a couple of rows from the front of a large table that was draped in a white cloth and empty except for a jug of water and a few glasses.

There were about 30 or so journalists seated around me; the atmosphere in the room was a combination of world-weariness and deep gloom. A few seats away from me I recognised the features of Ron Wills, the *Daily Mirror* boxing correspondent who had hung up on me a week or so ago. He was sitting with a notebook on his lap talking to Colin Hart, the *Sun* reporter whose name had adorned the story about Michael Watson I had sold to the paper. They both seemed bored.

Then Nigel Benn arrived. He was accompanied by his suavely-dressed advisor Ambrose Mendy and a smaller pale-skinned man. All three wore well-cut designer suits. Benn was also sporting a pair of expensive looking shades and looked, well, he looked exactly like the Nigel Benn that I had seen knocking people senseless on the TV, except for the fact that his Mohican had disappeared and had been replaced by a style that bore more than a passing resemblance to Mendy's well-groomed coiffure. Benn was smiling broadly, obviously enjoying the attention. As he moved slowly towards the centre of the table and took a seat he exchanged a few quips with the journalists who had been patiently awaiting his arrival.

Then another group of people shuffled quietly into the room. They were all black and all looked nervous, especially the tallest of the group. He had, I was soon to discover, every reason to be nervous: his name was Mike Chilambe, unheard of in this country but the middleweight champion of all of Africa no less – and Benn's next opponent. As he reached the table he shook hands awkwardly with the man who was scheduled to punch him in the face in a week's time; Benn looked the other man in the eye and his grin grew broader.

I pulled out my own notebook and began scribbling as Mendy took to the stage. Mendy spoke for about ten minutes. He spoke with the self-assurance of someone who obviously appreciated hearing the sound of his own voice. Yet he said nothing. His words were all recognisable, and I suppose he managed to get across to the newsman some of the more salient points relating to the reason why he had called the press conference. Somewhere in the endless flow of grandiloquence could be perceived, for example, the date and location of Benn's next fight. Similarly, if you allowed yourself to concentrate for a moment or two, it was possible to extract the name of Benn's proposed opponent from the infinite supply of non sequiturs that were being pumped in the onlookers' general direction. If you didn't think too hard Mendy's sentences appeared to make sense. And yet somehow they didn't.

I was not to know it at the time but Mendy would later confess to me that he had based his communication techniques on the American promoter, Don King. Indeed, the similarities between the American convicted murder with the electric shock hair-do and streetwise ex-con from north London were only too apparent. Both were black men in a business traditionally controlled by the white man. Both used flamboyance as a weapon; their words were an eclectic combination of misnomer and malapropism, liberally splattered with artifice, untruth and blatant lies. Most of the press seemed to have little time for Mendy and his elegant brand of multi-syllabic bullshit; however, there was no question that as a boxing agent Mendy was a formidable proposition. Since quitting his post as press agent to Frank Warren, Mendy had quickly become something of a minor celebrity himself.

As well as Benn and a few other lesser-known names from the world of boxing, he was also acting as agent for a number of footballers, including the future England captain Paul Ince and the Fashanu brothers; a couple of budding pop singers and various topless models, including Page Three 'stunnas' Suzanne Mitzi and Kathy Lloyd. While not quite being the stuff of legends, Mendy's extravagant parties, which he usually held at a restaurant in Stratford, were unmissable affairs. Only the very best food and the very best champagne were served at such events, embellishments that had not gone unnoticed by certain sections of the press, who vied like courtiers at Nero's imperial palace for Mendy's favour and the party invite that could come with it. There was, however, a more sinister undercurrent to his activities: rumours, for example, concerning the manner in which he financed his ostentatious lifestyle; whispers of drugs and guns. In the interests of keeping myself away from the law courts, such rumours, I have to say, have always been and will always remain completely unsubstantiated.

And there was his 'Black Pack': on the face of it a modern-day tribute to Sinatra's Rat Pack, in which – save for a few honorary Black Packers such as footballer Chris Waddle – a group of non-Caucasian movers and shakers would regularly get together, presumably, to engage in general revelry, merriment and back patting.

Certainly Mendy himself made little attempt to disassociate his name from the darker elements of society. Indeed, there was more than a suggestion that he actively encouraged such rumours in an attempt to embellish his already not inconsiderable charisma and mystique. The whole of his life seemed shrouded in a potent mixture of ambiguity and bare-faced gall.

On my first visit to the offices of Mendy's grandly named World Sports Corporation some months later, for example, which I had been told were located close to London Bridge, I spent a good half an hour walking up and down the street unable to find a building that corresponded in any way to the address I had been given. The reason for this turned out to be simple: Mendy was operating from the London address of the Papua and New Guinea embassy; somehow this former north London ragamuffin had managed to get himself elected as cultural attaché to that country. There was a twinkle in Mendy's eye when I expressed my surprise at this unusual scenario; and I could only chuckle when he informed me that this international designation had enabled him to become Britain's biggest importer of pistachio nuts. Of course, his enemies who claim that pistachio nuts were not the only foreign commodity that Mendy was importing. Allegedly.

I was not to know it at the time, sitting there at that press conference in my black cap with my arse hanging out of my jeans, but Mendy and I would eventually become close. In fact, I could even go so far as to say that we would become friends. Indeed, he would prove to be scintillating company: intelligent and self-deprecating enough to realise that most people were not taken in by his bombast, yet blessed – or cursed – with a natural arrogance that suggested he was ready to take over the world. Before we became friends, however, we would first be enemies.

Mendy finished his non-speech and sat down to muted bemusement from the rest of the room. Then the smaller man I had seen at Mendy's side earlier got up to speak. This time, by virtue of their inherent simplicity, the words made a little more sense. They were couched in the street jargon of an east London market trader. And the press got their story.

With a nod from the small man, a bag was brought to the table. It contained a filthy bundle of dead animal skins, which were then pushed in the direction of Mike Chilambe. Looking ever more uncomfortable, the African fighter pulled the flea-bitten package over his head. Lights flashed and camera motors whirred as Chilambe climbed wearily to his feet draped in the tatty lion skin. 'Ladies and gentlemen,' continued the small man, seemingly unconcerned by the fact that the inhabitants of the room were all male, 'may I present to you Mike Chilambe – the African Lion!' In the next morning's newspapers this would be line that would be carried on the back pages of most of the tabloids, 'Benn to fight African Lion!' And most of the press men gathered there that morning were happily aware that they had done their job.

The press conference came to an end and the mood in the room began to change as drinks and assorted goodies were served. This, I was to learn, was an established part of press conference protocol and the real reason that most of the media actually bothered to turn up. Then, for no apparent reason, the small man who had earlier been at the podium moved toward me and held out his hand. 'I've not seen you around before,' he said. Somewhat startled, I reciprocated the gesture and gave him my name, explaining sheepishly that I was on the payroll of the *Sunday Sport*. The other man's face lit up 'Really,' he grinned. 'I love that paper. My name's Frank Maloney – do you get to work with all those girls, then?'

One thing about boxing people you probably do not know about is that almost to a man they are all extremely friendly and personable people – particularly boxing promoters. I mean it. Indeed, apart from Hare Krishna disciples at airports and drug dealers, I have never come across a group of people who are just so darned approachable, so willing to embrace the company of strangers, so keen to ensure that you are comfortable in their presence. There's actually something rather unnatural and unwholesome about the whole thing. Of course, I say this from the perspective of, I suppose, a boxing person; and, although I know that this is not the case, it may well be that others in the less immediate vicinity of a boxing promoter's aspirations and ambitions are treated somewhat differently.

There are probably other reasons for such heart-warming approachability: sceptics might suggest that it has something to do with the fact that most people who are involved in boxing are ego driven and, therefore, only too happy to cast their fame about at every available opportunity; others might rightfully assert that if you're a boxing manager or promoter the act of being friendly with the press is a time-honoured means of ensuring that punters get to hear about the fight you happen to be putting on. Whatever the case, my opening exchanges with Frank Maloney did much to put me at my ease that morning.

I'm sure Frank himself will not be too offended when I tell you that on first acquaintance he is far from the most impressive person you are ever likely to meet. Indeed, many sports reporters have made a healthy living trading on this fact when compiling the numerous accounts that have since appeared in the newspapers which tell the story of the back street urchin that done good. However, he is not to be underestimated. Certainly, I, as well as everybody else present, had no way of knowing at the time that Maloney was on his way to becoming one of the most influential figures in British boxing: the man who would one day guide the career of Britain's first heavyweight champion for over a century. All I could see was a small man in a small suit whose eyes barely reached my shoulders, and whose accent could easily have been lifted from Kath's Caff in *EastEnders*.

'Any time you want a story for your paper just give me ring,' said Maloney, handing me his card. 'Come over to my pub and have a drink with me some time.'

I left the press conference and found a telephone box. I called the sports editor of the *Sunday Sport* and told him of the morning's events. 'Did you get an angle?' he asked obtusely.

'Not really,' I replied. 'The only thing that was mentioned was that Benn's opponent's nickname is the African Lion.'

There was a moment's silence and then the other person's response was so unexpected and so loud that I was forced to pull the telephone earpiece away from my head. 'The African Lion!' cried the man from the *Sport*. 'What a terrific headline! Superb!'

Then there was a further spell of silence; I could almost hear the rapid beat of the sports editor's heart. 'Get back to Maloney,' he urged abruptly. 'Ask him if we can get a photo of Chilambe wrestling a lion!'

%% %% %% %%

Things were moving fast now. As well as getting to meet Michael Watson, selling a story about him to *The Sun* and being offered a job with a newspaper that had discovered a double decker bus in the North Pole, I was now making new contacts in boxing almost every day. Most of this, I have to say was down to Eric Seccombe who, since our first meeting, seemed to have adopted me as a second son and was making it his duty to introduce me to everybody that he knew in the sport. A couple of times a week he would drive his black cab over to my flat in Finsbury Park and, with me sharing the back seat with Michael Watson, would take us to see fights.

I must admit to being more than a little overwhelmed by what was happening to me. It had, after all, only been three months since I had discovered the typewriter in the squat and decided to become A.J. Leibling. And little over three weeks had passed since I had escaped from the squat and the lifestyle that had been taking years off my life expectancy. And here I was being chauffeured around town by a boxer who was ranked in the world's top ten, shaking the hands of people I had grown up watching on TV, sharing jokes with Frank Bruno and Gary Mason and Mickey Duff and Terry Lawless. If this was boxing's way of illustrating how much of my youth had been frittered away chasing silly, juvenile dreams, it was making its point with some acuity.

Twelfth Rule Of Boxing: Fame Is The Drug

A boxer's primary motivation is fame. Although many will insist otherwise, a place in history is what they are really fighting for. The inflated fees that come with the job may go some way to healing the cuts and bruises that a boxer inevitably picks up at his place of work, but he is never fighting solely for money. He is fighting for posterity. He is fighting to become a legend.

Professional prize-fighters often refer to their predecessors in terms that pagan man may have used to describe his gods. When a boxer such as current WBO featherweight champion Naseem Hamed talks of emulating his idol, Muhammad Ali, he is not alluding to the tragic figure of today whom we spoke of earlier. Instead, he is remembering Ali at his peak: the beautifully proportioned athlete from the 1960s whose image will always remain frozen in time. Hamed is not alone in this use of selective memory: for even though the boxing world is littered with an abundance of reminders of a fighter's mortality, his gaze will seldom fall upon the corporeal.

Some boxers are so certain of their destinies that they will go to extraordinary lengths to convince others of their omnipotence. World middleweight champion Marvin Hagler, for instance, possessed sufficient self-confidence to think nothing of adding the prefix 'Marvelous' to his name by deed pole. While, in the arrogant bombast of fighters such as the aforementioned Hamed and others of his ilk, we are only hearing the echoes of words that have been uttered ad infinitum throughout the ages.

Boxers step into the ring to fight other men because – until they are violently persuaded otherwise – they believe themselves to be immortal. When boxers alternatively refer to themselves as 'invincible', as 'superhuman', as 'The Greatest', as 'The King' they are merely defining the scope of their own ambitions. In a boxer's case, fame really is the drug: unfortunately far too many of them will become hopeless addicts before reality is allowed to assert itself.

14

Betrayal

AT 10am on 7 March 1989, wearing the first suit I had ever purchased in my life, a dark blue polyester effort which had cost the princely sum of £30 and looked like it could well have numbered Norman Wisdom among its former owners, I finally began my new career as the boxing correspondent of the *Sunday Sport*. My responsibility was to provide boxing-related features of an appropriate length and atheistic quality to nestle comfortably between advertisements for 0898 numbers, baldness remedies and battery operated sexual implements that the *Sunday Sport*'s proprietor, one David Sullivan, elected to adorn his newspaper with.

Sullivan, a small man who liked to dress in white, endowing him with the appearance of a kind of miniature Marty from *Randall and Hopkirk (Deceased)*, had built an empire on soiled tissue paper. He had once been the lover of the late Mary Millington who, before her untimely death in 1979, had starred in a number of soft porn flicks, including the semi-legendary *Deep Throat*.

While still at university Sullivan had allegedly served notice of his entrepreneurial tendencies by starting a mail order business which supplied pornographic bubblegum cards to anyone with a taste for such exotica. Within a decade he had become one of the richest men in the country.

Sullivan's success owed little to quality, the appeal of his publications was distinctly below waist level. Almost single-handedly he had been responsible for taking away the soft focus and airbrushing of traditional American sex magazines such as *Playboy* and *Penthouse* and replacing their idealised view of womanhood with images of a decidedly meatier nature. If you bought a copy of one of Sullivan's soft-porn mags the term 'centre spread' had an entirely different meaning to the one used by its American counterparts.

Sullivan was also a boxing fan and liked to entertain top fighters and managers among the elegant marble columns and lush white interiors of his airport-sized country mansion. Accompanied by a fanfare of naked flesh, he had launched the *Sunday Sport* in the mid-1980s but despite the diet of oversized breasts and celebrity exposés that the paper served up for its readers, Sullivan had seen circulation figures dwindle until the *Sport*'s editor, one 28-year-old Drew Robertson, had hit upon the idea of following the example set by America's *National Enquirer*. Headlines such as, 'WORLD WAR II BOMBER FOUND ON MOON', 'KILLER PLANT STALKS QUEEN MUM', and 'GIRL CHOKES ON BLOWJOB' soon provided the publication's unlikely salvation and even went so far as to attract a more middle-class, trendier readership who, instead of discreetly concealing the newspaper between the pages of the *Sunday Times* when they picked it up at the newsagents, could now reply, 'Because it's a laugh, isn't it?' when asked why they were carrying a newspaper that contained an average of six naked breasts per page (currently the average 'nipple count' is around 60 per issue).

Now David Sullivan was my employer, and although I very much doubt that he even knew who I was, along with boxing he was indirectly responsible for the quite unprecedented transformation in my recent fortunes. For the first time in years I now had a steady job with a regular income. All of a sudden I could afford to do things that only a few months ago would have been quite beyond my scope; simple things – things that everyone takes for granted like going to the cinema or eating at a restaurant, taking the occasional cab ride, buying clothes. It was like a whole new universe had been opened up to me; one, it has to be said, that was surprisingly easy to grow accustomed to. However, I was soon to discover that holding down the position at the *Sport* held its own particular kind of price.

Upon entering the newspaper's offices, which were close to the Old Street tube station in London, I was immediately hit by that deep sense of disappointment which often grips visitors to the *Sunday Sport*'s offices when they realise that the reception desk is not manned – or womanned – by a lusty menagerie of semi-naked busty blondes ready to 'do it five times a night' with an assortment of textile magnates, politicians and grey-skinned extraterrestrials. In fact, the majority of my new colleagues would not have been out of place sitting in an accountant's office. One or two even appeared to be asleep at their desks.

Soon I was introduced to my fellow reporters in the sports department and given a short lesson in the newspaper's journalistic etiquette.

'At the *Sunday Sport*,' I was told by a northern accent that was destined to become gratingly familiar to me, 'we don't use commas, we don't use semi-colons, all our paragraphs are once sentence long, we use lots of exclamation marks and we like lots of capital letters.'

Or, in other words:

We DON'T use commas!

We DON'T use semi-colons!

All our PARAGRAPHS are one sentence long!

We use LOTS of exclamation marks!!!!!

AND we like lots of CAPITAL LETTERS!

In reality, however, working as a reporter at the *Sport* required no journalistic ability whatsoever; the real bulk of the writing came from the subs' desk, who took whatever they were presented with and magically transformed it into *Sport*-esque whether you liked it or not. Ninety-nine times out of a hundred the article that appeared in the newspaper on Sunday morning with your by-line beneath it bore little or no resemblance to the copy you had originally supplied.

The owner of the northern accent was called Tony Livesey. Strangely enough, he also hailed from Burnley and, like myself, had moved to London looking for work a few years earlier. At 24 his ambition was matched only by his aggressive pursuit of anything that remotely resembled a story. Although he was by no means an expert on sport he was employed by the newspaper as its sports editor; he was in charge of a team of three full-time reporters and a network of freelancers that, as well as the great Bobby Moore, included a number of retired footballers such as Frank Worthington and Stan Bowles. Livesey, as they say, drank with the right people and ate with the right people. By the time he was 30 he would be editing a national newspaper; two years later he would be at the helm of the *Sunday Sport*'s daily incarnation, before going on to minor celebrity status with a surprisingly accomplished appearance as panellist on the BBC 2 satirical quiz show *Have I Got News For You*.

'What's happenin' in boxing this week?' was the first question that the northern accent asked me that morning when we had finished my *Sunday Sport* grammar lesson.

'Nothing much, really,' I shrugged, it being a relatively quiet week in the world of boxing – no major fights, no minor controversies, no real stories floating about on which I could cut my 'journalistic' teeth. 'There's a heavyweight named Derek Williams fighting soon but that's about it.'

'What's he like?'

'He's not bad,' I replied, 'probably good enough to fight for the British title one day.'

'Give him a ring, then,' said Livesey. 'See if you can get him to say something interesting.'

Before starting at the newspaper I had been advised to purchase a small portable tape recorder and a sucker microphone that could be used to record telephone conversations. This instrument was fairly essential: not only was it far easier than trying to write down what the subject of your interview was saying, it also acted as a fail-safe in the not-uncommon event of the newspaper being sued by the subject of your interview. Feeling surprisingly professional, I took out my new toy and prepared to record my first interview with a boxer for the *Sunday Sport*. I called Williams's number and a sleepy voice with just a hint of Jamaican answered.

Derek 'Sweet D' Williams lived in a council flat in Hackney; it had been Michael Watson and Eric Seccombe who had first introduced me to him on a visit to the Carnaby Street gym, where he was sparring somewhat unsatisfactorily with a fighter named Proud Kilimanjaro. Since then I had bumped into Williams a couple of times at fights and was on nodding terms with him. He was an impressive physical specimen: standing some 6ft 4in tall and weighing over 15st; in a dark alleyway he would definitely be one to avoid.

He was, however, largely ignored by the public and, though still at a relatively early stage in his career, had already lost a fight to a nobody. Although he would eventually hold the European heavyweight title for a brief period in 1991 before losing it to Lennox Lewis, as a prospect Williams was perceived by those in the know as not so much hot as mildly lukewarm. Despite appearances, however, he was a very gentle man, politely spoken and friendly to anyone that came near him. However, so few reporters had bothered to talk to him that he immediately recognised my voice.

'Hi, Derek,' I called down the telephone. 'How's the preparation for your next fight going?'

'Good,' he replied. 'Yeah – good.'

'Listen, Derek the *Sunday Sport* want to do a feature on you for Sunday's paper – would you mind if I asked a few questions?'

'No – go ahead.'

'Okay – let's start by asking you the name of your next opponent?'

'I dunno, my manager hasn't told me his name yet.'

'Oh, right. What about after this fight – who are you looking to fight in the future? Mason? Bruno?'

'Yeah, I'm gonna be fighting those guys sooner or later.'

'Do you think that you could beat them?'

'Yeah – I'll beat anybody that they put in front of me. Mason... Bruno...'

'What about Mike Tyson?'

'Yeah, I could beat Tyson. No problem.'

This line of questioning continued unabated for several minutes. Until it began to dawn on me that unlike some fighters, who were able to make going to the bathroom sound like a some kind of superhuman feat, it was not within Williams's powers to say anything that might come across as even mildly interesting on the printed page. He was not a natural self-promoter in the way that Naseem Hamed is today, nor did he have the deep, cloying voice that was the trademark of housewives' favourite Frank Bruno. I was beginning to understand why most reporters had steered clear of him and gone off in search of more compelling quarry.

It was, however, my first day in a new job and, naturally, I wanted to come up with something that would impress my employers. In desperation I tried another approach: I would simply keep him talking, make him relax: get him to speak about anything in the hope that something vaguely printable might emerge. 'What about fans?' I asked. 'Do you have a large following?'

'Yeah,' answered Williams, suddenly growing more animated. 'I have hundreds of fans – I get girls queuing up outside the dressing room after my fights.'

This apparently innocent comment, I was soon to learn, was to be a BIG mistake for Derek 'Sweet D' Williams and myself in more ways than one.

※ ※ ※ ※

'What de say?' said The Northern Accent when I finally got off the phone.

'Not a lot, I'm afraid,' I replied, deciding that honestly was the best policy. 'He doesn't know who he's fighting next and didn't have anything remotely interesting to say.'

The Northern Accent frowned; his nostrils flared and he eyed me with a look of deep suspicion. 'Do us a favour, will you?' he announced. 'Type out what he said and let us have a look at it.'

With a shrug I followed my instructions and turned my attention to the battered old manual typewriter that sat gathering dust at my newly-appointed desk. About 20 minutes later I handed a transcript of my interview with Derek 'Sweet D' Williams to The Northern Accent.

It was not long before I felt an urgent tapping at my shoulder and hot breath on my neck.

'This stuff is dynamite!' exclaimed The Northern Accent, visibly shaking with excitement. 'You've got to get him on the phone again!'

I cannot really recall what my exact response to this comment was as I tried to find some means of comprehending my sports editor's words. Was I really so naive? Was I missing something? How could The Northern Accent possibly conclude that there might be anything remotely exciting in my nondescript interview with Derek Williams? Surely all I had produced was just a bunch of banal questions accompanied by equally banal answers. Perhaps I wasn't cut out for my new career.

The Northern Accent drew closer to me and spoke again. This time his voice was almost a whisper. 'Ask him if he ever sleeps with any of his fans,' he said conspiratorially.

I looked at my watch. It was 11.15am. I had been working in my new job for just 75 minutes and already here I was faced with my first moral dilemma. 'I can't do that,' I stuttered awkwardly.

'Why not?' asked The Northern Accent.

'Because it's...' I searched my mind and tried to procure an answer to this question. 'Because it's got nothing to do with boxing,' I said blandly.

'What do you mean it's got nothing to do with boxing? Of course its about boxing. It's boxing news isn't it?'

I quickly concluded that there were two ways in which I could react to this statement. I could do what The Northern Accent demanded, get back on the phone and ask Williams about his sexual habits, or I could stand up in front of the whole office and tell my sports editor to go fuck himself. There is little doubt that the latter reaction would have made me feel a whole lot better about myself, but images of north London squats and drink-crazed wrecking sessions were still fresh in my mind. I wasn't ready to return to that just yet and so, to my eternal shame, I did the dishonourable thing.

Yet even as I was picking up the phone and pressing redial, my mind was already seeking hasty justifications for my forthcoming actions. In common with every journalist that has ever picked up a notebook I was looking for a way to lie: except on this occasion the person I would be lying to was myself. However, before I could find the excuse that would exonerate my future sins the voice of Derek 'Sweet D' Williams could be heard once more.

'Yeah. Hello,' he said.

'Hi Derek – it's Ian,' I declared jauntily.

'Hello again.'

'Listen Derek, we've been talking in the office about the piece I'm doing about you and I need to ask a few more questions.'

'No problem,' replied the boxer, obviously feeling flattered that a boxing writer working on a national newspaper had called him twice in one morning.

'It's that bit you mentioned about your fans,' I continued.

'What about them?' asked Derek.

'You did say that most of them were female?'

'Yeah – that's right.'

'Would you mind if I asked you a question?'

'What sort of question?'

'It's nothing really,' I lied. 'It's just that my sports editor would like to know if you ever end up in bed with any of your fans.'

'What's he want to know that for?'

'Well, he just feels that our story on you would have more impact if we could tell everyone how popular you are.'

'Oh, right.'

'So do you?'

'What?'

'Ever sleep with any of your fans?'

'Yeah – now and then.'

It was not the kind of conversation that I'd anticipated holding in my new career. I could feel my face redden and the anxious silences that followed this staccato line of inquiry were even beginning to unsettle Williams. I decided to hang up as quickly as possible.

'Okay Derek,' I said hastily. 'I think I've got everything I need – good luck with your fight.'

I put the phone down and caught my breath; I stole a glance at my colleagues seated beside me: Kevin, a large Scot who was responsible for putting the words on the football pages; Nich, a Charlie George lookalike who was a bit of a Jack-of-all-trades. I wondered if they were aware of what I had just done, I wondered if they even cared. How many times had they been forced to do something similar themselves.

'What de say?' said The Northern Accent as I slumped into my chair and attempted to regain some dignity. 'Did you get him to say that he beds his fans?'

'Yes,' I said weakly. 'I got him to say it.'

'Fantastic!' said the other man as a broad smile spread over his features. 'Type out the quotes and let us see them.'

Once again I did as instructed and returned to my typewriter and the bottle of Tippex that stood beside it. From the corner of my eye I could see that one of the reporters on the news desk was now slumped over his typewriter, snoring heavily.

It was over an hour before I saw The Northern Accent again. This time he made his way to my desk holding the transcript of my second interview with Derek 'Sweet D' Williams; there was a heavy frown on his face.

'I've been talking to Drew,' he explained. 'We both think these quotes aren't bad but they're just not good enough to go really big on.'

'But I got him to say that he sleeps with his fans,' I spluttered. 'Surely that's enough?'

'Not quite,' said The Northern Accent. 'We want you to call him back and ask him if they ever suck his dick.'

For a moment I thought I'd misheard The Northern Accent. By the tone of his voice he could have been telling me to call Williams back and ask him if he ever flossed his teeth. He spoke the sentence like it was the most natural thing in the world.

'You're kidding!' was my numbed response.

The other man shook his head slowly. 'No, I'm not kidding,' he said, 'go on – give him a ring and ask him.'

'I can't do that!' I protested.

'Why not?' said The Northern Accent.

'I can't do that!' I repeated stubbornly, hunching my shoulders. 'I just can't.'

'Course, you can – its not going to do any harm is it?'

'But what has it got to do with boxing?'

'It's a story innit? Everything's a story.'

Once more I considered the situation and those same two options immediately sprang to mind: Stay or go. Stay or go. Should I stay or should I go? I knew what the moral thing to do was but I had already discovered my price: it had taken less than a morning at the *Sunday Sport* for me to realise that I wanted the job – in particular, the salary that came with it – much more than I valued any principles I'd imagined I possessed. I rang Derek 'Sweet D' Williams for the third time.

'Another question for you, Derek, I'm afraid,' I said nervously.

'Yeah. What?'

I cleared my throat, 'Remember when you told me that you occasionally slept with your fans?'

'Yeah.'

'Well the sports editor... Well, he wants me to ask you a bit of a personal question about them.'

There was a silence.

'Are you still there, Derek?'

'Yeah.'

'He wants me to ask you if these girls, well, if these girls ever perform oral sex on you.'

'Oral sex?'

'Yes, you know… oral sex.'

'You mean blowjobs?'

'Well, yes – I suppose I do, actually.'

'Do they ever give me blow jobs? Is that what you're asking?'

'Yes, that's right.'

'Yeah, they do sometimes.'

Once again there was a silence as I tried to take in what had just happened. What did Williams think he was doing? Didn't he realise that he'd just admitted to an almost complete stranger that he allowed his fans to perform fellatio on him after fights? Was he mad? Did he have some kind of death wish?

'Are you sure about that, Derek?' I asked.

'Yeah,' he replied, 'they give me blow jobs.'

Then for a few moments Williams seemed to lose all sense of reason. His voice raised in pitch and his words became more urgent, there was no stopping the boxer as he proceeded to provide graphic detail about his amorous extra-curricular activities. Williams left nothing to the imagination; frequency, duration, size of – no aspect of his love-life remained untouched. When his soliloquy was finally over I felt that I knew more about 'Sweet D' than I'd ever wanted to know about any man.

By the time that I had said my goodbyes and put the telephone down on Williams, The Northern Accent was already standing at my shoulder. As I turned to face him, his hands were shaking in anticipation. 'What de say?' he asked again.

I looked down at my feet as I answered the question. 'Don't worry,' I mumbled sullenly. 'He said what you wanted him to say.'

'Did he?' chortled The Northern Accent, his face lighting up like a magnesium flare. 'Did he really say that his fans suck his dick?'

'Yes.'

'Honestly?'

'Yes.'

'Let me hear the tape!'

I wound back the cassette and replayed the part of the conversation that The Northern Accent wanted to hear.

'My God!' exclaimed the other man. 'He really did say it! Hold on a minute!'

With that The Northern Accent sailed off in the direction of the editor's office and disappeared for about half an hour or so. When he finally returned he grasped my hand in his and shook it firmly. He was smiling as he told me, 'Me and Drew think your story's superb!' he gushed. 'You've done a great day's work!'

It was lunchtime and I'd seldom been so confused in my life.

%% %% %% %%

After this episode things seemed to quieten down slightly. It was as if the whole event had been some kind of strange mind game; the more I thought about it the more I came to believe that The Northern Accent had actually been testing me, seeing how far I was prepared to go when pushed, attempting to mark his territory and establish who was boss. If this was indeed the case, I had proven to be a bit of a pushover; I had lost that particular battle of wills in unequivocal fashion – a first-round knockout. Still slightly dazed, I was left more or less alone and allowed to get on with the job that I assumed I'd be doing prior to beginning my term of duty at the *Sport*. I interviewed boxers, went to press conferences, visited gyms, went to more press conferences and attempted to write about boxing.

By the time that Sunday's paper came out, the publication, I might add, which contained my inaugural efforts as a professional tabloid sports journalist, I had almost forgotten that awkward and bizarre Monday morning. However, when I turned to the back pages and found my story nestling among a menagerie of pink nipples, I was forced to take in a deep gulp of air. Set in 120pt lettering that dominated a whole page was the headline, 'My gals call me Sweet Dick!'

Beneath a photograph of Derek 'Sweet D' Williams was a picture of myself and the words 'Exclusive report from Ian

"The Truth" Probert'. Such was my debut as a boxing writer – it had taken me less than a week to become the lowest of gutter journalists.

%% %% %% %%

Back in the office on Monday, it was not long before the telephone rang and I once again heard the voice of Derek Williams. This was the part that I'd been particularly dreading. How was I possibly going to defend my betrayal? All that Williams had wanted was to see his name in the paper and I – along with a little help from The Northern Accent – had turned him into the laughing stock. He wasn't going to be happy about it.

'Hi Derek,' I said timidly, 'did you see the paper on Sunday?'

'Yeah,' he replied.

'What did you think?' I asked.

'I thought it was a good article.'

Now, once again, it was my turn to be lost for words.

'Still there, Ian?' asked Williams.

'Yes. You mean you liked the article?'

'Yeah. It was good – all my friends liked it.'

'Really?'

'Yeah.'

Then Williams said something that was infinitely worse than any of the howls of outrage, unprintable curses or threats to my personal safety that I'd been expecting from him. 'The only person that didn't like it was my mum,' he muttered softly. 'I showed it to her and she got all upset about it.'

Thirteenth Rule Of Boxing: Boxers Like To Lie

Like the people who choose to write about them, boxers are all habitual liars; for this reason it is necessary to view with extreme suspicion anything you might read about a boxer's exploits. The history of the sport is littered with examples of fighters who have either lied or been lied about in order to sell fights, stake a claim at immortality or get their mugshot in the paper.

Take, for example, the celebrated story of how Muhammad Ali supposedly threw his Olympic gold medal into the Hudson River. According to literally thousands of book and newspaper accounts, the fighter did this after he had been denied service in a restaurant because of his colour. Indeed, Ali himself recreated this dramatic scene when playing the lead role in the film of his own life story, *The Greatest*, a 1978 Hollywood biopic which proved that, along with being one of the most phenomenal athletes of all time, Ali – even when playing himself – was also one of the lousiest actors.

This myth was perpetuated for over three decades, being discussed at length in Thomas Hauser's exhaustive 1991 authorised biography of the boxer, *Muhammad Ali: His Life And Times*, and rightly declared one of the defining moments in Ali's life. The reality, however, is possibly something quite different. According to writer David Miller's touching tribute to the fighter, *The Tao of Muhammad Ali*, published in 1996, the former champion simply lost his medal and invented the story to get himself a little publicity. Muhammad Ali? Publicity? Since when did Muhammad Ali ever need publicity?

In the words of an eager young press officer who had learned the script well, there is no such thing as enough publicity. Nor, for that matter, is there such an animal as bad publicity. I was told this once while sitting in the office of fight manager Frank Maloney, who as well as being at the reins of heavyweight champion Lennox Lewis's career, was later to enjoy an unlikely spell as celebrity columnist in, you probably guessed it, the *Sunday Sport*.

There is, of course, the possibility that in debunking such an essential part of his legend, Muhammad Ali may have been lying to David Miller. However, even if that is the case the very fact that the fighter was able to produce two such contrasting versions of this celebrated episode merely reiterates the fact that he, along with all boxers, is not adverse to stretching the truth when the occasion demands it.

So why do fighters feel the need to lie when so often the truth is far more extraordinary? The answer to this is quite simple: boxers lie because it is in their nature. They lie because the whole essence of the sport they participate in has its basis in untruth. To paraphrase the words of former light-heavyweight champion José Torres, when a fighter steps inside the ropes his first and only inclination is to lie: feinting a left and then throwing a right, making to jab to the body before launching a hook to the temple, pretending to feel no pain when the body feels like it is being torn apart. From their earliest days boxers are taught that to succeed it is first necessary to deceive.

Thanks in the main to fighters such as Ali, the act of lying has been extended to include all aspects of the pugilistic ritual. From the very first moment that a fight is made, the lies begin to flow like sticky treacle until a stage is quickly achieved in which it is impossible to distinguish fact from fiction. Overnight, fighters will inexplicably drop a few years from their age; perfectly plausible excuses will be invented to explain previous defeats; sparring partners will be produced at press conferences to reveal that their employer – often a known non-puncher – is all of a sudden hitting with the power of Mike Tyson (the only time that I ever had reason to believe this claim to be true was at a Mike Tyson press conference). Managers and promoters will tell you that they do this to sell their fights. However, I am yet to meet a fight figure who can provide me with positive proof that such overstatement has ever succeeded in selling a single extra ticket.

One must, therefore, keep an open mind when you are told that Roberto Duran once knocked out a horse with his bare fists, that Nicky Piper is member of Mensa, that Tommy Morrison is the nephew of Duke Wayne, that Nigel Benn is the cousin of England footballer Paul Ince, that George Foreman ingests 60lb of hamburger each day, that Terry Marsh is allergic to chocolate, that Steve Collins enlists the help of a hypnotist before his fights, that Evander Holyfield suffered a heart attack in the ring, or that Frank Bruno once trained with a ballet dancer. None of these facts are true and yet all of them are.

15

Circus in the Supertent

THERE is a point at the very end of the fight – as Nigel Benn squats on his haunches deciding whether or not it's worth getting up – which illustrates the fundamental difference between the vast majority of people who have ever earned a successful living writing about other people hitting each other and myself.

Most of you, I realise, will not own a copy of this particular fight on videotape so please permit me to reveal to you what I was doing at the very same moment that Benn was busily concluding that he'd rather not stand up and get punched again by Michael Watson.

If you freeze the tape at that precise instant you will see a blurred figure in the background jumping about with his arms waving wildly through the air as the referee counts Benn out. Dressed in a black suit and wearing an expression reminiscent of the central character in Edvard Munch's painting *The Scream*, that person is me.

I am standing at ringside in the front row of the press section and, before the disapproving eyes of my newspaper colleagues, I am screaming for all I am worth. And this, I am afraid to say, is the reason why my career as a boxing writer was destined to end in tears.

Like referees, judges and ACAS officials, boxing writers aren't really supposed to take sides. I suppose there is an obvious logic to this time-honoured precept, it being, for one thing, a quite fruitless task to attempt to sing the praises of any boxer you happen to be supporting in next morning's fight report when he has been knocked spark out by his opponent. Yet although I have read about and even known many boxing writers who have stuck up close friendships with professional prize-fighters, almost to a man they have been able to keep their personal preferences to themselves in the course of their duty. When the moment came, however, I found this impossible to do.

%, %, %, %,

Barely a month after beginning my job at the *Sunday Sport* a press conference was held at a London casino to announce that Nigel Benn – aka the Dark Destroyer – was, after all, finally prepared to settle his ongoing dispute with arch rival Michael Watson inside a boxing ring.

Among the journalists who had gathered to witness this announcement there was a general feeling of relief: even though a match-up between these two fighters was a surefire money-spinner, there were many who had feared that politics would ultimately prove to be too much of an obstacle. Also in the air was a feeling of genuine anticipation: being well on the way, by this time, to becoming a veteran of the boxing press conference circuit, it was an attitude that I had rarely encountered in the course of such occasions. The fact that a large proportion of Fleet Street's finest could scarcely withhold their excitement at the news seemed to suggest that this was to be no ordinary fight.

The press conference had been attended by both boxers and their respective managers. Also present were the fighters' trainers: Eric Seccombe sitting quietly to Watson's right, and the heavy-set Brian Lynch sitting to Benn's left. As usual, though, it had been Ambrose Mendy who had done most of the talking. As he stood there in his impeccable designer togs, arranging random syllables like the bastard offspring of a union between William Burroughs and Professor Stanley Unwin, I had found it difficult to tear my eyes away from the face of Watson's manager, Mickey Duff, who sat close to Mendy taking occasional sips from a glass of water and wearing a scarcely concealed expression of contempt. I could not have been the only member of the press there that day who found himself wondering what must have gone on behind closed doors to have persuaded Duff to share a table with Mendy.

The fight would take place on 21 May at Finsbury Park in something that Mendy described as a 'supertent', which would be specially erected for the occasion. Quite why this particular locality had been selected was never satisfactorily explained. Finsbury Park, after all, could hardly have been described as your traditional boxing venue, possessing, as it were, no traditional venue in which boxers could box. Holding the fight at a location such as Wembley or the Royal Albert Hall would surely have made far better sense. However, if there was a reason for this strange choice, Ambrose Mendy was keeping it to himself; perhaps, some speculated, he had a mate in Finsbury Park who could get hold of cheap supertents.

As Mendy continued his monologue, Watson and Benn would occasionally exchange shy little glances; as with many fighters in such a situation they appeared almost embarrassed to be there. However, when the time came for them to speak it was Benn who dominated their verbal exchanges; like an actor he had learned whatever lines that had been thrust upon him well. It was Benn who provided the most telling quotes that day and it was Benn's words that dominated the back pages the following morning.

I never liked Benn. Although if I was to bump into him in the street tomorrow you can be sure I would claim that the previous sentence was a typo, I could never bring myself to foster anything that remotely resembled affection for him.

Admittedly, we had got off to a bad start when we were first introduced. 'Ere, ain't you got small hands!' he had said with a sly grin; hardly, you will agree, the most effective means of endearing yourself to the person whose undersized hand you are shaking at that particular moment. But there were other reasons.

There was, for instance, the time when I had briefly interviewed him for the *Sport* and been subjected to a barrage of obscenities when I attempted to make the interview run on a little longer than scheduled. And there was his general demeanour – a trivial point on which to base one's personal opinion of someone, I admit – which seemed to belong to a person who genuinely possessed a natural vocation for punching other people in the face, whether they happened to be wearing boxing gloves or not. The main reason for my dislike of Benn on that day, however, was both ordinary and unsophisticated: I didn't like him because in little more than a month's time he would be attempting to punch Watson in the face.

Despite the fact that Watson's WBC world ranking was one place higher than his rival's, it was Benn whom the bookies were soon tipping to come out on top. As, for that matter, was anybody else with an opinion to offer. Quite how everybody had managed to reach this conclusion puzzled me at the time. Although Benn, unlike his Islington counterpart, was unbeaten and obviously possessed dynamite in his fists, the quality of opposition he had faced was several notches below the men that Watson had been in with. And even though I was aware that my opinions as to the likely outcome of the fight were probably distorted by the warm feelings that I held for Michael by this time, I was convinced that the fight was far from a forgone conclusion. For this reason I, along with Colin Hart of *The Sun* – who even correctly predicted the exact round in which Benn would fall – were among the only journalists who opted for a Watson victory in our pre-fight previews.

Two things to note if you think that I'm beginning to sound a little smug about this almost Nostradamus-like ability of mine to predict the outcome of boxing matches. Firstly, my comments in the *Sunday Sport* almost provoked a minor riot when The Northern Accent – who had routinely concluded that I would be opting for Benn (incidentally, a friend of the publisher, David Sullivan) – discovered what I had written. Indeed, were it not for the fact that I turned out to be right I rather suspect that my stay at the paper would have been even briefer than it actually ended up being. Secondly, the Watson-Benn fight turned out to be one of the few occasions that I would ever guess the result of a fight correctly.

(Holyfield-Tyson – who was it who was convinced that Evander Holyfield wouldn't even make it past round one? Starling-Honeyghan – who was it who said that Lloyd Honeyghan was going to blast out the American veteran in three? Collins-Eubank… Eubank-Benn… Robinson-McMillan…

I'd better stop here; the list of boxing matches in which I have been 100 per cent incorrect in my expert pre-fight assessments could go on forever. In fact, if you are a betting man – I'd better say person – give me a call and I'll guarantee that if you put some money on the boxer who I am not tipping to win the fight you'll go home with a tidy sum in your pocket. It never fails.

※ ※ ※ ※

The fight:

It was – somehow inevitably – a beautiful sunny evening as I strolled the 20 or so minutes from my flat in Finsbury Park to Ambrose Mendy's conveniently (for me) situated supertent. As I approached the entrance to this gigantic piece of tarpaulin, the crowds of people holding cans of lager grew thicker. 'Beennnnn!!!' they chanted in unison, passing posters advertising the fight which featured the head of their hero spliced on to the body of Michael Jackson in bondage gear, adorned with the legend 'Who's Bad? Nigeeelll!'

It had been four or five days since I had last seen Michael Watson, who had called around to my flat with Eric Seccombe in tow to tell the man whom Eric now referred to as 'our reporter' what Michael intended to do to Benn. He seemed untroubled by his upcoming ordeal and, in a small way, I was able to boost his confidence even further, when I told Watson the story of what had transpired between Benn and I at a press conference a day or so earlier.

On the occasion in question, I had been sitting near the front of the press seats sucking on one of my painfully-thin roll-ups when Benn had suddenly called out to me, 'Ere, put that out!' It was not an unreasonable request, I suppose; after all, when you've just spent six weeks working your body into peak condition the last thing you want to do as final preparation for a fight is fill your lungs with somebody else's tobacco fumes. Reluctantly, I had done as he demanded, perhaps flattering myself that Benn had singled me out for special attention because he knew that I was on the side of the man who was imminently scheduled to be aiming punches at him.

Then we both did something childish. Although I doubt that Benn even remembers those brief few seconds, we suddenly found ourselves slap bang in the middle of a staring contest – one of those psychological scuffles that you're bound to have had in the playground as a child, in which both combatants would gaze deep into each other's eyes and remain locked in that position until, with tears streaming down face, someone was eventually forced to surrender. This is what we found ourselves doing: Benn staring at me – me staring at Benn. It was silly, really, but nevertheless I was determined that I would not be the one to turn away first.

As it transpired I was evidently more determined than Benn who, after looking at me for a few moments with a puzzled expression on his face, shook his head and shot me a thin smile. Perhaps I was guilty of reading a little more into this situation than it truly deserved but Watson, nevertheless, was delighted with my story. 'You see what I mean?' he had chuckled, reminding me of how Benn had avoided his eyes in the now legendary Benn/Watson/Club incident.

In typically cowardly fashion, allow me to redress the balance a little: Nigel Benn, if you're out there reading this and already deciding that you feel like having a staring rematch, there's no need. Please accept my assurances that I have no doubts whatsoever that you will win every time.

Throughout the build-up to the fight Watson had played Andrew Ridgley to Benn's George Michael. While Watson stood quietly on the sidelines it was Benn who got all the attention and it was Benn who provided the most colourful rhetoric for the never ending conveyor belt of media types who wanted to feature him on their television programmes. More worryingly, it was Benn who came across as the most menacingly of the two fighters, as a chilling pre-fight interview conducted with professional footballer/television presenter Justin Fashanu demonstrated.

Fashanu, 'Twenty-two professional fights and you've had 22 knockouts. Does it not annoy you... Get on your nerves that people still say that the fighters you've fought have been nothing?'

Benn, 'It does annoy me, yeah, but, you know, after I dispose of Watson then they'll realise that, you know, that I'm for real. You know, we're not talking about just the punching power and the heart, the determination, the will to win – everything's there. It ain't about winning the world title, it's maintaining it. Like I said, I was going to win the world title and retire a multi-millionaire by the time I'm 28. And the way I'm going now I'm on course. And I ain't going to change it for anybody. I'm going to do it my way and in my own time.

'I give the public what they want to see. They don't want to see a ten-round boring fight. They want to see, like, five... six minutes of X-rated violence. That's what they come to see. And they know that they're going to get it when they come and watch me.'

Fashanu, 'Predictions?'

Benn, 'Predictions? I hope – I believe – that it will go four or five rounds but, you know, he is really going to get hurt. I tell you, I'm going to be hitting him so many times with the left, he's going to be crying out for a right. I'm telling you, he's in serious trouble because, you know, he's really been badmouthing me. Because I'm, you know, I'm really glad that the fight's happening because I don't want him slagging me off in the other corner, you know, him saying that he looked me in the eye and I looked away. [Turning to face camera] I guarantee that when I see you on the 21st Watson, you ain't going to have no eyes to look out of. I'm telling you – you are in serious trouble!'

%%% %%% %%% %%%

Inside the supertent, amid a frantic atmosphere, there appeared to be plenty of evidence of Ambrose Mendy's interpretation of what was supposed to happen inside supertents. Favoured journalists were treated to a pre-fight dinner that must have cost more per head than the amount that some of the undercard fighters would be earning that evening. Filling their mouths with exotic sweetmeats alongside us was an eclectic mixture of Black Packers and various A-, B-, C-, D- and E-list British celebrities. Sitting directly across from me, for example, was the West Ham and Scotland striker Frank McAvennie with his Page Three girlfriend beside him chomping delicately on a lobster claw. In the corner of the room you could see Brian May from Queen and his new paramour Angie from *EastEnders* (for whom he had just produced a truly horrendous pop single entitled 'Anyone Can Fall In Love', with lyrics set to the *EastEnders* theme tune); to the right there was that bloke from *The Bill* with the receding hairline talking to someone from *London's Burning*; to their right, filling their faces with bits of dripping meat, were most of the England football team; and just behind them were Michelle and Wicksey, also from *EastEnders*.

Mendy himself was dressed in a buttoned-down white suit which gave him the appearance of a fashion-conscious ringmaster, which, in a way, I suppose, is what he was. Every now and then his bearded face bobbed up from somewhere within the crowd of celebrity diners: he was smiling and confident and oozing charm from every scented pore. Staging an event of this magnitude was no small achievement for the man whom the BBBoC had forbidden from even standing in the corner of the fighter he represented. Mendy may have been the possessor of a prison record that apparently made him a leper in the eyes of the boxing establishment, but here he was, Britain's first black promoter and clearly enjoying every minute of it.

Of course, on paper it was Mendy's partner, Frank Maloney, whose name was printed at the top of the fight posters and it was also his hand which provided the signature at the bottom of all the fight contracts; however, the night belonged to Mendy, it was his boy who was just about go out there and move a significant step closer to a world title, and it was Mendy's imprint that was indelibly stamped into every detail of the show.

※ ※ ※ ※

Wearing a blue silk dressing gown with gold lapels, Michael Watson was the first to approach the ring. Accompanied by Mickey Duff, Eric Seccombe, his cuts man Denny Mancini and the sound of a distant reggae beat, he appeared a little shell-shocked as he nodded slowly to well-wishers in the crowd. With stomach suitably full, I had by now taken my seat among the press: I was lucky – I was only two rows from the front and close enough to see the steam rise from the preliminary fighters' shoulders. As the press ranks looked on, Watson climbed through the ropes and threw a cluster of punches into the air. Then I think he waved to me – although he could have been waving to someone sitting behind me – and I couldn't help wondering if my parents were watching the fight at home on TV and had noticed the boxer's gesture and, absurdly, had somehow spotted my face in the crowd.

Then Nigel Benn arrived. His entry was certainly grand, if a little home-made. First the lights inside the giant tent were dramatically dimmed and the sound of sirens echoed throughout the arena. Next, there was a roll of drums and more reggae music blared out. Finally, a singer's voice joined the booming bass line, advising the waiting masses that the person who was about to appear was, 'Dangerous! Danger-ous. I am danger-ous. Danger-o-ous.'

In the darkness, a solitary spotlight moved through the warm air and sought out a set of cardboard sliding doors that had been covered in silver foil and were held aloft by several pairs of hands which were clearly discernible throughout the arena. Next came the inevitable dry ice, through which 12 blokes with moustaches dressed in army uniforms marched into view (apparently members of Benn's former marine regiment). 'Danger-ous. I am danger-ous. Danger-o-ous.' They were followed by about 50 other blokes dressed in white track suits, some of whom I recognised from my visit to Mendy's Papua and New Guinea embassy. Then, almost as an afterthought, the boxer himself finally appeared.

Flanked by statuesque models bearing large Union Jacks, Benn was wearing what can only be described as a kind of silver space suit; it appeared to be made out of the same sort of material as the Action Man space suit that was all the rage among boys who liked to play with dolls in the late 1960s. It had a pointed hood and made Benn look more than a little foolish. Still, he soldiered on bravely, skipping his way towards the ring and awkwardly swinging his arms through the air in a style that was more John Major than John Travolta. Nevertheless, despite the foolishness of his attire, there was a look on Benn's face which left one in no doubt that he meant business. It was certainly not the expression of a man who believed that he would end the night minus the '0' part of his boxing record.

To a crescendo of cheers, Benn climbed into the ring and jogged around for a bit, as if unsure of what to do with himself next. Then his silver gown was removed and for a few moments he stood in his corner staring over at Watson. There was a half-smile on his face as he glowered at his rival; as Watson gamely tried to return the expression I found myself suddenly wondering what he was doing up there. Throughout the heavily hyped build-up to the fight, the notion that at one point Watson was going to have to actually stand in a boxing ring and exchange blows with Benn had somehow managed to escape me. Now as the two fighter stood there looking at each other like teenagers before an after-school scuffle, the reality of the situation finally hit home.

They continued in this position as a man in a suit with a microphone gave a brief description of each fighter's achievements for those in the audience who had forgotten the reason for this gathering. Again it was Benn who drew the loudest cheers as his perfect 22 fights/22 knockouts ratio was read out. Then, for the weight-conscious in attendance, both boxers' relative densities were duly revealed. Finally, the referee placed an arm around the two men's shoulders and drew them together for their instructions. Benn's glare seemed to deepen as he found himself inches away from the eyes of the man who had occupied the majority of his thoughts for the past few months. I was relieved that it wasn't me doing the staring this time.

All at once the ring emptied of all superfluous personnel and with the white shirt of the referee still separating the two fighters, there was a slight hush as the 8,000 or so people packed into Ambrose Mendy's supertent waited for the bell. Then it began.

Bobbing and weaving in a crab-like stance, Benn advanced towards Watson and looked for an opportunity to launch one of his bombs. Watson seemed wary as he waited for his opponent to make a move; yet even as he prepared to experience the power of the punches that had parted almost two dozen professional prize-fighters from their senses, he still found time to try a few of his own. Three of the prodding hooks that he managed to throw hit thin air but the other two found his opponent's rib cage. Then the first attack came: five… six… seven… eight punches thrown with venomous intent from Benn that had Watson frantically back-pedalling and trying to cover up any vulnerable parts of his body with arms and gloves. Then another six blows: a couple of hooks, a jab and several fierce overhand rights. In the ringside seats, Angie from EastEnders could be seen to punch the air in excitement.

Yet Watson was already doing better than many people had expected. Although he was on the retreat he was firing back; sneaky little hooks to the body and almost tender looking cuffs to Benn's head. He was fighting a canny fight: keeping close to his opponent to deny Benn the leverage he needed for his pile drivers, and using elbows and gloves to nullify most of Benn's close quarter attacks. It was a technique reminiscent of former heavyweight champion Floyd Patterson's 'peek-a-boo' style from the 1950s; one that had been successfully employed by American welterweight Marlon Starling a month or so earlier when he had unceremoniously stripped Britain's Lloyd Honeyghan of his WBC title and in doing so made the usual mockery of my pre-fight prediction.

But Benn was not to be deterred. Punch after punch whistled through the air as he pursued his rival around the ring. Most fell short or were deflected by Watson's arms but some hit the target, including a triplet of body shots that made people wince in their seats. The blows were received with an appreciative hum of anticipation from most of those watching in the crowd, but the sound could not drown out the voice of Watson's cuts man, Denny Mancini, who, since the fighters' opening exchanges, had been keeping up a constant chant of, 'C'mon Michael… C'mon Michael… C'mon Michael…' Watson gritted his teeth and tried to concentrate on avoiding the onslaught.

To many it was beginning to look like Watson was a little out of his depth. Although he was defending himself pluckily, it was Benn who continued to force the action. It was Benn who was throwing seven or eight crunching haymakers to Watson's two or three tentative little clips, and it was Benn who appeared to be having the most fun under the warm spotlights. With half a minute of the round to go the pair were locked in a lover's embrace: Benn resting his head under Watson's chin and pummelling away at the other man's body; Watson twisting and turning like an eel, attempting to find the blows that might force his opponent to take a backward step. By the time that the bell sounded both fighters were dripping with sweat. As they returned to their respective corners they shot each other a smile that had nothing whatsoever to do with friendliness or mutual camaraderie.

Round two: The confrontation continued as before – Benn marching forward with hunched shoulders and Watson beating a fidgety retreat. Yet already Benn was beginning to slow down; without his adrenaline burst of the previous round, he appeared to have slipped a gear. He was still throwing just as many punches, and most of then appeared just as lethal as they had done before, but there was something lacking. Watson seemed to have noticed this, too; although he continued to clamp his gloves around his ears like a pair of oversized red headphones, he was gradually becoming more ambitious. Now and then he began to up his attacks and force his opponent to consider defence for the first time. There was a hiss of surprise from Benn's supporters when an uppercut jerked the boxer's head back.

The punch, however, only had the effect of redoubling Benn's onslaught. Soon, his opponent was back in his familiar position on the ropes. This time, however, Watson was a little lax; perhaps his early success was making him overconfident, or maybe he was beginning to feel the frenetic pace that was being set by his rival. Whatever the reason, Benn's punches finally found their mark and it was now Watson's head that was being buffeted from side to side. Needless to say, the breakthrough only served to encourage Benn, who gave a grunt of defiance and continued to deliver his power punches.

It was not until the fourth round, however, that the complexion of the fight began to change. Although Watson's success rate had continued to rise in the previous three minutes, he was suddenly beginning to look stronger than his opponent. With a minute to go he threw a flurry of blows that drove Benn across the ring and into the ropes. Without warning, Benn's hands dangled by his sides and his face bore an expression of profound confusion as the other man caught him with a dozen unanswered punches. Sitting close to Benn's corner, Mendy looked on in concern as his fighter soaked up the blows.

Then, as if he had suddenly found the solution to a particularly difficult crossword clue, Benn shook his head and sprung back into action. Once again, it was Michael Watson's turn to retreat as Benn forced his tiring arms through the air and tried to find the knockout punch that would rescue the situation. But already it was too late. Now Angie from *EastEnders* was standing up in her seat and casting anxious glances at Brian May from Queen as Watson renewed his attacks. This time he moved to the centre of the ring and invited Benn to come at him, slipping his opponent's flailing fists and nailing him with hard, economical right hands that brought a grunt of pain from Benn. The energy seemed to be draining away from him as another 11 unanswered punches knocked Benn's muscled frame backwards. Yet even as Watson pursued his opponent, he still appeared wary; like everyone else he had seen Benn in this position before and knew that he was still, as that reggae beat had informed us all earlier in the evening, dangerous.

Watson was giving the erstwhile Dark Destroyer a boxing lesson; an impeccable demonstration of the art of hitting while not being hit. For every six or seven of Benn's blows that whistled harmlessly by Watson, he now received three or four painful reminders of who was winning this particular argument. As the bell sounded, you could sense that Benn realised he had met his match; for the first time that night he gave his opponent an appreciative tap with the back of his glove, as if to say, 'Hey, Michael – what do you say we call this one a draw?'

It was at the point that I began to forget who I was supposed to be. With a colleague from the *Sunday Telegraph* elbowing me angrily in the ribs I found myself all once out of my seat and jumping up and down like a madman. There was a chorus of disapproval from the press contingent as I showed my true colours and gave Watson a piece of carefully considered advice which I was sure would once and for all take the fight beyond Benn's reach. 'Get the bastard, Michael!' is, I believe, what I might have said.

Benn fought the next round as if he was swimming through treacle. Watson stood in the centre of the ring and watched his opponent's blows creep towards him in slow motion. For the first time in the fight he lowered the hands that had been protecting his face and traded punches with the man who had been stealing his headlines. At one point a right hand from Watson sent Benn spinning across the ring, from which position Jonathan Ross, Michelle and Wicksey from *EastEnders*, as well as pop singer Paul Young were able to witness at first hand the vacant look on their man's face. Inside the supertent, the sound of the crowd grew quieter and the rows of minor celebrities who had been recruited by Mendy stared forlornly into their laps.

The end came in the sixth round. By now Benn was looking a sorry sight; his breath came in short, laboured bursts and his right eye was beginning to close. Sensing victory, Watson forced himself upon his opponent and intensified his efforts. Then, during one particularly brutal exchange, he caught Benn on the side of his face with another right hand and his rival turned away clutching his eye. Once more, I found myself on my feet being shushed by other members of the press and screaming something indecipherable at Watson and his stricken rival. By this point everybody in the arena knew that the fight was over; turning away from an opponent after being punched in the face was, after all, something that boxers simply weren't supposed to do. It meant that either Benn was badly hurt or looking for an excuse that might help explain why he was just about to be beaten in the ring for the first time in his professional career.

The referee cradled Benn in his arms for a moment and took a look at the boxer's eye, which was now just a slit. Then he indicated to Benn that he could continue if he so desired. With commendable bravery the Dark Destroyer had one more go at Watson; summoning up energy from Lord knows where in his tired body, he flung himself in Watson's direction and threw a final cluster of punches. As he had done throughout the contest, Watson raised his gloves to his face and waited for Benn's onslaught to diminish. Then he stuck out a lazy jab, and then another, and then a pair of hooks that made Benn's head roll, and then three more jabs and then, finally, as Benn advanced wearily towards him, Watson threw one last jab, which caught his opponent flush in the face and knocked him backwards to the floor.

Benn's tumble to the canvas seemed to last several seconds. Although he was not unconscious, his facial caste appeared to suggest that he was half asleep. With legs sticking out into the air like a baby waiting for its nappy to be changed, Benn lay on the floor and wished he were somewhere else. From the fighter's corner could be heard the voice of Benn's trainer, Brian Lynch. 'Get up Nigel!' he called, as if the thought had not occurred to his fighter. 'Get up!'

Benn rose wearily to his feet at the count of ten, or rather, a milli-second or so before the referee's count reached ten. As I watched from ringside, spittle flying from my mouth and arms performing cartwheels, the referee shook his head and decided that Benn had taken enough punches that evening. Then he waved the fight over.

※ ※ ※ ※

Pandemonium. An overused word but the only way to describe what happened next as the ring suddenly flooded with people and Denny Mancini rushed to embrace Watson in a manner that recalled Heathcliffe's hillside encounter with Kathy. Before you could count to three the ring was overflowing with heaving bodies and the two fighters disappeared amid a melange of blurred colours and panting bodies. Commendably, it was the damaged features of Benn who was the first to emerge from the chaos. With a dignity that many people did not believe that he possessed, the vanquished Dark Destroyer elbowed his way through the throng and sought out the man who had just beaten him up. Then, not for the first time that evening, the pair embraced.

A brief collection of memories relating to the night when the man who had provided my unlikely entry into the surreal world of professional boxing put a temporary end to the career of Benn: I remember standing on the ring apron and being ordered to sit down by a heavily-built steward; I remember watching an exhausted and overwhelmed Watson struggling to force the words from his lips as the ITV cameras recorded his post-fight interview; I can still hear the yelp of pain from Mickey Duff when someone trod on his foot as the smiling manager watched his fighter soak up the acclaim; and I can remember calling something out to Watson as he cast a pair of tired but still startled eyes over the scene at ringside (for some inexplicable reason I yelled 'come here!' to him as more members of the press tugged at my jacket and implored me to take my seat, a sentence which, along with my frenzied image, was duly recorded by the television camera).

More poignant, is the memory of Frank Maloney standing outside the Portakabins in the grounds of the supertent that served as makeshift dressing rooms for the two fighters.

'You should see Nigel's face,' he said in sorrow to an intensely unsympathetic Mickey Duff, as he tried in vain to force his way into the victor's camp. 'His eye's in a terrible state.'

Fourteenth Rule Of Boxing: A Great Fight Is That Rarest Of Commodities

For a fight to be considered a truly great fight it must fulfil a number of criteria:

1. The fight must be contested between boxers of approximately equal ability, though not necessarily of similar style. In fact, the greater the contrast in technique and approach the more chance there is of the fight becoming a classic.

2. If not the best in their weight division, the two boxers must be as close to the best as possible. It also helps if neither competitor has been beaten in the ring before; a circumstance that is particularly compelling for boxing

fans, who will be able to watch as one of the fighters loses for the first time; or, to paraphrase the unbeaten Michael Spinks prior to his 93-second annihilation at the hands of the unbeaten Mike Tyson in 1989, when 'somebody's '0' goes'.

3. Although not compulsory, it is a distinct advantage if both boxers dislike one another. All the better if they are approximately the same age and have allowed their hatred to fester for some time. As well as ensuring that the two fighters are sufficiently motivated for the upcoming epic, this will guarantee that the fight crowd will be split into two distinct and partisan sections, thus providing the necessary atmosphere and background ambience required for such an event.

4. It is vital that the fight is finely balanced and exhibit sweeping changes in control. Take for an example of such a truly great fight the 1981 welterweight confrontation between 'Sugar' Ray Leonard and Thomas 'Hit Man' Hearns, which saw Hearns's aggressive power punching steal the early rounds as Leonard attempted to box; and culminated in a switch of identities as Hearns was forced to dance in the latter rounds and Leonard turn puncher.

5. The fight must be resolved with a knockout.

%% %% %% %%

While any one of these specifications would be enough to ensure that a fight is memorable, it is only within their full range that a boxing match can achieve true greatness. Would Muhammad Ali's historic defeat of George Foreman, for example, be perceived in the same manner had the two boxers not been quite so famous and fighting, instead of in the jungles of Zaire, on an undercard at the York Hall at Bethnal Green? Rather an ambitious suspension of disbelief, I readily admit, but nevertheless it is impossible not to hear the hoots and catcalls that would issue from that particular establishment at the sight of two heavyweights, one lying on the ropes and covering up while the other attempts to punch him, and the other trying to punch an immobile target yet never quite managing to succeed in this deceptively straightforward looking task.

Similarly, could the 1987 middleweight classic between Marvellous Marvin Hagler and 'Sugar' Ray Leonard really have been so exciting without the added stimuli provided by the fighters' bitter rivalry?

Like the world of professional football, boxing is divisionalised: and for anyone wishing to purchase a ticket to the World Cup Final he must first be prepared to sit through several equivalent rainy seasons' of Mansfield Town against York City. In boxing a truly great fight is a rare commodity indeed. Such a jewel is uncovered only once or twice in a generation and is to be treasured for all it is worth.

16

Love and War

HER name was Sarah Campbell. She was pretty and blonde and intense and had no small talent as a sculptor. She was in her early 20s when she died and I still have a sketch that I made of her a year before she left art college. In truth I could not really call her a friend – in fact, a large part of me suspected that she didn't even like me very much. We shared only a handful of conversations in the three years or so that I knew her and whenever we talked she made it fairly plain that there were other places she would rather be. She died in 1987 in the saddest, most ridiculous, most futile, most pointless manner one can imagine but whether she realises it or not, I will carry a small part of Sarah inside me until the time comes when it is my own turn to die.

Sarah was working as a barmaid in a quiet country pub on the night of the accident. Her boyfriend had been sitting across from her at the bar and they had argued. He had stormed out of the pub and she had chased after him into the darkness where he had been able to stand and watch as the car appeared from nowhere and ploughed into Sarah, killing her instantly.

Who knows what Sarah would have gone on to achieve had the driver of that car not elected to be on that particular stretch of deserted road at that precise moment in her life? Maybe she would have fulfilled her childhood dream and become a famous artist, creating objects of beauty and enriching the lives of other people; or perhaps she might have remained working at that bar, got married, had children – all that sort of thing. We shall never know. All that remains of Sarah, the girl I once sat and sketched as she struggled to paint a self-portrait on the top floor of the painting studio all those years ago, is a handful of dust and a collage of memories shared by a scattering of people dotted around this slowly revolving ball of mud and water that we call home.

There will be family photographs, of course; already fading and no doubt stained with tears, they will show a happy, smiling, pretty little face staring expectantly out at the world; hungry for adventure and thirsty for life, unaware of the death sentence hanging over her. There will as well be school photographs: Sarah aged eight – reasonable at sport, not bad at English, top of the class at art; Sarah at 14 – a crush on David Cassidy, puberty already turning her into a woman, still top of the class at art. Perhaps there are even videos or old Super-8 movies that can let us see again her movements and hear her voice just one more time. There are also the lives that she touched and the people whose lives she changed. Somewhere – I have no idea where – is her boyfriend, now ten years older but quite unable – I am sure – to rid himself of the memory of Sarah; racked by the guilt of that night; knowing that but for their stupid, stupid argument she would still be a living, breathing human being.

There is the driver of the car that crushed her body and the sleepless nights he has spent thinking of those terrified eyes staring out into the headlights. And there are her parents – although again I have no idea whether they are alive or dead – who will await with equal dread the anniversary of her birth and the anniversary of her death; a piece of stone somewhere with Sarah's name carved into it, a stack of sketches and a few plaster sculptures their only mementoes of the life of their so talented daughter.

For my part I will remember her smell and the way that her nose tapered to a point. And if I should ever forget I still have that drawing of her, although it is difficult not to feel guilty whenever I look at it. Somehow those few pencil lines scraped across an A2 page seem hopelessly inadequate and I often ask myself how I would have approached the drawing in the knowledge that Sarah had but a year to live. Would I have painted my tribute to the memory of her in oils and placed it in a gilt edged frame? Would I have insisted that she sit for hours so that I could get to know her better, find out more about who Sarah was before she died? Could I have somehow made a difference? Could the set of circumstances that conspired to place Sarah and the driver of that car on a collision course that night have been prevented by something I that could have done – no matter how insignificant?

I am aware, of course, that thoughts such as these serve no purpose; the fact is that I had no way of knowing that Sarah was destined to die that night. Had I have known it would have been a simple matter for me to have stood outside the pub at that crucial moment and stop her as she pursued her boyfriend.

Perhaps even a phone call from me warning her to be careful that night would have been sufficient: the driver would have passed by and gone home to eat his tea, Sarah and her boyfriend would have made up and gone back inside the pub, and I wouldn't be sitting her now lamenting a life that will never be lived.

Fifteenth Rule Of Boxing: Boxing Is Not For Vegans

The concept of mortality is something that must be confronted head on by those who spend any of their time watching boxing. When two highly-trained athletes step into the ring prepared to use their gloved fists to beat each other into unconsciousness, death and tragedy are never too far from the horizon. For this reason, anyone who has the temerity to tell you that boxing is a safe pastime is either lying, dangerously stupid, or on the payroll of the British Boxing Board of Control.

Boxing is the most hazardous sport (although, as always, I hesitate to call it a sport) on the face of the earth, of that there is no room for dispute. Despite statistics which show us that, pound-for-pound, there are more motor racing drivers injured, maimed or killed than boxers, there is no other recreational activity in existence whose contestants deliberately set out to inflict physical damage on one another. Although motor racing may occasionally endure harsh headlines when a spectacular crash claims one of its participants, at least the drivers are all facing in the same direction when the green light flickers on; they don't come roaring towards each other from opposite sides of the road.

When you watch boxing you are left in no doubt as to its inherent dangers. When the fighters return to their corners at the end of each round there is in their faces ample evidence that they are taking far more than a Sunday stroll. Boxing is not for vegetarians or vegans; to attend a boxing match is to bear witness to some of man's most basic and primitive instincts. The struggle to survive and the battle to prevail come bathed in blood and snot – and if you sit too close to the ring there is a fair chance that you will take some home on your shirt.

The knowledge that what is happening is for real acts as both repellent and enticement to those who follow boxing. Yet despite a set of ropes and a legacy of tradition that exists to transmit the impression that the onlooker is somehow detached from what is going on inside the boxing ring, the relationship between the fighters and the people who pay money to watch them perform is intimate, complex and ultimately interwoven. For just as the referee, dressed in white shirt and elegant bow tie – his uniform of public conscience – has it within his power to bring a fight to a close at any time if a boxer appears to be taking too much punishment, so it is possible for the observer to exert a similar influence over the proceedings.

In Bob Dylan's 'Who Killed Davey Moore', his requiem for a fighter who died in the ring in 1962, the singer speculates that it was not only the fists of the other boxer that were to blame for the tragedy, but also the referee, the fighter's manager, the boxing writers who were paid to report on the fight, the audience present at the boxing arena and all of those who watched the doomed contest on TV – and for the most part he is probably right. For without the combination of minor and major roles played by all of these people, the set of circumstances that led to the death of that young man might have been avoided. Dylan, who is himself often in attendance at major boxing events, declares that to condone is to actively encourage. However indirect his involvement and however ardent his denials, the boxing fan should, therefore, be aware that when blood is being spilled in the ring it is being spilled because of his desire to see it being spilled.

The closer one gravitates towards the nucleus of boxing the more pungent the aroma of tragedy. There is not a boxer alive who does not bear the physical and mental scars of his trade: calloused hands, horribly deformed 'cauliflower ears', brows made Neanderthal by the calcium deposits built up from the blows they receive, slurred words, detached retinas; such impairments are carried like trophies and serve as constant reminders of a boxer's quest for immortality – for there are surely not enough coins in the Royal Mint sufficient to provide adequate compensation for such self-mutilation. When injury and death are endured as unfortunate by-products of their craft boxers must surely be fighting for more than money.

※ ※ ※ ※

I had been working for the *Sunday Sport* for a little under three months when I met the person who was destined to provide my first reminder of just how high the stakes can be for a professional prize-fighter. The boxer on a collision course with catastrophe was a young black middleweight known as Rod Douglas. Douglas was in his early 20s when our paths first crossed and, as well as dominating his division during his amateur days, had won the gold medal at the 1986 Commonwealth Games – an achievement rightfully deemed several notches above noteworthy by those in the know. For this reason Douglas was perceived in boxing as a future champion and, since his professional debut in 1988, had shared the same manager as Michael Watson.

On the day that I first met Douglas he was not a happy man. Like Watson, his mind was preoccupied with thoughts of Nigel Benn, who was still two months away from that fateful night at the supertent. Having defeated Benn as an amateur, Douglas simply could not understand why his rival was grabbing all the headlines while he remained buried in obscurity.

There was a cancer of resentment growing inside Douglas's washboard stomach when we sat down to talk in his three-storey terraced house in Bow. He had plenty to say about his Benn, which I was sure would please my superiors at the *Sunday Sport*. Prior to my arrival, The Northern Accent had instructed me, 'Try and see what you can get out of Douglas.' His hope was that I could encourage Douglas to criticise Benn or, in the words of my superior, 'Ger him to slag off Benn so's we can do a big splash in Sunday's paper!' With his three-year-old son, Tyson, wearing boxing gloves and cheerfully teeing off at my shins as we spoke, I turned on my tape recorder and attempted to follow my brief.

Douglas, it transpired, could have been one of any number of professional boxers that I had come into contact with during my brief tenure with the *Sport*. He was simple – though not in an unintelligent way – honest, hard-working and blessed with that kind of gentle humility that is noticeable in so many fighters. Not for the first time when meeting a boxer it came as something as a surprise that Douglas bore little resemblance to the man who between the ropes seemed to have a divine love affair with violence. Of course, he looked more or less the same: features slightly dulled by the thousands of punches that he had taken since he first stepped on to the boxing conveyor belt while little more than a child, eyes clear and sharp and bleached white, faint scar tissue buried within the eyebrows, body rock solid with muscles that would give the impression of being carved from oak were you to touch them.

To the untrained eye, however, Douglas could have been anybody: a dentist, a social worker, somebody who sat at the next desk in the office. In fact, the only aspect of his appearance that hinted of his unusual occupation was the haircut: cropped short like a five o'clock shadow and shaven away at the sides in the manner of Rocky's arch enemy Mr T; a stylistic device intended to unsettle the Mexican roadsweepers he had, to paraphrase Muhammad Ali, been 'beatin' up on' for the past couple of years.

Douglas's problem was that nobody knew who he was. As a result he was still a bit-player in boxing and his appearance in Sunday's newspaper was likely to be insubstantial unless we could discover something about him that could titillate the readers' appetite for jingoism.

Even Max Clifford would have had problems making a star out of Douglas. Without wishing to sound heartless, he just wasn't the type. His personality, his demeanour, the way that his shoulders hunched as he spoke; none of these attributes suggested that one was in the presence of a potential superstar. Most damning of all was his voice: a slight lisp that muffled his words and would prove a major disadvantage in those all important post-match televised interviews. Such, however, is boxing – where personality and physical appearance so often take precedence over ability.

'Nigel Benn stole my haircut!' This was the line that I eventually coaxed out of the fighter, and the line that appeared above Douglas's story and – regrettably –above a large picture of Benn in the newspaper a few days later. In their infinite wisdom, the powers that be at the *Sunday Sport* had decided that Douglas simply wasn't interesting enough to merit a story that contained a photograph of him. Their solution had been a standard newspaper ploy: they had simply run his quotes beneath an image of the man that Douglas had slagged off and turned the whole thing into a Benn story.

Perhaps understandably, Douglas was none to pleased when he called me to complain on Monday morning. 'You've done me over!' he exclaimed. 'Why've you got a picture of Benn instead of me? You reporters are all the same – you're all bastards!'

This, you may well appreciate, left me in rather an awkward position. The fact that I had written the piece in good faith, also expecting to see it accompanied by a photograph of Douglas, meant nothing to him. However, as far as Douglas was concerned he had been wronged – and I was the perpetrator. There is little doubt that to many of you reading this the notion that Douglas could get so upset because a picture of Benn had been used instead of one of his own may seem petty and trivial, but I can still understand Douglas's outrage. When boxing is your life, when boxing and all the fame and glory that is supposed to accompany it has been the only thing that you have thought about for most of your years on this planet, every setback, however minor, takes on an extraordinary significance that is beyond the comprehension of most people. As he spat insults at me over the phone, I could sense that Douglas was close to tears, that spluttering voice of his could scarcely hold itself together, and I was left feeling like I was the Devil.

%% %% %% %%

I tried to make amends. I promised to follow Douglas's progress and ensure that his fights always got a mention in the paper. This olive branch seemed to do the trick: 40 words every month at the bottom of the *Sunday Sport*'s boxing page turned Douglas into a friend. I grew to like him a great deal; his sense of humour, his habit of taking a sneaky cigarette every so often when his manager wasn't looking. Then disaster struck.

As Christmas 1989 approached, Douglas was given the opportunity to move into the big time. His opponent was to be Herol Graham, the current British middleweight champion, a man whom many considered to be in decline but who was, nevertheless, still a formidable fighter. This was to be one of Douglas's manager Mickey Duff's famous gambles, a trademark mixture of experience, instinct and guessology that had five years earlier turned the unknown and untameable British welterweight Kirkland Laing into Jack the Giant Killer when he defeated the murderous Roberto Duran under the harsh lights of Las Vegas.

LOVE AND WAR

The flash of inspiration that had seen another welterweight, John H. Stracey, travel to Mexico to take the undisputed world title from the seemingly invincible José Napoles in 1975; a gambit of similar nature to the one that Duff had lain to witness an unknown Lloyd Honeyghan demoralise and humiliate Don Curry in a car park in Nevada before an audience of admiring fans and starstruck boxing writers who were all so convinced that Curry was destined for greatness. Mickey Duff liked a challenge, he liked nothing more than to put one of his fighters into the lion's den before licking his lips and counting the bundles of cash that regularly fell into his hands via the bookmakers. Except this time the stake was Douglas's career. For just as there were many so-called experts who were predicting a win for the younger man, there were others – myself among them – who feared that Douglas was about to receive a lesson that he might never forget.

Douglas came into the fight a slight outsider at the bookies, which may have been the way that Mickey Duff had perceived that things might go. Herol Graham was in his early 30s and slower than he had been in his heyday of only four or five years earlier. Nevertheless, he was a true original, with a style that was often misinterpreted as, well, stylish, when in fact it could have been better described as awkward. As a younger man Graham had boasted that his reactions were such that no man could ever lay a fist on him. To demonstrate this, his habit had been to stalk the pubs and clubs of Sheffield, and with hands tied behind his back, challenge people to hit him. They never could.

Nor for that matter could Douglas, who spent ten rounds chasing Graham around the ring before tiring himself out and succumbing to a flurry of punches from the older man that saw him counted out in the tenth round. Yet even as Duff tore up his betting slip and counted the cost of his misplaced optimism, you could see that something was not quite right with Douglas. There was something in his eyes, something about the vacant look that he gave as he sat down panting in his corner and attempted to regain his senses. As Graham celebrated what amounted to a reaffirmation of his own skills, those sitting at ringside were already casting anxious glances in the direction of Douglas.

Douglas collapsed and was put in an ambulance before being driven to St Bartholemew's Hospital. Within the hour surgeons had sliced away a piece from his skull and were delving into his brain with variety of chrome-plated medical instruments. After over four hours on the operating table they finally found what they were looking for: a tiny globule of blood, smaller than a pinhead, that had formed when Graham's fists had smashed his opponent's brain against the lining of his skull; it was now lodged in to a tiny artery, blocking the flow of blood and starving Douglas's brain of oxygen.

The extent of Douglas's injuries were such that 20 years ago he would have been a condemned man. Then, the decision to switch off the life support machine would have been the responsibility of his wife, Sue. Now he was a lucky man; he would live – he would be able to lead a healthy life. He would also never box again.

After several weeks in intensive care Douglas finally returned home with his head now completely shaven and wearing a silver cap that had been riveted to his skull to protect the hole in his head from the elements. Enough people had already told him that he was fortunate to be able to walk out of that hospital but he was, naturally, inconsolable. His life had changed in a manner that he could never have imagined even in his darkest nightmares. Instead of a superbly-conditioned athlete well on the way to generating more money than his bank manager could ever conceive of, Douglas was just one of Thatcher's three million: he was a young black man with no real qualifications, the quality that defined him, that set him apart from everybody else, savagely ripped away from him. Aged 23 he was a has-been, worse still he was an invalid: he had been advised that even stepping inside a gym could potentially end his life.

Boxing tried to rally around him. The BBC gave him some work sitting alongside Harry Carpenter commentating

on other fighters; close enough to the sweet jar to touch it —
we cannot, of course, even begin to imagine what was going
through Douglas's mind while he was doing this. Inevitably,
however, his new occupation was short-lived, the ex-boxer's
unwieldy voice saw to that, his slight lisp was amplified ten-fold
by the television microphones. Apparently people rang in to
complain: they could not understand what Douglas was saying.

17

The Man with Two Faces

I WAS sitting on the tube on the way back to the office from yet another press conference when I saw him. He was in his early 20s, I guess, and if you viewed his face from the right-hand side he looked perfectly normal; there was nothing exceptional about him at all: he was not particularly handsome, he was not particularly ugly, his was not a face that would stand out from the crowd. However, if you happened to be sitting to his left it was an entirely different story. From this position the young man was horribly deformed. Ugly bumps and twisted scar tissue jutted out from his face at uneven angles and his eye was fused tightly shut, giving him the appearance of a latter-day John Merrick. Whatever had caused these terrible disfigurations, I have no idea; I was just relieved that it wasn't me sitting there in that carriage full of people who were carefully looking the other way.

I described this sad spectacle to The Northern Accent when I got back to the office and immediately regretted doing so. For a moment he was angry at me for not having spoken to the man in the tube train with the deformed face. Then he composed himself and scurried over to the news desk, from where a reporter was hurriedly despatched in an attempt to locate this unfortunate person. I sat and watched as The Northern Accent stood in the centre of the office; his eyes burned brightly as he anticipated the story that would undoubtedly make the front page of Sunday's paper. Already he was composing headlines, 'We'll call it "THE MAN with two faces!"' he exclaimed excitedly.

%%%%

At the beginning of August 1989 – barely five months after becoming the *Sunday Sport*'s unlikeliest boxing correspondent – I finally did what I should have done on my very first morning at the paper: I walked out. I'd had enough of the place. I simply couldn't justify working there any more.

Despite everything, however, my decision to call it a day had not been an easy one to make. For a boxing fan who had fallen on his feet, the job had been perfect in so many respects. Not only did I receive front-row tickets for any fight that I felt like attending, and not only did I spend my days meeting and talking with some of the most famous boxers and fight figures in the world, but I also got paid a salary for doing so.

I got paid a salary for sitting behind a desk with a phone in one hand and trying to track down my heroes from the past and present. I got paid a salary for attending press conferences and weigh-ins and sparring sessions that were frequented by people who I would once have chased for an autograph. Most of all, someone was actually paying for me to sit at ringside and watch the people I had admired for most of my life go about their business in full CinemaScope.

Yet it's interesting to note how the alabaster glow of fame can be so quickly dimmed. For me it was only a matter of weeks before I began to treat my daily contact with the idols of millions with a degree of nonchalance that bordered on disdain. In that short time I had gone from someone who had visibly trembled when first introduced at ringside to Lloyd Honeyghan, to someone who now refused to answer the phone to Lloyd Honeyghan when the boxer called the office because he was busy talking to somebody more famous than Lloyd Honeyghan. I started to understand why most of my fellow journalists went around with a look on their faces which suggested that the dog had just eaten the budgie.

They'd seen it all before, of course: they'd had more than enough time to grow bored of the endless conveyor belt of up and coming fighters who continued to repeat the same mistakes as their predecessors. Most of them had long since forgotten the reasons that had originally drawn them into seeking a career among the people who were paid to punch each other. It was just a job to them. And although it was infinitely more stimulating than counting the bricks in an architect's office or pulling corks out of bottles, it was becoming just a job to me.

%, %, %, %,

Although there were far too many reasons behind my decision to resign from the *Sunday Sport*, what finally forced my hand was when the paper decided to run an innocuous interview I had conducted with the IBF flyweight world champion Dave 'Boy' McAuley accompanied by a photograph of the boxer that had been taken at a weigh-in. The picture in question depicted an embarrassed looking and bollock-naked McAuley shivering on some scales and covering his genitals with both hands. Being one of those fighters who always seemed to have difficulty making the stipulated weight for the division in which he fought, McAuley must have been forced to strip down to such a state of undress in order to come in at 112lb.

One of only two Britons who held versions of a world title at the time, McAuley had been wary when we had first spoken over the telephone. He was familiar with the *Sunday Sport*'s reputation for over-exaggeration and had only consented to appear within its pages on the strict understanding that there would be no stitch-ups. I knew that he would be disappointed when he opened up Sunday's paper and saw that photograph.

My attempts, however, to persuade The Northern Accent to select an alternative accompanying image proved fruitless. Even when I explained that McAuley was a world champion and that publishing the picture would probably mean that he would never speak to the paper again, my sports editor refused to budge. In the end I made him an ultimatum: I would give him until 6pm and if he had not changed his mind I would resign, taking the story with me.

Please forgive me if it appears that I am trying to paint too noble a picture of myself, for that is not the case. The simple truth is that I should never have been working at the *Sunday Sport* in the first place. Although, as you may by now have gleaned from the pages of this book, I have not in the past been adverse to telling the odd lie or two in order to further my cause, by now I realised that I had well and truly met my match. When it came to the business of deception I was a novice compared to most of the journalists who earned their living in the employ of David Sullivan. It was simply no contest.

Yet to look at the people who spent their time fabricating stories that had as much to do with reality as the proportions of some of the bare breasts that were to be found in the pages of the newspaper they represented, you would never have guessed how they earned the money to pay for their mortgages. Most were still in their early 20s and as fresh-faced as a college leaver. Most were politely spoken and doted on their wives and children. And most were extremely affable company when sitting on a bar stool after work. It was only when they clicked into hack mode that one felt one's stomach begin to churn. When they were chasing some hapless celeb around the country, these young men and women were transformed. When they had the spurned mistress of a soccer star at the other end of a telephone line they became transfixed by a desire to outrage and humiliate. Their body language altered, their shoulders tensed and their faces twisted into a snarl.

I felt myself changing, too. Although I had so far managed to avoid being coerced into producing another world exclusive of the 'Sweet Dick' variety, I had somehow managed to forget the reasons that had first drawn me to boxing when my father had burst into my bedroom that morning more than 15 years earlier. I tried lying to myself. I tried telling myself that it was far better that someone like me was sitting behind that desk in the *Sport*'s offices, than someone who would have drawn satisfaction from producing stories that set out to demean some of the people that I most admired in the world. I would go to parties and find myself drawn into long elaborate discussions as to the nature of the work that I was undertaking in order to finance my new, elevated, standard of living. Yet although I tried to find a means of justifying the manner in which I spent my days, I never really could. There was simply no way that I could defend my contribution to a publication which revelled in bringing such misery to the lives of the people that it chose to feature among the bearded ladies and 50st milkmen and oversized knockers. So I had to leave.

There are those, of course, who will argue that such a reaction to the publication's list of misdemeanours is merely indicative of a person who is severely lacking in a sense of humour. Indeed, it is usually with wit that many of the *Sport*'s more articulate defenders are able to provide entirely convincing arguments in defence of their newspaper. They will tell you that their stories are not to be taken seriously; that in comparison to rivals such as the *News of the World* and *The Sun*, their tales of obesity and the misadventures of the rich and famous hurt no one. But I have been present when the victims of these moral invasions have shed tears of shame and outrage on the telephone to a leering reporter. And I have also been there to hear the mocking laughter that reverberated around the office when the *Sunday Sport*'s editorial team celebrated the public humiliation of yet another fallen star.

※ ※ ※ ※

Six o'clock came and went and so did I. When it became clear the sports editor was not prepared to change his mind about that picture of Dave 'Boy' McAuley I quietly packed up my possessions and bade a long overdue farewell to the *Sunday Sport*. I received a telephone call the next morning telling me that if I reconsidered my decision there was still a job there for me. But I said no. Even though I was aware that I had just kissed goodbye to a career that I could scarcely have dreamed of only a year earlier, I just did not want to work for the *Sunday Sport* that much.

On the other hand, however, it has to be said that my quitting the job was not that big a deal: leaving a job that they are not happy in is, after all, something that hundreds of people in London do every week. At least, however, I could console myself that I had saved McAuley the embarrassment that the newspaper had planned to thrust upon his shoulders. I should, as the song says, have known better – my former employers were just not that stupid. Nevertheless, it was still something of a shock when I picked up a copy of Sunday's newspaper to discover that my interview with the Irish boxer – along with that photograph – had been run. Somebody else's name was on the by-line and the wording of the piece had been altered slightly, but the newspaper had managed to get its own way. Furthermore, it had taken them only days to find a replacement for me.

%. %. %. %.

So now it was back to the shitty jobs. Even though I had been working as a professional boxing journalist for practically a year, and even though I had in that time somehow managed to accrue a network of contacts in the business that stretched around the world, I was far from optimistic about my chances of continuing to earn a living in the same way. By telephone and in person I had conducted interviews with boxers of the stature of Larry Holmes, George Foreman, Evander Holyfield, Michael Nunn and Thomas Hearns. Yet I suspected that this would stand for nothing if I approached another newspaper and showed them clippings of the eventual resting place of these dialogues. I had little choice: my brief experience of what it was like to be part of the boxing circus would have to remain just that – an experience: something I could tell the grandchildren about when I was an old man.

Boxing, however, was not quite ready to give up that easily.

A couple of days after quitting my job at the *Sport*, I received a phone call. It was from the publishers of a new glossy boxing magazine that had been launched in this country three months earlier. The magazine was called *Boxing Monthly* and I remembered that I had been present at a press conference held to celebrate the launch. The person at the other end of the line explained that due to the success of the magazine they had decided to launch a weekly incarnation. They were looking for an editor – how was I fixed at the moment?

Sixteenth Rule Of Boxing: Everyone Loves A Knockout

To suggest that everyone loves a knockout is, of course, something of an overstatement. In reality, at that crucial moment when a boxer suffers what writer Joyce Carol Oates has described as a 'symbolic death' in the ring there are many people who will find themselves watching the brutal spectacle with less than enthusiasm. These will include fans of the fighter who is just about to see stars, relatives, corner men, management and, naturally, the recipient of the knockout blow himself.

The knockout – the act of one man hitting another in the head with his clenched fist so hard that the person being hit in the head with a clenched fist is rendered unconsciousness – is one of boxing's principle attractions. It is also the most compelling reminder that boxing's claim that it is in any way related to other sporting pastimes that involve strips of leather and pieces of wood is dubious at the very least. People who watch boxing watch boxing to see a knockout; of course, they will tell you that this is not the only reason that they choose to be party to a ritual that has been responsible for the lives of so many of its participants. They will talk about defence strategies and beautiful combinations and whatever other reason they evoke for their decision to watch two people share a beating in the ring, but in truth the knockout blow is what most people are in attendance for.

Indeed, knockout specialists occupy a special place in the hearts of most boxing fans. For many people the concussive exploits of fighters such as Mike Tyson, Joe Louis, George Foreman, Nigel Benn, Thomas Hearns, Julian Jackson, Naseem Hamed, Archie Moore and Earnie Shavers represent boxing in its most refined state. That these knockout specialists have shown themselves capable of separating another man from his senses on a regular basis is a source of enduring fascination.

The knockout blow allows onlookers to be party to the real time dismemberment of one of mankind's biggest taboos. It is shocking to observe but at the same time savagely compelling. It is boxing's most unequivocal demonstration of its independence from the laws which govern our society – and although many may find themselves watching this barbarous act through the cracks in their fingers, they will be unable to turn away from that moment in which a fighter experiences what Muhammad Ali has described as the 'black void'. Even though the punchline will seldom elicit a laugh, people love to see a knockout. It's what boxing is all about. Don't let anyone tell you otherwise.

18

The Omega

'WHO you fawwww?' drawled an American accent from beside me as we sat peering through the darkness towards the glittering lights of the ring.

'Watson,' I replied, turning to face my questioner, who I could see was wearing a sweatshirt with the word 'Bodysnatcher' printed neatly across it.

'Your boy ain't got a chance,' said another voice sitting nearby. 'He's goin' be broken into pieces.'

There were three of them in all. All of them black and all part of the entourage that Mike McCallum had brought over with him from America to provide moral support for the first defence of his WBA middleweight crown at London's Albert Hall. They had been with him 11 months earlier at this same venue, and like me had watched McCallum capture the vacant title in a hard fought points win over Britain's Herol Graham. In his previous fight Graham had been able to make Rod Douglas look like an amateur but McCallum had given 'Bomber' a taste of what it was like to mix it at the highest level.

Graham had ended the fight with one eye closed and so exhausted that he was barely able to stand on legs that were made of jelly. Now it was Michael Watson's turn to see if he could cope with McCallum's famed body shots.

McCallum was a highly accomplished boxer. Although there was little doubt that his fists carried concussive power, he was a fighter who preferred to work to the body. He was a throwback to another era; the era which many in boxing will tell you was superior in every respect to its modern incarnation. McCallum was what people liked to refer to as a 'scientific' boxer: he would take a look at you, dissect your weaknesses and sooner or later find a way to make you suffer. At least, he'd managed to do this on 36 out of 37 occasions since he had turned professional in 1981, the only blot on his record being a points loss to the WBA middleweight champion Sumbu Kalambay two years earlier. I, however, was sure that in Michael Watson he was about to meet his match.

'I don't think so,' I confidently informed the three men. 'McCallum's too old and Watson's defence is too good.'

'You're talkin' BS,' one of them continued. 'You'll see – soon it's gonna be Bodysnatcher time!'

※ ※ ※ ※

I suppose I should have sensed that Michael Watson was destined to remember the next half an hour or so with very different feelings to the recollections of his night of triumph almost a year earlier in Ambrose Mendy's supertent. He was, after all, featured in the centre pages of the boxing paper I had been editing for the last six months. And it was my pre-fight prediction which confidently told our dwindling readership that Watson was about to become the country's first middleweight champion since Alan Minter. Yet another one of my famous 100 per cent incorrect boxing predictions, I'm afraid.

A chance to test his skills against McCallum was the reward that Watson had eventually received for the victory over Nigel Benn that had somehow still not quite managed to turn him into a star. Since that thrilling night, the boxer had been forced to endure a series of cancellations and training injuries which meant that by the time he finally climbed into the ring to attempt to fulfil his childhood dream he had not fought for almost 11 months. Yet while Watson had spent that period fighting boredom instead of other men, I, on the other hand had been far from idle.

In addition to becoming the editor of Britain's only weekly colour newspaper, I was now also selling my words to a clutch of other publications around the world; as well as this I was getting paid money to occasionally appear on television and give my expert opinions about the latest big fight. And if this was not enough I was also Watson's agent. My life had become completely transformed and it was all down to one thing: boxing.

For those of you who are beginning to tire of the seemingly endless tide of good fortune that had carried me along since I first decided to use that typewriter to write about boxing, you will be relieved to hear that I was about to receive my comeuppance. In under a year I had, after all, gone from Islington squatter to boxing writer to boxing reporter and, finally, to editor of a weekly boxing paper. Things like that aren't supposed to happen. I knew that. Boxing knew that. And within months everybody else would be aware of this fact.

※ ※ ※ ※

By round two it was clear that Watson was in big trouble. He was still strong and he was still gamely attempting to stick to a fight plan that was intended to allow his older opponent to tire himself out before Watson would take over, but things were going badly wrong. McCallum seemed to punch with twice the speed of Watson: hard, sickening blows, carefully delivered and designed to sap the life force of his rival. Furthermore, his renowned body shots were ripping through his opponent's defence at will.

'Bodysnatcher time!' yelled the three men standing beside me in unison and smiling self-satisfied smiles. 'Bodysnatcher time!'

By this time, Watson had become more than just a boxer to me, I had come to view his career almost with a sense of symbolism. Fate seemed to have linked us together since we had first met in that gym a year earlier: he had been the up-and-coming fighter and I had been the up-and-coming writer – somehow our careers were interlinked. And now I could only sit and watch as his hopes and aspirations were violently torn to shreds.

'You don't know what you're taking about,' laughed one of the men, shooting me a triumphant grin as Watson's ribs shuddered under the onslaught of yet another accurate volley of body shots.

Watson's mother was sitting just in front of me as her son continued his downward slide. Her face was emotionless and I found myself marvelling at how she seemed to be handling what was happening above her so much better than I was. For a moment I felt like turning to my three gloating neighbours and telling them to be quiet: didn't they know that his mum could hear them? I understood, however, that such a gesture would have been treated with the contempt it deserved; after all, who was I to deny this trio of Americans the satisfaction of watching their man complete a famous victory – was I not the person who had been happily baying for Benn's blood when I had been sitting in their position only 11 months earlier?

Watson lasted until the 11th round before he finally succumbed to a sustained assault that forced the air from his lungs. He had enjoyed minor successes during the course of the fight but in reality he had always been second best. He was the student and McCallum was the master. Watson had fought with bravery that took him beyond endurance, and at the appropriate moment McCallum had confirmed his class by being able to move up a gear and apply the finishing touches to a flawless display. In the final three minutes of the fight the American had thrown more than 130 punches; in one vicious display of persistence McCallum had hit his opponent with some 62 (by my reckoning) unanswered blows. And before Watson's body had collapsed into a heap on the canvas, the Islington boxer had been hit with a further 22.

Watson lay on the floor for several very worrying minutes before he was finally pulled to his feet and allowed to slump wearily into his stool. A terrible silence had descended over the Albert Hall as the crowd waited to see if he would recover. It was the second time in only six months that I had been forced to look on as fate decided whether a man that I knew would live or die. But if Rod Douglas had been the hors d'oeuvre to my approaching moment of self-revelation, somehow this was the main course. In between casting anxious glances at Watson's mother, who remained motionless in her seat, I found myself wondering what I was doing in that famous theatre. How had I been able to sit and watch as two men attempted to beat themselves into submission? How could I sit there in my smart suit and tie as blood streamed from Michael Watson's nose and his eye swelled to the size of a golf ball?

It was a long overdue attack of conscience because suddenly it was not a game. Over the past year I had seen countless boxers endure pain in the ring and watched even more suffer in the course of their profession on my television set at home. I had managed to do this while somehow being able to overlook the reality of the situation.

But this was different. This was somebody who was close to me up there bleeding over that canvas. How could I sit and do nothing when the man who had provided my entrance ticket to the world of boxing was having the life systematically beaten out of him?

With the benefit of hindsight it is easy to speculate that the systematic hammering that Watson took at the hands of McCallum should have told us something. Boxing people will tell you that a fighter will never really recover from such a beating; even though his wounds will eventually heal he will never be the same fighter. Personally, I'm not completely convinced by the wisdom of this old axiom but nevertheless one would have to be a fool not to look at back the events of that night and realise that a warning signal of sorts was being flashed at us. For me, though, Watson's defeat signalled the beginning of a decline in appetite that would soon force me to take a serious look at the way in which I lived my life. Ultimately, it would compel to me to sue for a divorce from the fight game.

%. %. %. %.

Before we go any further, however, it's only reasonable that I provide you the background to the story of how I came to be Michael Watson's agent, if only to provide a cautionary warning should you ever decide that it's something you'd quite fancy doing. It was a kind of mutual thing. It came as a result of numerous conversations between the boxer, his trainer and I. As ever, Michael was looking for someone who possessed the ability to get his name in the newspapers. And as I was now in charge of my very own newspaper, his decision to ask me to take on the task was a fairly natural one to take.

The paper I was editing was called *Boxing Weekly*. Perhaps not surprisingly, it was about boxing and hit the streets when possible every seven days. Although there was already an existing weekly trade paper – the long-established *Boxing News* – it had been hoped that our publication would appeal to a different audience than the one that our rivals catered for. We launched in February 1990 with a press conference at the Thomas A. Beckett, a famous boxing pub in the East End run by a former fighter named Gary Davison, where, before a motley collection of active and inactive professional prize-fighters, I had given a spluttering speech outlining the newspaper's atheistic manifesto.

To the day I cannot believe that the publishers of *Boxing Weekly* chose to select me as editor for their paper. I'll tell you straight away that I wasn't the first choice for the job. Indeed, to my knowledge at least three other people had rejected the post long before the money men had turned to me in desperation. In many ways, however, their decision to offer the role to the former boxing reporter of the *Sunday Sport* should have told me enough about the publishers' grasp of reality to have been at least compelled to use even a little common sense before I committed myself to such a lofty position. But I needed a job and I saw no reason to look a gift horse in the mouth.

From the very start, however, things were doomed. Not only was I patently under-qualified for the post, but the majority of the staff that had also been hired by publishers were even less well-suited. To assist me in the task of writing and compiling boxing's newest mouthpiece, I was given a 17-year-old school-leaver who had never even seen a typewriter before; a 22-year-old university graduate who had not been employed since finishing his education; and a man who, up until recently, had been working in a pizza restaurant. This trio of reinvented sports journalists had been selected not so much for their wealth of experience or depth of pugilistic knowledge, but by virtue of their inherent cheapness. My publishers, I was about to learn to my detriment, had very little choice but to run the newspaper on a shoe-string.

I won't bore you with the whys and wherefores of newspaper publishing, suffice to say that a publication's chances of success are dependent on a number of factors. These include marketing; the sale of advertising, potential audience and the quality of journalist employed by the paper. In *Boxing Weekly*'s case, marketing was minimal; the sale of advertising was practically non-existent, as was our assumed potential audience; and, more importantly, the quality of writing contained within the pages was everything that you could expect from four hastily assembled individuals still wearing their journalistic 'L' plates. Within months, our circulation had gone from a high of 13,000 to a low of 2,000; bills were being left unpaid, contributors remained unpaid, staff salaries were regularly late and money was being lost at an unacceptable rate.

Yet at the same time boxing still seemed determined to present me with as many opportunities as possible. On an almost daily basis I received visits from all manner of misfits and starstruck wheeler-dealers who came to my office with get-rich quick schemes. It was as if I was being allowed to experience at first-hand the social flotsam and jetsam that are traditionally drawn to the sport's practitioners like moths to a flame.

One morning, for example, I received a mysterious phone call asking me to be at a London hotel at a certain hour, where I was met by a group of decidedly unwholesome looking middle-aged men who were apparently about to create their own boxing governing body. Tentatively entitled – if I remember correctly – the NBO (the National Boxing Organisation, or something like that, I presume), I was informed that the headquarters of this fraternity would be situated, inexplicably, in the Bahamas, and was invited to become a director. I suppose the rationale behind this unexpected offer was that, as editor of a boxing magazine, I was in a position to legitimise such a venture.

The perpetrators of this scheme, it was explained to me, intended to nominate their own boxing champions and charge a hefty fee for the privilege of competing in NBO title fights. Needless to say, I made my excuses and left.

Then there was the time that I was asked to become part of a syndicate that was being assembled to sponsor the career of a young welterweight who was just about to turn pro. For the measly sum of £10,000, I was informed, I would receive ten per cent of the boxer's future earnings. Maybe I was over-dressed at the time, certainly I must have been sending out the wrong signals; whatever the reason, I have no idea how anyone could have taken one look at me and concluded that I had a disposable income of that nature. Once again, I politely declined this kind proposal, which was fortunate because the fighter in question went on to lose two of his first three fights before sinking into obscurity.

Yet there were some offers that I did not reject. Although for legal reasons my co-conspirators will have to remain nameless, I did actually wind up becoming a director of a promotional company that specialised in handling the public affairs of boxers. Thus, as well as being the agent for Michael Watson, I was employed in a similar capacity for a number of other fighters, including Duke McKenzie, Kirkland Laing and Darren Dyer. I have to stress that my involvement in this scheme was minimal. Most of the fighters that the company represented seemed to be concerned with only one thing: for whatever reason, they were all gripped by a desire to sit behind the wheel of a sponsored car with their name painted along its side. Even though the majority of the boxers that we briefly represented already owned their own cars, there was something about the prestige of being given a brand new one for free that appealed to their egos – to them it was an indication that they had really arrived, that they were now stars.

My participation in such ventures was also a clear indication that I had bitten off more than I could chew. And although I soldiered on as best I could for the rest of the year I could not stop my devotion to boxing from being steadily drained away from me. As the newspaper's circulation figures continued to drop so did my energies. Suddenly, it was no longer so much of a thrill to keep company with the people who had once been on my bedroom wall. Taken away from a two-dimensional television screen, these people were all too human; they were exactly the same as you and I.

Although it really shouldn't have come as any great surprise to me, the characters who inhabited the fight game were no different from any other group of people that you would meet in any other walk of life. Some were nasty evil bastards that instinct forced you to keep a discreet distance from; some were all round nice guys, who were a pleasure to be with; but most were just ordinary average people with wives and kids and dandruff and mortgages to worry about. It was only when they came under the scrutiny of the cameraman's lens that the way in which they elected to earn their keep took on a different significance.

Suddenly, everything seemed too much like hard work. Whereas at the height of my obsession I had been enthusiastically attending every boxing show that I could – sometimes going to three or more shows a week – the whole ritualistic monotony of these occasions seemed to sap my strength. It was the way that nine times out of ten you could accurately predict who was going to win the undercard fights; it was the endless procession of punched-up has-beens and never-will-bes who marched before you to receive their statutory beatings from the house fighters. It was the same faces: the silent ranks of depressed pressmen who took their seats and sullenly recorded the night's events, having little choice but to use the same words they had been using for decades; it was the smiling managers who slunk towards you and shook your hand and slipped you a quote for next week's paper. And it was the bewildered eyes of the boxers themselves, who never quite managed to give the impression that they were any more comfortable in the midst of the mad circus that surrounded them than you were yourself.

It was the phone calls late at night from boxing's double dealers. 'What's this you've been saying about my boy?' anonymous voices would demand. It was the brown envelopes with the neat red ribbons delivered to your door containing letters from lawyers complaining about something you have written and threatening to make you pay dearly for your impudence.

This was not what boxing was about to me; all I had really wanted to do was sit on the sidelines and hope to be there on those rare occasions when a spark of greatness briefly shone. I just wanted to watch boxing.

As the months went by I found myself looking forward with dread to another night at the Albert Hall or York Hall or Battersea Town Hall. Eventually, I found myself doing what I had done as a teenager: sitting and watching my one-time heroes slug it out in the safety of my front room. You could say that I had overdosed on boxing. It no longer gave me any pleasure. Now that I was living at the heart of a sport that had so often been a kind of emotional crutch for me I was only too aware of the poison that coursed through its veins. Slowly I looked around for a means of escape; I sat and contemplated what it would be like to stop writing about people hitting each. However, before I had any chance of reaching a conclusion, boxing made the decision for me. Before I could jump, boxing gave me a well-deserved and long overdue push and suddenly it was all over.

Purely by coincidence, on the day that I was sacked from *Boxing Weekly*, Margaret Thatcher also left the Conservative Party. Quite what the significance of my telling you this is, I know not, other than to say that we had both underestimated our rivals. But while the Iron Maiden's tearful goodbye to Number 10 had been splashed over the front pages for the world to see, my retreat from the world of boxing went without a whimper. As had happened all those years ago when I was a waiter in the Grand Hotel, I was called into an office by two men in suits and told that my services were no longer required. The sacking came as both a surprise and a relief to me.

After I left, the paper survived for two more issues before the publishers decided to stop pouring bad money after bad. But I was already long gone. For whatever reason, it has always been a habit of mine to avoid lengthy goodbyes – and that is how it was with boxing. I gathered up my belongings, severed all ties with the ridiculous promotional company that I was a director of, threw away my record books, and buggered off.

%% %% %% %%

Ultimately, I left boxing because it was a world that I never really felt part of. While I had probably come to understood as well as anyone else the mechanics of Budd Schulberg's 'microcosm of life', I could not find it in myself to spend the rest of my life with my head under boxing's bonnet. Although it was easy to fall under the spell of these young men who tortured their bodies and battled each other for the right to put their hands on the most temporary of prizes, there was a large portion of me that knew that what I was witnessing was wrong.

I lost touch with Michael Watson, although in truth we had been drifting apart since the Nigel Benn fight. And I stopped talking to others of his ilk who had been part of my life for the last couple of years; people like Kirkland Laing, the man who had once beaten Roberto Duran and was now my occasional opponent at the pool table; and poor Rod Douglas, both a survivor and a victim of the sport that he loved. I found work that didn't involve blood and snot and spit bucket carriers. I decided that from that day forth my involvement with boxing would not go beyond the sanctuary of my front door.

Seventeenth Rule Of Boxing: Boxing Will Eat Itself

For a pastime which, by its very nature, insists that its participants achieve a state of physical well-being that borders on perfection, boxing is curiously inattentive when it comes to watching its own back. This may have something to do with the quality of parasite that the sport is wont to attract but there are other reasons. At the time of writing, boxing is in the midst of a decline which threatens to put an end to its very existence. This is not because people have decided that they no longer want to bear witness to the sometimes thrilling spectacle of one man hitting another for money (indeed, terrestrial viewing figures for major fights over the past decade are second only to football); rather it is because boxing itself no longer wants anyone to see them.

The roots of boxing's decline can be traced back to the early 1980s and the advent in America of pay-per-view cable channels. Indeed, it is significant that before the money men considered charging their subscribers a fee for the privilege of watching a movie or a sporting event, it was with boxing that they elected to test the waters. On both sides of the Atlantic it was boxing that was used as the yardstick for the medium's profit-making potential; and when people showed that they were prepared to pay in their millions to watch top-line fighters go about their business, boxing's fate was already sealed.

It was television which also demanded that every fight selected for broadcast came with a title attached to it. And when the marketing men realised that more people were predisposed to tune-in if there was a title at stake, boxing was more that willing to oblige. The fact that there was only a finite number of titles that could be handed out to its performers was of little consequence to boxing. With the minimum of effort it simply created a few more.

By the end of the decade there were four separate organisations vying for the right to call their leading exponents world champions. During the 1990s, countless other self-appointed governing bodies also emerged. With acronyms such as the WBO, WBA, WBC, WBF, IBF, IBO, IBC and IBU they are known in the fight business as the 'Alphabet Boys'. There is usually no real qualification required to become an Alphabet Boy; anyone who has ever swept away the sawdust from the corner of a gym and knows how to use a photocopier is entitled to become a member of this club. Indeed, to operate in this country, a self-appointed body of this nature does not even require the permission of the British Boxing Board of Control (although it will usually grant it when push comes to shove), which, after all, is itself self-appointed. But that's another issue.

In addition to the plethora of back-street organisations that are willing to let a fighter live the lie that he is the best in the world, the nature of what is considered to be a title has also undergone some transformation. Whereas in the uncluttered panacea of yesteryear there were only eight world titles, and likewise only eight national titles available to boxers, there are nowadays literally hundreds of 'interim' titles, including international titles and intercontinental titles, and even pentacontinental titles. Yet while this rapid growth of tinsel championships may have pleased television punters it has only succeeded in diminishing boxing's most glittering prize.

There have never been so many boxers walking around calling themselves world champions as there are today. Under the watchful eye of the camera lens, it is now possible for whole truckloads of fighters who – to borrow the words of Larry Holmes, are not fit to lace up the boots of their predecessors – to slip into a championship belt. And what of the real champions? They are still about, for sure; and every bit as good as the men who came before them. People from America such as Roy Jones and Oscar de la Hoya; people like our own Naseem Hamed and Lennox Lewis. People whose talents deserve to be celebrated yet whose names remain submerged in an ocean of non-entities and under-achievers.

As we approach the end of the millennium, and professional boxing as defined by the Marquis of Queensbury prepares to celebrate its centennial, it is both a sad fact and a damning indictment of the sport that there is no one fighter alive today who can universally lay claim to the right to call himself champion of the world in the weight division in which he competes. There are boxers, of course – including the four names I have already mentioned – who can quite justifiably be regarded as leading lights in their respective divisions; some of them even own belts of one form or another to provide partial proof of their proficiency. There is, however, always going to be someone else out there with his own tawdry title who will be prepared to dispute this point. When boxing itself cannot even name its own champions how can it expect anything different from anybody else?

Boxing is dying a slow death because it has sold its soul to the remote control. It has sacrificed its survival for the dollar sign. When the sport's leading exponents remain uncrowned and anonymous; when its future champions are starved of both exposure and financial support; when its governing bodies are composed of the corrupt and the incompetent; and when its proud traditions are steadily eroded by the cynical and the exploitative, there can be no salvation for the sport. Boxing will die. It might take a while for it to happen, but it will die. I just hope I am not around to hear its death rattle.

19

The Long Goodbye

But still boxing refused to go away.

⁄⁄ ⁄⁄ ⁄⁄ ⁄⁄

I had been out socialising that night and had set the video timer to record the fight. It was Michael Watson's third attempt to win a world title, and for the second time his opponent was to be Chris Eubank. The eccentric Brighton-based boxer had won a hotly disputed points victory over Watson when the pair had fought for the WBO middleweight title in June 1991. Now, only three months later they were at it again, this time fighting for the right to be called WBO super-middleweight champion.

It had been more than 18 months since I had communicated in any way with anyone from the world of boxing. I was now living an ordinary life with an ordinary job and interacting with ordinary people. I was 28 and, like my ill-fated famous artist/director schemes, the couple of years that I spent in boxing seemed part of some distant dream. Nevertheless, I could not deny that I had much to be grateful to boxing for; it had, after all, dragged me from the pit and shown me a real way to survive. I knew for a fact that I wouldn't have been living an ordinary life with an ordinary job and interacting with ordinary people if boxing had not interceded when it did.

Being able to view one's heroes at a respectable distance also allowed some of the excitement I had once held for the sport to slowly return. It was far more comfortable to be able to watch these people batter themselves into submission before a baying crowd if you were holding a can of beer in your hand and sitting on your nice comfortable sofa in your nice comfortable living room. In the sanctuary of the cathode ray tube these images of violence became sanitised; you could no longer feel the punches and hear the scarcely concealed grunts of pain. Gradually, I came to enjoy boxing from the perspective of my teenage years, when the spectacle of two men fighting each other to a standstill had seemed wildly exciting – as far away from the mundane as you could possibly get.

There was, however, still a part of me that viewed Watson's crusade to reach the top as somehow personal. Although I had not seen or spoken to him since the Mike McCallum fight I had followed his progress as he endeavoured to return from that horrific defeat. I'd seen him on television a couple of times: I had seen him in action against an Australian named Craig Trotter, who Watson had completely outclassed before rendering unconscious in the sixth round; and I had watched as he valiantly took Eubank as close to the edge as humanly possible in a fight that many people thought Watson had won.

That I had elected to hit the town that night rather than watch Watson's third world title attempt live on television says much about my feelings regarding the sport at the time. Yet even though I would once have viewed such indifference with contempt, I was still interested enough in Watson's fate to make sure that the first thing I did when I got home was to flick on the Ceefax and find out who had won.

In many ways, there can be no better means of demonstrating boxing's ability to both excite and repel than in the last three or four seconds of round 11 of Watson's second attempt to be better than Eubank. There can also be no more comprehensive method of proving that in boxing, glory and tragedy all too often come manacled together at the ankles. Perversely, those frozen few moments represent boxing in its purest form. In the time that it would take most of us to light a cigarette, the destinies of two human beings had been decided in unequivocal fashion. Three seconds of mayhem were all that it took to turn Eubank from a beaten fighter, with reputation and future earning capacity in tatters, into a winner; and to transform Watson from a person who was just about to achieve all the glory he had ever dreamed about into someone who would never fight again.

I read the Ceefax and tried to take in what was happening. I flicked over to ITV and scanned their report of the night's events. According to what I read Watson had collapsed immediately after the fight and had been taken to St Bartholomew's Hospital in London, where he was currently undergoing brain surgery.

What could I do? I considered for a moment calling Watson's former trainer Eric Seccombe, but quickly concluded that it would be a futile gesture – we had, after all, not spoken for the best part of two years. I thought about taking a taxi down to the hospital but I knew that the place would already be full of reporters and exploding flash bulbs. However much I may have endeavoured to protest my innocence I knew that I would have been regarded as just one of many.

In the end I did something which, I believe, is both unforgivable and understandable: I flicked on the video recorder and rewound the tape to the start of the fight and I sat down and watched it. Although there would be many who would rightly suggest that such an action places one on a par with those people who buy videotapes of executions, in my defence I have to say that I did not watch the fight with an iota of morbid curiosity. Although we were no longer part of each other's lives I still considered Watson a friend, and I had no wish whatsoever to see him get hurt. I watched the video recording because I had to. It wasn't because there was a part of me which was optimistically hoping that, come the fateful moment, Eubank would somehow forget to throw that lethal uppercut and Watson would see out the rest of the fight and be crowned champion. I watched it simply because I had to.

※ ※ ※ ※

Two days later I went to visit Watson. I had left it this long because I had been hoping that the circus outside his hospital ward would have subsided a little by then. Although he was still in a coma I felt that I had to put in an appearance.

I told none of the people who questioned me as I made my way through the building that I was a reporter. I said I was a friend and eventually was taken to a waiting room and told to sit down. There was only one other person in this room. She was wearing a patterned scarf around her head and smoking a cigarette. It was Watson's wife.

I can't remember what we talked about in the five or ten minutes we spent together in that room. Although she had seen me in Watson's company on a number of occasions she had very little recollection of who I was. I was just one of the hundreds of strangers we had avoided her eyes over the past 48 hours. In a day or two those eyes would be featured on the front page of one of those tabloids, courtesy of an eager snapper who happened to be pointing his telescopic lens at the window of the waiting room while Watson's wife had been taking some fresh air.

※ ※ ※ ※

I went back a second time, although I didn't really expect to be any more successful in getting to see Watson than I had been on my first visit, when I had been told after waiting for an hour that I would have to leave. I was glad in a way, I suppose. I didn't really want to see Watson lying on a hospital bed, covered in wires and surrounded by machinery; I just went there to be a little closer to him because there was nothing else I could have done.

Eighteenth Rule Of Boxing: There Is No Place In A Civilised Society For Boxing

You didn't really think I'd let you get this far without even a cursory attempt at answering the question I have been carefully avoiding asking since I first sat down and decided not to write about boxing for you? I think we know each other better than that. You didn't really believe that I would let you sit through the half-baked quasi-biography of a man who has done absolutely nothing without making at least some effort to furnish you with an explanation?

You've heard me moan on about boxers and their doomed destinies, and you've also listened to me whimper with excitement at some of their exploits. You've tapped your feet in boredom as I've harped on about the mistreatment of boxers and the lies that they tell, and you have withheld more than your fair share of doleful yawns as I've endeavoured to skirt around the issue by taking the longest and most un-scenic of possible routes. Now it's time to cut to the chase: boxing is wrong. There, I've said it.

There can be no place in a civilised society for an activity provided exclusively for the entertainment of the masses which places its main protagonists in clear danger of losing their lives. Such an activity was no more acceptable when the Romans were feeding Christians to the lions and it is no more acceptable today.

I am aware, of course, of all the counter arguments; indeed, I have employed them myself on far too many occasions. I know that nobody is forcing the boxers to climb into the ring and hit each other until somebody gives in; yet if you look at the poverty from which the vast majority of them spring you have to wonder how much say they really have in the matter. I realise, as well, that if boxing were made illegal many fighters would have no choice but to do their job under conditions that have very little to do with the Marquis of Queensbury; nevertheless, despite the existence of its more socially acceptable elder brother, bare-knuckle fighting continues to find an audience among the seedy back streets.

I know, too, that boxing has been able to allow many people to live a life that would have been unthinkable were it not for their ability to hit other people accurately and hard; yet at the same time, if we were to weigh up the cost in human suffering to the recipients of these blows we would find that the scales told rather a conclusive tale. I've heard all these arguments before and however valid they might appear, they tend to fall flat on their faces when a boxer loses his life. There is simply no way that this can be defended.

Yet I've sat and watched as two men risked their lives for my pleasure. I've lost count of the number of times I've done this. Little ol' moral me has gasped and yelped and screamed along with the best of them. I have enjoyed boxing. I have felt myself consumed by thrill of this ritual. I still do to this day.

When I said before that there can be no place in a civilised society for an activity such as boxing, I meant every word. What I didn't say, however, was that it should be banned. And what I didn't mean to imply is that we live in a society that can be in any way described as civilised. Yes, in an ideal world boxing should be consigned to the trash can that contains the remnants of other equally abhorrent pastimes such as badger baiting, bull-fighting and seal culling. Yes, to idly look on as a man is beaten to within an inch of losing his life is not something that a society which brought us the Teletubbies really ought to be doing.

Yet I would suggest that before society elects to make an example of boxing there are plenty of other things that it should be worrying its head about. Prior to ridding itself of the sport that is not a sport, which gives us all a glimpse of our species' most primitive and primeval urges, society could turn its attention to more the pressing concerns that continue to impede the development of civilised man. More immediate problems such as mass poverty and mass unemployment. Or murder... Or rape... Or drugs... Or racism...Or child pornography... Or pollution... The hole in the ozone layer... Jeffrey Archer... The Royal Family... People who listen to personal stereos in tube trains... Sexism... Organised religion... Global warming... Bug-ridden software... Homophobia... Young male singing bands with names like Boys II Men... Nuclear disarmament... World-wide recession... Ivory traders... Genocide... Television licence fees... Exploitative landlords... Joyriders... Fur coats...

Chris Evans... Corrupt politicians... Pub opening hours...
The felling of the rain forests... Cancer... Heart-disease...
Baldness... Dodgy curries... People who write confessional
novels about sport...

20

No Escape

Eight years later:

In the spare room that serves as both a makeshift office and an occasional bedroom for guests, I have an entire wall that is lined with shelves holding videotapes. Visitors to this room are apt to express surprise when they enter. Those who do not already know me quickly tend to reach the conclusion that my girlfriend and I must be ardent film enthusiasts; some even press their noses against the lines and lines of carefully labelled and numbered tapes in the hope of picking out a long forgotten favourite movie. It is at this point that there is usually a moment of silence followed by a look of puzzlement. Then the questions begin.

At the time of writing, my collection of video recordings of people hitting each other is such that it would take some 59 consecutive days and nights for me to be able to sit with my feet up in front of the television and watch them all. I know this because I have just counted them and used a calculator to reach this absurd figure.

Most of the boxing matches that I have for one reason or another decided to commit to videotape I am fairly sure that I will never watch again. Indeed, I would imagine that a surprisingly large percentage of them have never been watched by anyone, including myself. But they're there nevertheless:

Duke McKenzie against someone called Sonny Long in 1986; Derek 'Sweet D' Williams versus the hopelessly inept Al Evans in 1989; Gary Mason knocking over a flabby American named Terry Armstrong in that same year; Johnny Nelson's mind-numbing 12-round draw with Carlos DeLeon in 1990. The list just goes on and on.

This video collection represents one of the very few orderly features of my life. In contrast to the socks that are thrown haphazardly towards the laundry basket; the drawers filled with buttons, loose change, long-expired tube tickets and the piles of unlabelled cassette tapes that I keep meaning to get around to sorting, my recordings of semi-naked men hitting each other are afforded the kind of respect that I usually reserve for the more delicate parts of my anatomy.

Indeed, I have in the past even gone to such lengths as to sit down and teach myself to write custom databases so that I may be able to tap a name into my computer and instantly receive an alphabetic listing of the fights that I possess involving that person. It is, however, an incomplete listing. Having realised that attempting to keep this database up to date would soon become a full-time job, I eventually lost interest in maintaining my records. Nevertheless by switching from the word processor that I am using now and keying in a name at random, let's say Jones, into the database search facility I can tell you that – as if anyone would really want to know – I possess video recordings of the following fights that involve fighters with the surname Jones:

Date	Contest	Result	Opponent	Highlights/full
13.03.63	Muhammad Ali	Wpts10	Doug Jones	Highlights
13.03.63	Muhammad Ali	Wpts10	Doug Jones	Full
31.03.80	Larry Holmes	KO8	Leroy Jones	Full
09.07.89	Edwin Rosario	KO6	Anthony Jones	Full
22.03.90	Lennox Lewis	KO3	Calvin Jones	Full
22.05.93	Roy Jones	Wpts12	Bernard Hopkins	Full

Except already I'm beginning to feel a little piqued. Because I know that the preceding list makes no mention of fighters such a Junior Jones or Paul 'Silky' Jones, and includes only one of Roy Jones's contests, a fighter of whom I know for a fact I possess at least two dozen or so of his fights on videotape. So now I'm tempted to choose another name – perhaps, Ali or Holmes or Tyson or Hearns or Leonard. But that would be cheating.

Of course, buried among the reels and reels of dross are a few genuine jewels that I am sure from time to time I will be tempted to relive again. Indeed, there will always be a place in my heart for such scintillating classics as, to name but a fistful: George Foreman's five-round war with Ron Lyle in 1975; Marvin Hagler's staggeringly exciting three-round knockout of Thomas Hearns in 1985; Hearns' two-round annihilation of Roberto Duran in 1984 (which contains, quite simply, the most devastating punch that I have ever witnessed); and, inevitably, Muhammad Ali's momentous meeting with George Foreman in Zaïre in 1974.

Fights of this calibre are, however, few and far between. But this, I am sure you will understand, is not the point. For although I am in possession of hundreds and hundreds of recordings of boxing non-entities fighting boxing non-entities in nothing contests, there is a part of me that is happy to let them share my life.

It's lucky for you, I suppose, that I'm not a real obsessive: a friend of mine in his early 50s has a similar if rather more extensive collection of videos of people hitting each other – he once worked out that it would take him over six months of steady viewing to watch them all, something he tells me he intends to do when he reaches retirement.

On the wall of my living room there are more shelves: these are home to some 70 or 80 different books about people hitting each other. Sometimes there are several copies of the same book; and occasionally I own both the hardback and paperback incarnations of a particular title. In contrast to the videos, I can honestly claim to have read most of these books; some of them are even written by people that I know. However, in common with the videos there are but a handful of them that I am ever likely to want to read again. And yet still they sit there gathering dust.

Last but not least, in the cupboard in the hallway that was originally conceived as a cloakroom, the coats have been pushed to one side and their place taken by three precariously constructed tower blocks comprised of copies of old boxing magazines. These tottering columns contain several rainforests' worth of compacted paper, and even though from time to time I am inspired to attempt to bring some order to them, I know that I am fighting a losing battle. Like the videos and the books, the vast majority of these magazines – the combined work of possibly thousands of people over a period that stretches back to the 1950s – will probably never be read by anyone.

So why am I telling you this?

I'm telling you this because I'm trying, in a half-hearted way, to redress the balance. To let you know that despite all my protestations to the contrary, I remain as much a slave to boxing as I ever was. Sure, the obsession may have tapered off slightly. Whereas, for example, there was once a time when I considered it an unforgivable breach of protocol if I failed to commit to videotape even a single second of television airtime that contained the merest mention of boxing, these days I am more selective in my choice of memento. Part of the reason for this is the emergence of satellite television which, until their relatively recent decision to curtail their boxing coverage, meant that the dangerously over committed boxing fanatic would have to buy two or three videotapes a week in order to keep up with their broadcast output. Other reasons have to do with lack of space and the fact that I have grown weary of the chase.

In many ways it would have been all so much easier if, for instance, the focus for this peculiar obsession, had fallen upon something like, say, *Doctor Who*. If this had been the case I could have seen an end to my journey. There being a finite number of episodes to collect on videotape, I could have cheerfully purchased the two hundred or so that are available and that would have been it. Oh, but that would be forgetting the books… and the novelettes… and the comics… and actually, I read on the Ceefax the other day that they're in the process of negotiating the rights for a new series with Eddie Izzard(?!) cast in the role of ninth Doctor. So maybe that's not a very good analogy. Or maybe it is. For in truth there is never really an end to an obsession, just lots and lots of false endings and lots and lots of denials.

Which is why I already know that I would be lying to myself and lying to you if I told you that what happened yesterday had anything to do with fate. Sure, we can all play the game that television boffin James Burke used to play on that programme of his in the late 1970s (it was called something like *Consequences* if my memory serves me right), in which he would postulate that some medieval monk tripping over a cat in an Italian abbey in the seventh century eventually led to the invention of the microwave oven; or that some bloke in France with a headache in 1704 was eventually responsible for the famine in the Sudan during the mid-1980s. These things may be fun but they are pointless fun.

In this manner I could tell you that my going to the cinema and watching a Woody Allen movie entitled *Mighty Aphrodite* in 1995, which had clarinettist Benny Goodman playing a song called 'Whispering' accompanying the closing credits and led me to take up the clarinet at the ripe old age of 34, which in turn compelled me two years later to take a stroll down to the local music shop for replacement reeds only to discover that the shop was closed for redecoration, which in turn obliged me to walk a further half a mile down the road to a pawn shop that I knew sold second-hand musical instruments, which in turn enabled me to meet and talk with former British middleweight title challenger Rod Douglas for the first time in around eight years.

%% %% %% %%

I was just about to leave the shop when he yelled out my name. Apparently he had called by to look for a stereo for his flat. At first I didn't hear him, my mind was a little preoccupied with the thought that I had finally put the finishing touches to this book. I was feeling relieved that I would no longer have to sit in front of this computer and attempt to not write about boxing. Then he moved closer behind me through the sunlight and called my name again.

I turned around and did not know who he was at first. He was shaven-headed and wearing a blue string vest and jeans. For a moment all I saw was a really hard looking black man heading right towards me with a determined look on his face. Then I recognised his features and felt a shovel-like hand grasp my own.

I suggested we find a nearby café and go for a cup of tea and as we crossed the road my eyes were drawn to the enormous scar on the left hand side of his head; it was shaped like a 'C' – as in 'C' for constant reminder of Douglas's brush with death all those years ago, and 'C' for constant reminder of who Douglas could have been. As we walked, he revealed that he had recently moved to the Islington area and was, in fact, living fairly close to my own flat. 'I do some building work for a mate,' he replied when I asked him what he was up to.

We reached a café and settled into some seats and he pulled out a packet of cigarettes and offered them to me. He was still smoking – but then he'd always been one for having a crafty fag, even when he was supposed to training for a fight. Despite this, however, he was in tremendous shape. If anything he looked even better and even younger than he had in his boxing days. Paradoxically, in spite of that evil looking scar it seemed to me that he had turned out to be one of boxing's more palatable survivors. There were no tell-tale marks around the eyes, his nose was straight and true, and only his marvellous physique gave away any hint of what he used to do to earn a living.

Then he asked me what I was doing with myself and I told him about my boxing book that is not about boxing; I even mentioned that he was in it.

'Is it about when we fell out?' he laughed, referring to that *Sunday Sport* stitch-up involving Douglas, Nigel Benn and the haircut that they both claimed to have invented.

We reminisced for a while, pulling out old names from the past, until I eventually suggested that we arrange to meet one evening in the future for a beer. At this point Rod began to look a little cagey.

'I work most evenings so that would be difficult,' he said.

'What do you do?' I asked.

'I'm an entrance supervisor at Metropolis – it's the best lap dancing club in the country,' he replied.

'You mean a bouncer?' I said.

'No,' he smiled, 'I'm an entrance supervisor.'

We both found ourselves laughing out loud and then I asked him if he still went to the fights.

'Not really,' he shrugged. 'Not since I stopped working for the Board.'

Soon after his ring injury, you may remember, Douglas had been employed by the British Boxing Board of Control. He had been given some kind of clerical job, a position which, although applauding the Board's compassion, I had at the time inwardly suspected would not be a long-term career move.

'I really loved that job,' Rod continued, 'but they were taking the piss. There was no money in it. One day I went to John Morris and showed him my outgoings and how much they were paying me but...'

His voice trailed off with a trace of sadness as the drinks we had ordered were brought to our table. It was a voice that I had heard many times before in many different locations: in a west London gym in 1997 with ex-featherweight champion Colin McMillan trying to keep a brave face as he struggled to come to terms with the grim reality that his career as a fighter was over; in a cluttered council flat in Hackney in 1993 as ex-British welterweight champion Kirkland Laing was made to realise that his crazy relationship with the boxing ring was about to come to an end.

'Do you ever feel tempted to make a comeback?' I asked.

'Not any more,' he replied. 'Now that I'm 33 I know that I'm too old to be boxing – mind you a couple of years ago I would have liked to if I could.'

'Not when there's people like Foreman fighting at 50,' I reminded him.

'The only thing that I really miss,' Rod continued, 'is getting in the ring for a good tear-up. For a lot of fighters it's like they've died when they finished fighting. Some of them can't handle it. But I don't miss the money or the fame – I just miss having a good old-fashioned tear-up.'

Rod handed me another cigarette and I asked him how his children were, remembering how when I had first visited his house in Bow back in 1989 his youngest son had been wearing tiny boxing gloves and using my shins as a punch bag.

'Tyson's nine now – he's an academic,' Rod replied proudly. 'TeeJay is the oldest – he's 15 now, I named him after the boxer TeeJay. Remember him? Then there's RJ – he's named after me.'

I thought back to the last occasion I'd seen Rod. It had to have been around the time that he was still getting sporadic work as a boxing co-commentator. I say sporadic work but in actual fact I doubt that he ever enjoyed more than a handful of appearances in that role.

By that point he had probably been out of the ring for about a year but already his appearance was beginning to show tell-tale signs of decline. Having been forbidden by his condition to set foot in a gym, Rod must have added about a stone to his weight and carried a girth that seemed to have been surgically grafted on to his athlete's physique. When you bumped into him at a fight it was hard to think of what to say to a man who had just seen his future ripped away from him in such cruel manner. You could sense that whatever you chose to tell him he would have already heard a dozen times before. Even the most optimistic among those who encountered this troubled man found it difficult to predict any kind of future for Douglas.

'I'm going to have to go now,' said Rod, interrupting my remembrances with a smile that sat on top of a torso that seemed to have been miraculously restored to its former splendour. 'I'm going home for a shit, shower and a shave and them I'm going out on the town tonight.'

I thought of Rod's children, and of the number of times since his enforced retirement from boxing that speaking their names had been a bitter reminder of what he could have been. Tyson the academic, named after a man who was to spend time in prison for rape and later bite the ear off another man; TeeJay, named after the former British cruiserweight champion – Lord knows where he is now; and RJ, named after his once famous dad.

'Listen,' I persisted. 'We really should have a drink some time.'

Rod moved over to the shop counter and asked for paper and a pen. He tore the paper in two and gave one half to me to write my telephone number on, on the other he wrote his own. I noticed that he took great care over his signature, as if it was something that he had spent a lot of time developing. In my mind I could see the 14-year-old Douglas sitting at the table practising the elaborate twists and curls of an autograph that would one day be coveted by so many.

'You'll have to come down the club,' he said as we shook hands for the final time. 'You'll really enjoy yourself – I'll get you a girl who will make your toes curl up.'

※ ※ ※ ※

So there we have it. Am I guilty of watching far too many episodes of *The X-Files* or was Woody Allen really responsible for easing me back into the path of a boxer able to procure for me a girl capable of making my toes curl up? The more rational among you could probably do me a great favour by pointing out that my accidentally bumping into an ex-fighter named Rod Douglas on an Islington high street on the day that I finished writing a book that is not about boxing has nothing to do with fate; you could tell me that there is nothing unusual about a one-time boxing writer meeting a one-time boxer that he used to know.

And you would, of course, be right – for, as I outlined earlier, I would be lying if I were to claim that the ties that bind me to the sport of boxing are anything other than self-woven. Like Hannibal Lecter and his collection of pickled body parts, I carry with me far too many trophies of my sometimes fatal obsession.

Epilogue

THE telephone rings and a voice with a French accent speaks my name. It's Julie's father, which is unusual because in the course of a relationship that has lasted seven years he has never before actually called solely to speak to me.

'What's the name of the boxer who beat Mike Tyson?' he asks.

The plot thickens. Julie's father – like Julie – is French and as far as I know has limited knowledge of my connections with boxing. The fact that I used to be a boxing writer may or may not have surfaced during one of those uncomfortable 'meet the girlfriend's family' occasions but I couldn't swear to it. But already my mind is ticking over.

'Do you mean Evander Holyfield?' I reply, knowing that, due to his dilettante knowledge of the sport, he could not possibly be referring to 'Buster' Douglas, the other man who beat Mike Tyson.

'Yes, that's right,' he says.

Julie's father has just turned 60 and according to what I've been told, was something of a big cheese in the advertising business in France during the 1970s and 1980s. Recently he's started a new company, a PA company, the function of which, although it's probably been explained to me on a number of occasions, I've never really quite managed to take in.

Julie's father tells me that he's doing some kind of deal with Holyfield's people. That Holyfield is jetting over to France for a meeting.

'Of course, you'll be there,' he says.

Afterword

CONGRATULATIONS. Unless you've skipped to the end you've just managed to reach the final page, digital or otherwise, of *Rope Burns*. I don't offer such applause lightly, because if I were in your shoes I'm not sure that I would have been able to finish it at all. This is not any half-hearted attempt at false modesty on my part. Because I've got nothing to be falsely modest about. Having just read *Rope Burns* myself for the first time since I finished work on it almost 20 years ago, well, let's put it this way: it's nothing to write home about. In actual fact, as I mentioned earlier I think you'll agree that more than anything it's a sort of diary, a primitive form of diary at that. And like most diaries it should have been kept hidden under a pile of clothes in a drawer somewhere, well out of the way of prying eyes.

I think that by now you've probably picked up on the fact that I'm not a fan of the book. It's poorly written in my opinion. It was executed under duress. It was a book about boxing that I didn't want to be about boxing. And it's certainly not the sort of thing I'd be reading unless I really had to. If there is anything going for it, however, it's the fact that it's a kind of time capsule: still contemporary enough as to be vaguely comprehensible but written sufficiently long enough ago to be a curio, to tug a little at the heart-strings, to belong to days gone by when all we had was Teletext, Ceefax and Mike Morris's moustache on GMTV. When my own personal YouTube was a spare room stacked

270

with wall-to-wall boxing videos, mostly pirated by a bloke who sold them in the classifieds for a tenner a shot.

For me it's difficult to read the book without cringing. Was I really so concerned about losing my hair that I would expose my insecurities so universally in print? Did I really imagine that anyone would be interested in a few crusty anecdotes about art college and some frankly sordid tales based upon my days as a squatter? And what was I really trying to say when I wrote about my father's shoes?

Having just finished writing the sequel to *Rope Burns*, which I'm calling *Dangerous*, I'm now aware that the story of those ridiculous platform shoes actually hinted at something a whole lot darker. If anything I may really have been sending out a subconscious message to my father: A *lot* more about him in *Dangerous*. If you can bear it.

As far as I know, however, that subconscious message never reached him because my father apparently never read the book. Never even knew I'd written it, in actual fact. Of course, now that I have a child of my own I naturally find this astonishing. If Sofia ever managed to one day find her name written down the spine of a book I'd be cheering from the rafters, that's if we had any rafters to cheer from. But that's the sort of father I had: a Labour councillor, a potential future Lord Mayor of Weston-Super-Mare I'm given to believe, obsessed, apparently, on protecting the poor and needy while simultaneously refusing to give the time of day to anybody close to him who happened to be needy and poor themselves.

So how come, if *Rope Burns* is so bad, I've written a sequel? Well I'd like to be able to say it was because of public demand but that would be blatantly untrue. And I'd also like to be able to say it's because I've suddenly rediscovered my love of boxing. But that would only be partially true. I think the real reason has to do with me unlocking something inside me that needed to be unlocked, was crying out to be freed, was screaming to be liberated. This, I must assure you, is not me being faux enigmatic in order to do a blatant bit of marketing for *Dangerous* but you will understand what I'm talking about if you ever do feel the urge to look at a copy of *Rope Burns*'s younger brother. There are people out there who regularly e-mail and tweet at me who are apparently keen to do just this.

In the meantime let me try to round things off by telling you the chain of events that led me to consider *Rope Burns part deux:* It so happened that at around the end of the 1980s – just as I began working in boxing, as it happens – I began experiencing regular fainting spells. These usually occurred in the middle of the night, often after an evening of heavy drinking, and frequently resulted in me hurting myself by falling down the stairs or collapsing on tiled bathroom floors.

I had no way of knowing it at the time but this was one of the first symptoms of hypothyroidism. In other words my thyroid gland was fucking up and not producing enough hormones for my body to operate efficiently. Over the years this condition somehow conspired to remain undiagnosed and I gradually fell to pieces: I grew enormously fat, I partially lost my hearing and sense of smell and taste, I developed avascular necrosis of the hip, the soles of my feet split apart, I got terrible psoriasis and eczema. There were lots of other symptoms, too, both major and minor. Most of all, though, I became very, very depressed: so depressed that I thought I was dying. So depressed that listening to Joy Division records became a happy, carefree, liberating experience for me. At the same time I also lost the ability to concentrate, meaning that the world was spared any further literary efforts on my part. I can't say that the world seemed particularly bothered about this at the time.

Then, in 2013, I was finally diagnosed after more than a decade of barely functioning. I received the replacement hormones that my body had been crying out for and I could finally work again. You can read all about it if you search for me on *The Guardian*'s website.

This coincided with me suddenly beginning to receive those messages from people about *Rope Burns* that I waffled on about 300 or so pages ago. And occasionally, would you believe, plaudits! Plaudits! Why only the other day, Matt Christie, the talented editor of *Boxing News,* even tells me that *Rope Burns* is a 'classic'. While I have the strong feeling that Matt was being a little over polite that evening, my conclusion is that classics simply ain't what they used to be. You can judge for yourself.

One of the people who contacted me around that time ran a boxing website. He asked me if I was interested in writing something for it. After I'd fished my dentures out of my cappuccino I thought about it for a long time and eventually told him I'd do it. Thus, armed with an iPad instead of a pencil (what a fool! I quickly discovered it's very difficult to write in a notepad using an iPad instead of a pencil!) I turned up in an east London gym and met my first boxer in two decades or so. Reprinted in the appendix to this book is the article I produced on that day. It's called 'The Look Of Love' and features a young professional boxer named Frank Buglioni.

The second article I produced actually ended up, in slightly fucked-up form, in *Boxing Monthly*. This one is called 'A Fork In The Road' and deals with the imminent death of my father, told via a second interview with Buglioni.

Neither of these articles are likely to win any awards but they form an important part of my own story, my personal journey as it were. They also segue nicely from *Rope Burns* into *Dangerous,* in which the flippant, tongue-in-cheek, try-to-tell-a-joke-at-all-costs tone of the former is replaced by the altogether more grown up, sombre and, I hope and believe, soul searching, introspective approach of the latter.

Be lucky.

Ian Probert
June 2016

Appendix

The Look of Love

EVERYTHING is cyclical: we're born, we procreate, we die. A plant sheds its seeds, the seeds germinate and mature, the plant sheds its own seeds. Everything is cyclical but never more so than in championship boxing.

A championship boxer enters the ring at a young age. He has a distinguished amateur career. He turns pro and wins domestic honours. He's fed a faded former champion or two for experience and a notch on his ring record. He wins world honours. He defends his title. He loses his title. He's fodder for the next champion and becomes a notch on their ring record. And so the world turns. Everything is cyclical.

※ ※ ※ ※

In the days before iPods and tablets and Twitter I was part of the cycle when I met my first boxer. Well, in actual fact it was my third boxer but I'm not counting Alan Minter and Chris Sanigar because in my role as wine waiter I was there to serve them not write about them. In the days when mobile phones were a luxury that only the very rich or very crooked could afford I met my first boxer. His name was Michael Watson.

I met him in a gym in London's Carnaby Street. It's gone now. The gym was run by renowned cornerman Dennie Mancini: gruff, of Italian stock, a heart of pure gold. He's dead now. Occasionally, boxing figures such as Mickey Duff and Terry Lawless would call in to inspect their wares. They're dead, too.

In those days Michael was on the rise. He'd won all but one of his fights, including a victory over the highly-rated American 'Dangerous' Don Lee. Michael and the people around him were all aware that he could be The One. I watched him train and he watched me watch him. Afterwards we talked and got on well. We were both about the same age. We struck up a friendship.

Standing beside him at all times was a taxi-driver named Eric Seccombe. Like Michael and myself, Eric lived in Islington. Eric had known Michael since he was a boy and was employed as his trainer. His affection for the younger man was palpable. It was so omnipresent that you could have reached out and scooped up a handful of that affection. When you spoke to _his_ Michael you always felt it was an intrusion. At all times in Eric's eyes was a look of pure devotion, of love, if you will.

In the years to follow I was to see that expression many times. In the eyes of Emmanuel Steward as he talked to me about Thomas Hearns. In Angelo Dundee's when he spoke of Ali. In Brendan Ingle's eyes when he mentioned his beloved Bomber. I could go on.

Leap forward a quarter of a century and I see that look of love once more. It's not directed at me. Naturally it's not. It's directed at a young boxer named Frank Buglioni and it's coming from his trainer Mark Tibbs, the son of – are we allowed to say the legendary – Jimmy Tibbs?

And this is because boxing is all about love. Love and hate and war. The love of one man for another that allows him to reach over and gently caress his fighter's face; to wipe the grease from the other man's eyes with a tenderness only matched by a lover or a parent. The hatred and despair that one man feels for another when a paltry half-an-hour or so is the dividing line between success or failure. And war: the shared experience of battle and blood that both unites and separates.

※ ※ ※ ※

Boxing is cyclical and no one can escape the cycle. I've entered the Twilight Zone. I'm like one of the Pevensie kids returning to Narnia. Twenty-five years later and I'm standing in a gym in Canning Town to meet Frank Buglioni (pronounced without the 'g', I keep telling myself) and to spend a little time with a boxer for the first time since the late 1990s when I watched the aforementioned Herol 'Bomber' Graham prepare for a fight with the American Vinnie Pazienza.

It's a big, big deal for me. Many years ago I was the editor of a paper thin periodical entitled *Boxing Weekly*. Boxing was my life back then. When I wasn't writing about it or watching it I was out socialising with some of the many friends that I made in the sport. Chief among these was Michael Watson. As many people are aware Michael was almost fatally injured during a world title fight with Chris Eubank. It was because of this that I questioned my fascination with boxing and came to the conclusion that I couldn't write about boxing without being complicit in its repercussions. Check out Bob Dylan's 'Who Killed Davey Moore,' for a far clearer picture than I could ever paint. So I wrote a book about why I was not going to write about boxing anymore. And then I stopped writing about boxing. Until now. And I'm not sure why.

※ ※ ※ ※

I walk through the gym and recognise Frank Buglioni. He is sweating it out on an exercise bike. We shake hands and I'm immediately struck by this young man's easy going nature, and his quiet confidence. We chat for a while and I tell him my story. About how he's the first boxer I've interviewed for a lifetime; about how I was unsure what to talk about. About how I've decided that the best thing to do is simply talk about boxing: talk about boxers and fights that we like. And that's what we agree to do.

But first there is work to do. For both of us. I have my camera and I walk around the gym taking snaps of the fighters. A small part of me expects to be recognised but nobody does. Not even Mark Tibbs, son of Jimmy and almost a father to Frank. I tell him I remember seeing him fight at the York

Hall as a young man. I watch as his protégé spars a couple of rounds, first with impressively-muscled light-heavyweight Ovil Mckenzie and then with a boxer named Eddie McDonagh. Buglioni's work is serious and scrupulous.

Just as with Michael Watson all those years ago, there is an air of expectation. Buglioni and his team mean business: they are in no doubt that barring unforeseen roadblocks their boxer is going to the very top of the hill. And there is that look. Always there is that look.

Buglioni with no G finishes his morning's work and heads for the shower. I sit and drink coffee and inhale the community atmosphere of the gym. Twenty minutes later he is sitting across from me and I begin at the beginning because there is nowhere else I can start: How did he get into boxing?

'I wasn't a natural athlete. When I was about 12 a friend of my dad's son had just done a little boxing and asked if I wanted to try it. I jumped at the chance, gave it a go. I remember the coach saying I could whack and I was fit. I improved very quickly.

'I started training with Mark Tibbs. I went down to spar with Billy Jo Saunders who was with Mark and Jimmy Tibbs. I think we did eights rounds straight off and I think Mark saw something in me, decided to take me on the pads. I think we clicked straight away. I like the fact that Mark went in my corner and gave me advice, gloved me up and I thought "that's a good man". Straight away I had trust and respect for him. He taught me certain things and they worked. And I thought if I'm gonna turn pro its gonna be with Mark.'

At close quarters Buglioni looks nothing like a boxer. Some people are already likening him to a boxing version of David Beckham. He's already done a little modelling. How does he feel about people hitting that as yet unmarked face of his and how will he take it when somebody beats him?

'I had my first amateur fight at 15. I won it. It was a good old tear-up. I got hit loads of times. Do you know what? It didn't bother me. Didn't bother me at all.

'I won my second fight. My first defeat came in my third fight. It was in the junior ABAs I fought a guy there with 30-

plus fights. I put up a good fight. He beat me on a majority. It was a close close one. I was gutted but I was hungry to get and rectify it.

'I've been rocked a couple of times but never hurt. I think body shots hurt more than a head shot. I'm confident in my heart and my chin and my ability to dig deep when it matters.

'I more competitive with certain people. Like my brother, when we play a bit of table tennis we're really competitive against each other. We're very evenly matched. But I'm only really competitive with boxing. I don't like losing the sprints in training I like to try my hardest. But I listen to Mark. If he comes and says, "Listen I want you to block and move and don't worry winning the sparring," then I'll do it.'

He's good company, is Frank Buglioni. If I was going to meet my first boxer for 17-odd years I couldn't have picked a nicer bloke. I tell him how much I envy him. How I envy the fact that he has a goal in life and that everything he does is geared towards achieving that goal. And I think about the cycle. I ask him if he ever wonders what will happen should that goal be reached.

'Not really. I'm enjoying the present so much that I don't really look too far into the future. I take it week by week. I've got good people around me. I've got trust in them. World champion is the goal. If I didn't think I could be a world champion I wouldn't be doing boxing. It's too hard a sport.'

It's a short interview but worthwhile. We shake hands and I wish him the best. Frank mentions that Eric Seccombe sometimes pops into the gym and offers advice. And the connection between Watson and myself and Buglioni is established.

And already I'm worried for him in the way that I used to worry for Watson. Because every time you meet a boxer you can't help but worry about them. Well I can't anyway. As Frank exits, Mark Tibbs enters and takes a seat at the table. We chat for a while and I remind him that back in the dusty recesses of history we did meet a couple of times. He talks about Frank of course and again that look creeps into his eyes. I can see that he worries about Frank too.

A Fork in the Road

THE sun is hotter than a George Foreman grill set to 11. But no amount of dazzling June sunlight which creeps incongruously over the pile of discarded fast food packaging decorating the entrance to the TKO Gym in London's Canning Town will ever make it look attractive. It's here – via a comedy detour courtesy of Apple's seriously fucked-up Maps app – that I find myself preparing for one of those fork in the road moments that we all have to deal with at certain times in our lives. This is how I describe my thoughts when I enter that gym and come face to face with a young super-middleweight prize-fighter named Frank Buglioni. And we both know exactly what I'm talking about.

'We knew it was the biggest step up in my career to date. We knew he was a very good opponent but knew that he falls apart after about six or seven rounds,' an eloquent, focused Buglioni tells me. 'He's 39 years old so I had the youth on him but I didn't box to my strengths. I think I could have put the pressure on earlier, settled him down a little bit, made him wary rather than trying to lull him into a false sense of security and catch him with counters.'

A quick recap for the untold billions out there in Twitter land there who quite justifiably couldn't give a flying tweet about either one of us, me and Frank that is: earlier this year the then unbeaten WBO European super-middleweight champion had the dubious privilege of being the subject of the first interview I had conducted with a boxer for more than two largely empty decades. One for the future, intimated my shimmering purple prose to a ringing fanfare of trumpets. Going places, I gushed. A genuine contender.

That Frank promptly suffered his first professional defeat in the ring should not have come as a surprise to someone like me, who considers himself unfeasibly fortunate to have drawn Australia in the World Cup sweepstake. But lose he did. Unequivocally so. Taught a lesson in manners by a wily old coyote named Sergey Khomitsky. An OAP in boxing terms, the have-gloves-will-travel Belarusian could easily qualify for the boxing equivalent of a free bus pass (although perhaps not in these days of Foreman and Hopkins et al). Someone whom Frank should have been able to speedily return to his mobility chair if our would-be contender is to be taken as seriously as he wants to be.

But since when did anything really ever go according to plan? Certainly not for Frank and certainly not for the likes of you and me. Which neatly brings me to that fork in the road I mentioned earlier.

It's fork in the road time for Frank because he's GOT to win his next fight, preferably in a manner that can erase those YouTube images of our hero taking far too many punches for his own good before being pulled out of the fight by his wholly sensible and merciful trainer Mark Tibbs. Buglioni MUST win this fight – to lose would set his career in an unpalatable direction, along a pathway that anybody who happens to be 24 and harbouring ambitions to be a world champion will want to avoid at all costs.

And it's fork in the road time for me because my father is just about to die. Just over a week away from dying, in fact. And I don't know what to do with myself other than to sit here at four in the morning and write about boxers. Which is kind of ironic really because I have a strong suspicion that on a subconscious level I only write about – have only <u>ever</u> written about – boxers to try to impress my father. And although he'll never read this one – I can't actually say for certain that he's ever read much of what I've written – I've got to do it.

A FORK IN THE ROAD

Fortunately for Buglioni when it comes to getting back on to the yellow brick road the odds are heavily stacked in his favour. Charged with the responsibility of rehabilitating chipped chins and bruised egos is one Sam Couzens. Even Herodotus himself would have trouble bigging up the qualifications of Couzens. Nobody is pretending that the Hampshire-based fighter is anything more than a 'W' to sit atop the 'L TKO 6' that currently besmirches Buglioni's ring record. Nevertheless, when people are throwing punches at each other's heads for hard cash it's never a good idea to start counting chickens.

Unfortunately for my father the odds are rather heavily stacked against him being in a position to watch Buglioni climb into the ring on 16 July at London's York Hall ready to put the hurt on Couzens. Life for him is 24 hours of concentrated misery followed by another 24 hours of the same followed by another. And at the risk of intruding upon what is supposed to be an article about people who punch each other for a living, I'm not there and won't be there to try to lessen that misery. He doesn't want to see me and I don't want to see him. And it's at times like this, inevitably, that one is forced to wonder how things ever managed to turn out this way.

It is my father who is responsible for this love/hate relationship I have with boxing. It was his enthusiasm for the sport which I am reluctant to call a sport that long ago compelled me to consider that there might be magic lurking behind the blood and sweat and snot. It was his excitement that carried me along through the long, hot, mainly miserable summers of my youth. It was probably the one thing that we ever really had in common other than the battles we waged against one another.

'You just know in their eyes. I hit him with a shot and his back leg gave way a little bit. And I went in and threw a few shots and he held.' In a distinctly unglamorous back-room Buglioni tucks in to a home-made pasta salad and reflects on what went wrong that night in April. 'When I was hurt I didn't have that experience. I didn't hold. I didn't tie him up. I tried to fight when my coordination and timing wasn't there. And that's what happened in the sixth round. He caught me with a good shot and I went with him a little bit. And then he caught me with exactly the same left hook round the side and on the chin again.'

There is no animosity in Buglioni's words. He doesn't hate the man who damaged his unblemished record. There is a refreshing absence of hostility. But then why shouldn't there be? We sometimes tend to overlook the fact that boxing is nine-tenths business and nine-tenths artifice. But then who's counting? And without wishing to dial in the clichés Buglioni seems to view that night as little more than a bad day at the office. He's simply relieved to live to fight another day.

'It didn't hurt,' he insists. 'Obviously my legs went, my coordination went and the ropes probably kept me up but I didn't go down. In the corner of my eye I saw the referee and I thought, "Don't jump in! Don't jump in!" I was still thinking, although obviously I couldn't defend myself.'

A couple of weeks earlier Frank had contacted me via Facebook asking if I'd like to come back and conduct a follow-up interview with him. The strange thing was that at exactly the same time I'd been contacting him through Facebook to suggest the same. Perhaps deep down both of us knew we had unfinished business. Back in the 1990s when two men shared the same experience – generally physically it has to be said – they might have called it an 'Ulrika' moment.

'My trainer stopped the fight because he knew that fella could have finished me and done more damage,' Frank continues. 'I'm not naive – I know he could have done that. I was in no position to continue at that time. He said, "It's over. We'll come again." And I remember him saying, "Walk back to the corner – you're walking out." And that's probably why I'm so confident and I've come back so strong. Because I walked out of that ring. I wasn't put on my arse.'

I watch Buglioni work on the pads. There is a marked difference between the man I see now and the man who was training for the Khomitsky defence. On that earlier occasion it was notable – even to my uncultured eye – that Buglioni seemed to lack aggression. Nothing too discernible – one certainly could not have accused him of going through the motions – but there was a sense that the boxer might just have temporarily forgotten about the life and death nature of the world that he inhabits. There is none of that now. There is a meanness to Buglioni's punches that occasionally makes me wince from the sidelines as he throws them.

'My mindset has changed,' he explains. 'When I train now, I train to hurt people. I wasn't doing that previously. I was boxing nice, I was landing good shots but if I hurt anyone I would take a step back.

'Things have changed now. If I hurt someone I jump on them. If they're in the ring with me they're getting it. I'm in there to hurt people. And if I get beat so be it but they'll know they've been in a fight. There's no way they're coming out unscathed against me. They'll have to kill me to beat me.'

Such time-honoured boxing rhetoric inevitably draws me back to my father and I struggle to concentrate as images flash by of the two of us perched in front of the TV yelling at Alan Minter as Marvin Hagler brutally exposes the British middleweight champion before being showered with bottles and cans. The perennial abuse that my father was wont to hurl at that great underachiever Joe Bugner as he pranced his way to yet another points loss against yet another mid-range American. There are so many moments that we shared together at the shrine of that fuzzy analogue screen: Stracey's win over Napoles. Stracey's loss to Dave 'Boy' Green. Green's shocking one-punch KO at the fists of Ray Leonard; Kenny Norton's frankly outrageous loss to Ali in their third fight. Some of those men have gone now but the memories are indelible.

Boxing was one of the very few things on which my father and I grudgingly walked a common ground. He was a soldier and then a copper and then a white collar worker at a local factory. Latterly he was a Labour councillor. My brother was a soldier and is still a copper. I was the black sheep. I liked to see myself as an artist but never the twain and all that. He didn't understand me and I didn't understand him. It was as if we both spoke a different language, with boxing being an occasional but all too fleeting translator.

The rest of the time we were at it like two heavyweight rivals. Him hurling the blows, both verbal and otherwise. Me ducking under their slipstream. Me erecting an impregnable defence that left him pondering and no doubt regretting the mistakes that we all make when we are young men.

'I still live with my parents. Me and my brother are still at home and my sister lives around the corner. We're a close family.' Buglioni's relationship with his own father is thankfully somewhat less destructive. 'We didn't sleep that night. Me and my dad sat and watched the fight back. We came to the conclusion that I need to rectify this loss and come back a better fighter and that this could be the making of me. I said if I could fight that fella right now I would.'

I'm full of big ideas, me. I tell Frank that he needs to have an iconic image. That an iconic image is what will get people talking about him. As if I know anything at all.

And for reasons that will become all too obvious I have it in my mind to get him to recreate that famous *Esquire* cover shot of Muhammad Ali as St Sebastian. And Frank is just so nice, so accommodating, that he agrees to my scheme without hesitation. I warn him that he might look a prat in front of his fellow fighters but he doesn't care. And this is just one of the very many reasons that I am reminded how lucky, how fortunate I am to spend even a little time with one of these extraordinary people; this curious species who risk their lives and their future health looking for some sort of gold at the end of the rainbow. About how, almost to a man, you will seldom come across a nicer breed of person.

This is the incredible dichotomy inherent in boxing: that these individuals, who choose to express themselves through bouts of controlled violence that is so often frightening to behold, that is frequently way beyond the boundaries of what our society deems to be acceptable behaviour, are generally more at peace with themselves than many of us will ever be. A small part of me wishes that my father was standing beside me to witness at first hand the tangible aura of tranquility that glows from Buglioni. And yet another part of me is probably aware that I'm taking no small advantage of somebody who is slowly, I think, becoming a friend. Because actually it's me who should be standing there looking a prat in front of the other boxers. It's my flabby body that those arrows should really be aimed at.

There I go again. All too often in the past people have accused me of using boxing as a device to allow me to harp on about myself. But it's Buglioni who clearly deserves the last word before heading towards his own fork in the road to destiny.

'I take a lot of positives from the defeat: My chin is decent. He caught me with two absolute peaches and I was on the ropes and he was throwing right hands at will. And I was still on my feet. And I see that as a good sign,' he looks me in the eye earnestly as he tells me this. 'Since turning pro I've never been the underdog. And I'm a dangerous underdog. I like to be at the back of the pack chasing. This has brought out another side of me and I'm spiteful. Everything I hit I'm hitting to hurt. I'm not going through the motions with anything. I'm in there to end careers.'

Postscript

I BEGAN writing this less than a week before my father died. A part of me is, of course, already deeply regretting that I wasn't there to to support him as his body withered away and succumbed to the truly awful incurable medical condition known as motor neurone disease. I hadn't seen him for maybe two years after what in retrospect was always bound to be a frankly silly falling out that isn't worth going into here. Over the years there had been many such trivial arguments and long periods in which we studiously avoided seeing each other. I think both of us realised that our superficial bickering masked a deeper chasm that often threatened to rend our father/son relationship into shreds. I believe it's not that uncommon.

One of the many things I've taken from him is boxing, another is music, which I guess aren't such bad gifts to receive from anybody. And it is to boxing – and you – that I must apologise. On too many occasions I've found myself hijacking the sport as a means of exorcising inner demons. And I'm doing it again right now. I hope you'll understand.